This book has _____ *College of* _____

by the author ____ **MADE IN WASHINGTON**
illustrates the involvement of the United States government and governments of other nations in matters influencing the production, marketing and distribution of food. Political forces within nations, including our own, continue to impact relative prosperity of the agricultural sector. The author intends this publication to document the manner in which governments influence the flow of agricultural commodities in the world and also the quality of the diets around the globe.

MADE IN WASHINGTON

MADE IN WASHINGTON

*Food Policy and the
Political Expedient*

Clarence D. Palmby

**I
P
P** THE INTERSTATE Printers & Publishers, Inc.

Danville, Illinois

MADE IN WASHINGTON

Library of Congress Catalog Card No. 84-82282

1 2 3
4 5 6
7 8 9

ISBN 0-8134-2482-8

Preface

This is a review of U.S. agricultural policy in the last 50 years, seen from the unique perspective of one privileged to serve both governmental and private sectors in this country and abroad during a watershed period of global political, economic and social change.

A study of the nation's agricultural economy must of necessity consider those political actions at the heart of farm policy. The record will show that agriculture—the largest and most basic American industry—has often been a target and, frequently, a casualty of fragmented information and flawed decisions.

Time and again, actions and legislation by the federal government have eroded the foundation of our free market system. Yet, on other occasions, that same government has intentionally reduced its involvement in the agricultural economy.

A carrot and stick policy? Not likely . . . more a climate of uncertainty fueled by political expediency.

It is not uncommon for politicians, elected and appointed officials and others to be classified as market-oriented, that is, in favor of price determination through the free exercise of the market forces encompassing supply and demand. But conversely, the same label is applied to those in opposition to the natural interaction of those same market forces.

Clearly, there is confusion. In many instances, the concept of market orientation is misused. This book examines that question in exploring the full meaning of market forces and their impact on the operating ease of this country's most fundamental economic precept.

The much used expression, "Two steps forward and one step backward," hardly marks the true progress of those dedicated to maintaining a reasonably free agricultural sector. More accurate would be, "One step forward and one step backward."

Freedom to plant specific crops, as determined by hundreds of thousands of farmers on the basis of expected financial return, has been the gleaming cornerstone of a market-oriented agriculture. Equally important is the freedom of millions of consumers to register their likes and dislikes for a virtually limitless supply of food in the marketplace. Between the producer and consumer in the United States, a vast network of entrepreneurs add place, time and form utility to farm products. A favorable operating climate for these risk-takers, processors and investors is another key building block of a market-oriented agriculture.

Because food is so vital a commodity, each and every person has a stake in policies having to do with food production, processing and distribution. As the population of the world has grown—now totaling over 4½ billion—those policies are increasingly important.

The United States of America is endowed with great natural agricultural resources, generally dependable rainfall over much of its surface, water for irrigation in other areas and climate conducive to favorable plant and animal growth. In addition, this nation is blessed with internal waterway transportation systems second to none.

Despite those advantages—plus a well educated, well trained agricultural production, processing and distribution system—the entire sector is subject to problems. Weather is often unpredictable and disheartening. Abnormally large harvests often depress prices and resultant incomes.

Such supply/demand situations are tailor-made for political intervention. Legislators are always eager to court voters with proposals to alleviate short- or long-term farm income problems.

Market intervention by central planners is not a new phenomenon. Economists, elected officials, farmers, marketers and government administrators seem never to agree on the most desirable level of government intervention in the marketplace. Some favor outright establishment of farm prices by government, accompanied by production and marketing quotas. Others favor minimum loan rates or price supports. Still others expound the theory of no market intervention whatsoever.

The Charter Act authorizing Commodity Credit Corporation (CCC), the government entity established 50 years ago with later revisions for the purpose of financing farm programs and related activities, makes it relatively easy for the Congress or the executive branch to intervene in grain and other commodity markets. Legal intervention may be authorized even without an appropriation of funds, with reimbursement usually following specific program authorization. This mechanism has enabled CCC to intervene on short notice. In the absence of the CCC, intervention would be difficult, if not impossible.

The agricultural sector, as compared to others in the total economy, has performed well. The nation has reaped the advantages of abundance. More than 8,000 different food items are available in the supermarket at prices requiring a lower percentage of take-home pay than in any other nation.

U.S. export earnings from agricultural commodities far in excess of imports has become legendary.

Agriculture's success has attracted attention of lawmakers because it is deemed politically wise to be involved with such positive stories. Unfortunately, results of political or diplomatic actions have often been more disruptive than supportive of normal market forces. The attendant imbalance between supply and demand has had far-reaching negative effects.

Early in my work career, I came to two conclusions regarding involvement of the U.S. Department of Agriculture (USDA), or any other agency of government, in the marketing of grain and other non-perishable commodities.

First, I believed producers would fare far better and perform more responsibly by projecting and acting upon commodity prices as determined by free forces than under central government fiat. But I also appreciated the volatility of production and prices one year to another.

Second, and with hands on knowledge of the impact of price supports (at some level) and their consequences on farmers in the 1930s, I learned one lesson well. The precise level of price support or loan level, as announced for an ensuing wheat or corn crop, almost immediately equated into the per bushel production cost for the next year's crop. Simply stated, "Established farmers expanded operations or committed capital consistent with the new price guarantee."

As a youth, with an eye to a farming career, I found the idea of politicians eulogizing the greatness of higher and higher price supports hollow and self-defeating. Now, 50 years later, I still cannot understand why more thinking people do not grasp this basic truism.

The impact of higher and higher guaranteed cereal prices on cost per unit of production of those cereals in the European Economic Community (EEC) and Japan will be discussed.

Maybe it is possible only for people directly involved in production, transportation, processing and distribution of food and other farm products to fully understand why personal involvement in agriculture is absolutely necessary for a successful enterprise. Socialist countries almost without exception seemingly have demonstrated their inability to "buy" production efficiency.

A market-oriented agricultural policy must, of necessity, include a freedom to plant concept. This can best serve the nation and the agricultural community within the framework of a global market.

The Agricultural Act of 1970 provided for suspension of producer marketing quotas for cotton and wheat—two of the original so-called basic commodities. Suspension of marketing quotas was legislated with an eye toward normalizing trade in farm products on a global basis.

Events leading to normalizing such trade with the People's Republic of China, the USSR and other socialist countries by President Nixon will be discussed in the book, as will the actions taken by government leading to feed grain sales by exporters to the Soviet Union in 1971.

Grain exports in 1972 and subsequent years and the growing pains experienced by the United States in servicing a world market in times of scarcity will be described.

Relatively minor actions designed to allow free market forces to better reflect total use and exports in their entirety will be explained.

A history of agricultural policy indicates that there are few new programs or techniques through which CCC or the government interferes with marketing machinery, thereby impacting price. A scheme once tested and found wanting does not mean it will not be tried again. New players in the policy field are often reluctant to learn from lessons learned in past years.

Ill-conceived government intervention in the marketplace, taken for the purpose of enhancing producer income from specific commodities, historically have resulted in unpredicted price gyrations of other food items which in one way or another relate to those basic commodities. If the message of the interrelationship of commodity prices and the sensitivity of those prices to the actions of policymakers and political leaders is better understood by the examples included in this book—then the effort expended will have been rewarded.

Table of Contents

☆ ☆

☆☆☆☆☆☆☆☆☆☆☆☆

CHAPTER 1

☆☆☆☆☆☆☆☆☆☆☆☆

The Formative Years

☆ ☆

"Prices are made in Washington."

During the decade of the 1930s, through the war years and into the 1950s and beyond, the spokesman for the Farmers Union Grain Terminal Association, the grain cooperative headquartered in St. Paul, Minnesota, was William "Bill" Thatcher. Mr. Thatcher ran the organization. He was an orator. He was a crowd pleaser. He was an effective organizer. His theme song, "Prices are made in Washington," meant prices for farm commodities.

Mr. Thatcher, through that long period of time, had a loyal following in Minnesota, the Dakotas and Montana, and in areas bordering those particular states. His organizational skill and his oratory were well known.

"Prices are made in Washington" was his favorite radio chant.

A spokesman expressing an opposing view to Mr. Thatcher during this volatile period for U.S. agriculture was Allan Kline, the most effective spokesman for the American Farm Bureau Federation (AFBF). Mr. Kline was second to no one as an effective lecturer, public speaker and thinker. He disagreed with Mr. Thatcher on most every issue having to do with government programs and the effect of such on farm prosperity. Mr. Kline believed government should be less involved in commodity markets. He thought of global markets in contrast to regional or national interests.

The National Farmers Union (NFU), a national general farm organization, was subsidized at that time by the Grain Terminal Association. The policies of the NFU were generally identical to those embraced by the cooperative.

The years following World War II saw an increase in the membership and power of the American Farm Bureau Federation. On the other hand, the NFU was vocal on agricultural policy issues and usually in opposition to the views of the AFBF. On the general issue of government involvement in agricultural affairs, including marketing of farm products, it seemed to me that the AFBF favored a retrenchment of government in such matters. It also was my opinion that the NFU favored and was comfortable with greater government involvement.

Also on the national front, the Grange was a factor of some importance in farm circles, but to this day I have never been able to comprehend where the Grange stands on many issues. Usually the organization stood somewhere in between the Farm Bureau and the Farmers Union.

It is not my intention to write a history of farm programs nor to trace in detail in a chronological manner the changing provisions of farm legislation. I leave that assignment to others. On the other hand, in order to discuss major policy changes and views having to do with agricultural production and marketing, I deem it desirable to capsulize the beginnings of programs and legislation as major government involvement in the business of agriculture came into being. Many price stabilization techniques have survived, in one form or another, over half a century.

The first major stabilization, The Agricultural Adjustment Act (AAA), or what was to become known as The Farm Program, became law under President Roosevelt and Secretary of Agriculture Wallace in May, 1933. The chief goal of the legislation was to restore the purchasing power of farm commodities to the 1909-1914 level. Hence, the word "parity" came into being, which in reality reflected the relationship between farm prices for commodities and the costs which prevailed in the 1909 to 1914 period.

Acreage allotment programs came into operation for cotton, wheat, corn, rice, peanuts, tobacco and sugar in a staggered manner over a three-year period, 1933 through 1935.

Commodity Credit Corporation was first established by executive order in October, 1933. (The CCC Charter Act which is the authority under which CCC now operates was approved by President Truman in June, 1948.)

The first nonrecourse commodity loans, whereby the commodity itself was the only security for the loan, were initiated by CCC in the fall of 1933. The loan on cotton that season was 10 cents per pound—slightly less than 70 percent of parity. The first corn loan level was 45 cents per bushel, which was about 60 percent of parity.

As a consequence of the Hoosac Mills (textiles) decision of the Supreme Court, the production control provisions of the AAA were invalidated in January, 1936. The production control provisions under AAA had been financed by processing taxes, and this is what was challenged in the courts.

The Hoosac Mills decision reflected the thinking of the Supreme Court in a test case working its way through the judicial system by the Hoosac Mills of New Jersey. The Supreme Court decision in addition to invalidating production control provisions of AAA determined the collection of processing taxes to be illegal. This famous Court decision was most instrumental in causing President Roosevelt to seek legislation to "pack the Supreme Court." He attempted to increase the number of jurors on the Court from 9 to 15. The Congress rejected the proposal, but the attempt to pack the Court rallied many forces against the New Deal. I can say, with strong conviction (nearly 50 years later) that the attempt to "pack the Supreme Court" was the most blatant power play attempt by any president in my working career.

In order to continue the production control programs, Congress enacted The Soil Conservation and Domestic Allotment Act which became law in February, 1936.

The Agricultural Marketing Agreement Act was enacted in 1937. This law, until this day, provides the legal basis for marketing agreements designed to establish and maintain orderly marketing conditions for certain agricultural commodities in interstate commerce.

Perhaps the most ambitious production control and price support program ever written was enacted in 1938. It became known as the Agricultural Adjustment Act of 1938. In reality, marketing control was substituted for production control. Marketing quota provisions for cotton, wheat, corn, rice and tobacco were included. The mandatory nonrecourse loan provision became the basis for the Ever-Normal Granary concept. All risk crop insurance authority was also included in the AAA of 1938. The secretary of agriculture was delegated rather broad discretion in determining the level of loan rates in the 1938 law. For example, the secretary was authorized to establish the cotton and wheat loans between 52 and 75 percent of parity.

In April, 1941, mandatory price support legislation for peanuts was enacted. The new law also contained provisions for establishing marketing quotas for peanuts.

The "Steagall Amendment," as a wartime measure, became law in July, 1941. This authority directed the secretary to support at not less than 85 percent of parity the prices of those nonbasic commodities for which he found it necessary to ask for an increase in production. Support prices for corn, cotton, peanuts, wheat, tobacco and rice (basic commodities) were raised by the amendment to not less than 90 percent of parity. (The author and sponsor of the Steagall Amendment was Congressman Bascomb Steagall—D.-Alabama.)

Wartime levels of price support were continued after the war for the stated purpose of assuring ample food for the devastated people in Europe and Asia. Prior to the time of expiration on December 31, 1948, Congress mandated price support loans for the 1949 crops of wheat, corn, cotton, rice, peanuts and tobacco at 90 percent of parity.

The following year, 1949, new legislation set the support prices for basic commodities at 90 percent of parity for the 1950 crop and between 80 and 90 percent for the 1951 crop.

Price supports for hogs, chickens and turkeys which had been in operation through the war years and beyond were discontinued in 1950. The price of milk and the products of milk continued to be supported from 60 to 90 percent of parity. This was accomplished by loans on, or purchase of, non-fat dry milk, butter and cheese. Hence the term, "manufactured milk products price support program." (One can only speculate, as I do, how much more rapidly varieties and types of cheeses would have been developed and marketed in the United States had the dairy industry been given the privilege of being free and subject to true market forces. But the industry manufactured the three basic items for CCC. Producers lost, as did millions of consumers.)

In 1948, the AFBF promoted flexible price supports for basic commodities, the specific dollar amount was to be based on level of carryovers and/or production. In 1949, the debate continued. On one side of the argument the AFBF recommended lowering support prices for the basic commodities when supply or carryover reached some predetermined level, whereas the National Farmers Union continued to recommend fixed support prices for the basic commodities.

As a farmer during this period of time, and one mostly interested in corn, livestock and soybeans, I found myself in growing sympathy with the views of Allan Kline and the AFBF. I was having problems with the proposals being promoted by the NFU. The reason was quite simple.

My problem at that time can best be illustrated by the farm program available to corn producers in most years following World War II. Provisions varied from year to year or from period to period as laws were written or amended. Generally, though, compliance with an acreage allotment on each farm was a requirement for price protection for corn produced on the farm—and then through a nonrecourse loan. A farmer using the loan provision was required to keep the corn in storage through the so-called loan period; after which, the Commodity Credit Corporation stood ready to take title and physical delivery of the corn in full payment of the loan.

Glaring weaknesses inherent with rigid corn acreage allotments and price supports became apparent—at least to me.

A fixed level of price support immediately resulted in a capitalization of the expected returns from that guaranteed price being seen in land prices. For one attempting to establish a more viable farm operation, I found that trend discouraging.

Secondly, and more importantly, the announced loan rate (floor price) almost automatically became the new per bushel cost of production for that year. A guaranteed price by its very nature encouraged the application of inputs such as fertilizer be applied to the level of diminishing returns. This elementary fact is really one of the simple truths of basic economics.

I found myself in opposition to such policies of rigidity and limited opportunity. I realized long before I made my first investment in agricultural land that opportunity to acquire or accumulate reasonable equity in a farming enterprise would more likely be accomplished if risk of failure be borne by me rather than the directors of farm programs.

I was in opposition to prices being made in Washington. It was abundantly clear, however, that powerful forces and many well meaning people, some engaged in agriculture and some with peripheral interest, favored the establishment of price by central planners.

Because of my feeling that the nation's agriculture would be best served by less rather than more federal government involvement, and because I agreed to serve, I was elected president of the Blue Earth County Farm Bureau in 1946 (the soil in the county is not really blue). I remained in that position for five years. Membership consisted of about 2,000 dues-paying members (most of whom were farmers, but some of the members were local business people).

As a county farm bureau president, I realized two truisms regarding political clout. The state farm bureau could effectively influence the Minnesota state legislature. The AFBF was extremely effective in *preventing* enactment of proposed legislature. But the AFBF was not particularly powerful in securing passage of proposals before the U.S.

Congress. This was not a negative situation in my thought process, because there were already too many laws anyway.

On the national political agricultural scene other developments seemed obvious. When the AFBF supported a proposal, the NFU opposed, and vice versa. Likewise, as the NFU supported a view, the AFBF adopted the opposite attitude.

My observation on political clout did not change as I became a member of the Minnesota Farm Bureau Board of Directors in 1951 and subsequently a member of the AFBF livestock committee (positions from which I resigned when I became a member of the Eisenhower administration in March, 1953).

The farm programs of the 1930s were generally popular with farmers in the United States. Farmers in the Midwest and South for which the early legislation was designed particularly latched on to the programs and administered them with enthusiasm and, generally, in a non-partisan manner.

The Agriculture Marketing Act of 1937, authorizing marketing orders, was tailor-made for California specialty crops.

The original Agricultural Adjustment Act (AAA) established the elected county and community committee system for the purpose of administrating farm programs enacted by the Congress. Across the Corn Belt the original committees were known as the "corn-hog committees" because of the benefits flowing to corn and hog farmers. To this day one may, on occasion, still hear comments such as "killing little pigs." Time, however, has dissipated the criticism of reducing pig numbers to improve prices, which was the thrust of the original corn-hog program.

What is of more than passing significance was the quality of leadership elected to the early county farm program committees. Many farmers who were recognized leaders in their communities served on the committee system. This enthusiastic attitude and general support continued through World War II days and to a degree beyond the mid-1940s. Then attitudes changed.

Somewhere around the midterm of Harry Truman one began to hear the term, "The *Federal* Farm Program." Prior to that time it was "*The* Farm Program" or "*Our* Farm Program." Several explanations may be given for the changing attitude, among which were prosperity on the farm, a new generation of farmers and a growing trend toward commercialization and away from the mental fixation that farming is a "way of life." The latter explanation is the most plausible. More and more farmers were feeling qualified and sufficiently confident to operate their farms as businesses, free of government dictation and direct program benefits.

By this period in history, under President Truman and Secretary of Agriculture Charles Brannan, the federal agency responsible for administering the farm program was known as the Production and Marketing Administration (PMA). Somewhat as a result of the Brannan direct deficiency payment proposals with emphasis on perishable commodities such as livestock products which were never enacted by the Congress, the PMA was branded as an extension of the Democratic administration and in some areas as an extension of the Democratic party. The politicizing of farm programs, whether in fact or in fiction, did work toward the defeat of Adlai Stevenson by General Eisenhower in the Midwest in 1952. Of course, many other factors were also at work.

From the standpoint of U.S. government involvement in farm policy, the 1952 election was indeed meaningful. The trend in rural areas to brand farm programs as federal farm programs was here to stay. The title *Our Program* was no longer commonplace. The most enthusiastic promoters for expanding farm programs were office seekers.

1953—STATE OF THE ART OF FARMING—CORN BELT

The national average per acre corn yield in 1952 was 40 bushels. This was 35 percent of what the productivity per acre was to be 30 years later in 1982, when the yield was 113 bushels.

Farming was in transition in 1953. Application of commercial fertilizer on agricultural land in the Corn Belt and Great Plains was mushrooming. Hybrid seeds were being improved each year. Commercial seed company plant breeders were outdoing one another in utilizing inbred lines and experimenting with various crosses.

Health products and growth stimulators for livestock and poultry were finding their niche.

Land prices were low. Capital was available for farm expansion but expectations were disciplined. A general good feeling prevailed in rural America, but on the farm level, the fissure between the proponents of farm programs with "teeth" were vocal, and those favoring less involvement of the federal government were likewise firm in their beliefs. The term "teeth" referred to the concept of enforcing fixed crop acreage allotments established at the national level. In program terminology, it meant marketing quotas for specific crops with severe economic penalties for non-compliance.

During the early 1950s, and even later into the decade and beyond, terminology so commonplace in rural areas had become part of the day-to-day vocabulary. Terms such as "conservation base," "diverted acres," "diversion," "loan level," "conversion," "delivery date," "compliance" and many more were common jargon.

Ezra Taft Benson became Secretary of Agriculture following the inauguration of General Eisenhower as president, January 20, 1953.

Mr. Benson, not a farm program enthusiast, was in unusual contrast to Mr. Brannan who had built the Production and Marketing Administration into an agency that overshadowed USDA itself. Mr. Benson dismantled PMA a few months after he took office. The chief function, however, continued on within the confines of the smaller agency which later was named the Commodity Stabilization Service (CSS). And at the state and county level, the Agricultural Stabilization and Conservation Service (ASCS). The chief function of the agency consisted of administering the production adjustment and price support programs—and the activities financed by the Commodity Credit Corporation, such being the custodian of the commodities owned by the corporation.

Mr. Benson, upon the recommendation of Senator Edward J. Thye (R.-Minnesota), appointed me chairman of the Minnesota PMA committee effective March 9, 1953. Each state PMA committee in the then 48 states consisted of three or more members. Minnesota had three. Charles Stickney, chairman and member of the Minnesota PMA committee of Sherburne County for many years, had resigned several weeks earlier; hence, Senator Thye was anxious to have the position filled. This appointment in Minnesota was the first in the nation under the new Republican administration and did receive more than passing notice. Subtly stated, PMA had become somewhat of a political entity. Interest in the farming community was quite high.

Senator Thye later revealed that he had received letters or applications in one form or another from more than 100 people expressing interest in the position of chairman of the state committee. Other than having been involved in many regional civic projects, my only claim to political office seeking had been membership on the local school board for seven years. I had, of course, supported General Eisenhower in his candidacy for the presidency.

Again, upon reflection 30 years later, I wonder why I agreed to accept the appointment. I had put together a viable general farming operation, including a money-making livestock enterprise. My wife and I and our family of three children were happy with farm and rural living.

Being chairman of the agency responsible for administering the farm program in Minnesota did not require our leaving the farm. It was a part-time job. It did require may resigning two advisory roles I had with the U.S. Department of Agriculture. One, as a member of the USDA research advisory committee and two, as a member of the Blue Earth County Farmers Home Administration (FmHA) advisory committee. This latter position had truly been educational and a lesson learned remains valuable to me even at this moment—namely, you do not do a young farmer or his family a favor by approving his application for an FmHA loan thereby enabling him to continue farming, or maybe to buy a farm, unless, and I repeat *unless*, there is *solid* evidence that the enterprise can become *economically viable*.

And so as chairman of the Minnesota PMA committee, shortly to become ASCS, a new chapter commenced. Rather quickly the committee of three was rounded out. My two new colleagues were Henry Bolstad of Lac Qui Parle County and Arnold G. "Gus" Hamnes of Marshall County. Both were recognized as highly successful farmers. I soon found them to be bright, fair and completely dependable.

As an aside and as mentioned earlier, national corn yields were increasing rapidly in the decade of the 1950s. Improved hybrids were performing well, and the use of commercial fertilizers was causing yields to further increase. Farmers in the "newer" farming areas were developing and expanding drainage systems.

Application of this new technology was making it possible for those adopting such practices to literally double their production. Introduction of new and improved methods has always been thus. Those pioneers adopting such practices first, particularly in the early years of development, managed to prosper, increase their farm size and move on towards a still greater degree of commercialization. A new type of farmer was emerging; a businessman with instincts for success!

THE SURPLUS PROBLEM

In the spring of 1953, the Commodity Credit Corporation owned 30 million bushels of grain—mostly corn—stored in CCC-owned bins in most major grain producing counties in Minnesota. The grain had been surrendered to the CCC by farmers as payment for loans secured under the price-support programs. Participating farmers were authorized to deliver commodity in full payment of the loans. Through the loan period, the grain had been stored on the farm as collateral.

Title to grain and the actual grain itself passing to CCC—and then coming to rest in hastily erected bins owned by CCC—was a rather new development. Actually, President Truman, himself in his bid for a full four-year term in 1948, blasted the Republican-controlled Congress for "doing nothing" by not appropriating funds to construct CCC storage as a home for grain forfeited by farmers to the government under the price-support program. Thus, in the four ensuing years (1949 through 1952) under President Truman, storage facilities had been erected in most major grain-producing counties within the state, as well as in other states.

In my many conversations with Senator Ed Thye and then somewhat ironically, years later with President-elect Nixon, I was advised that a politician or a politically appointed government official who has time to criticize his predecessors is not likely to be a constructive leader. I followed that advice of not finding fault with earlier actions, but I also discovered that one must become acquainted with decisions and policies as historically determined and developed. To do otherwise is not unlike an ostrich burying its proverbial head in the sand.

Quality of bin site stored corn in *some* counties left much to be desired. In the worst situations the corn had been placed in the bins (many of which were Quonset huts with a capacity of 30,000 to 50,000 bushels) through the use of makeshift equipment. Also, the corn had not been leveled in some bins, consequently, the cones or peaks were heating and caked. I later discovered this situation was not unique to Minnesota. Other Corn Belt states also had problems.

County committees, I discovered, were given considerable leeway in caring for bin sites and the contents—but less than enough funds and insufficient guidance to perform a good warehousing function. Let's face it—the government was in the grain business, and in a big way.

Not an uncommon attitude shared by a meaningful number of county committee persons reasoned that CCC-owned corn and other grain would never be used, so the sooner it spoiled and thereby lost its value the better off everyone would be. I understood that feeling of frustration, but much to Mr. Benson's credit, we in a supervisory capacity with responsibility for the government-owned commodities were expected to maintain quantity and quality. Grain was food!

In some instances, local cooperative and privately owned grain companies were not without blame in not adequately servicing CCC bin sites. They (the dealers) were hired to fill and empty as well as service a bin site. In some cases the bin site work was performed as the job of least importance. In other instances, as one would expect, the work performed by the grain trade was superb and conscientious. In a few of the counties, where the grain trade was less well organized or financed, county committees hired farmers and their equipment to work the CCC bin sites. In such cases it was not uncommon to see flight-type elevators (built to handle ear corn) utilized to fill the bins with shelled corn. Breakage oftentimes was severe.

We, on the state committee, agreed that Henry Bolstad take on the responsibility of whipping the Minnesota bin site operations into shape. It is a tribute to him and the county committees for the manner in which they accepted leadership and guidance in becoming good and trusted custodians.

The county committees helped develop uniform filling and emptying contracts with the grain trade in their respective counties or with farmers when that seemed more logical. Regular inspection schedules were developed, as was a meaningful log system for each bin site.

One decision, by we three on the state committee, still causes me to smile. Late in 1953 we were disappointed and a bit disgusted with a few members of the grain trade in their seeming lack of response to our request that they be more businesslike in their working bin sites. I requested permission from the head of the grain division, CSS, Washington, to buy 9-inch 42-foot augers for county committees to work the sites themselves.

We bought 40 augers and assigned them to several *appropriate* counties. It did the job. I received more criticism and more phone calls. I was dubbed a socialist and a conniver.

It now amuses me because my record of recommending or not recommending more or less government involvement speaks for itself as it did then. We had made our point. Any foot-dragging county committeeman enthusiastically became concerned with quality of grain owned by CCC, as did the trade—almost without exception.

The general attitude shared by many within the county and community system, and certainly many people on the street, looked upon government-owned grain as a liability, not an asset. "Drop it in the ocean" was not an uncommon remark. Anyone reading the hearings of the appropriation sub-committees would have reason to believe surplus grain and other commodities owned by the government must be one of the great calamities in the United States.

Few activities of state and county committees received greater attention than the matter of compliance. The state office had a compliance section head and a staff to write procedures for the county offices as well as to supervise all activities having to do with compliance with the several programs.

The county offices, likewise, had a compliance section. In most county offices, one member of the county committee on a part-time basis was responsible for overseeing the compliance program within

☆ *E. S. Gandrud, Owatonna, Minnesota, and the Gandy Wheel in 1936.*

the county. Acreage devoted to allotment crops such as corn and wheat had to be measured. The conservation base on each farm was checked.

After all, eligibility for price support payments to idle land or to divert agricultural land from production in a given year was dependent upon rigid compliance with specific crop-acreage allotments—as determined by county committees within guidelines established by statute or federal farm program administrators.

The Gandy Wheel had come into being.

Many years later in August, 1979, I visited with Mr. E. S. Gandrud in Owatonna, Minnesota. He was president and owner of the Gandy Company. Mr. Gandrud developed the 1-rod long iron wheel with a meter specifically for use in checking compliance with acreage control farm programs. He had the wheel patented in 1936.

The wheel was still in use in 1953. A common sight in the rural areas was an automobile with a Gandy Wheel aboard traveling from farm to farm to check compliance.

As time passed, Mr. Gandrud developed a precision-ground rubber-tired wheel with an enclosed gear drive, 5 feet in circumference with a resettable counter which reads directly in feet. In later years, farmers were trusted to certify compliance with program provisions.

I choose to call the period from the mid-1930s for the ensuing quarter of a century, when farm programs are discussed as the era of the "Gandy Wheel."

On the other side of the globe another emblem of a wheel had come into being—the Gandhi Wheel in India. Mahatma Gandhi developed it as an emblem denoting small cottage industries.

The two are coincidental and not related but of passing interest to the curious.

After three years as chairman of the Minnesota ASCS committee, I became Associate Director, Grain Division, CSS, in the U.S. Department of Agriculture, Washington, D.C.

Lloyd Case was director of the division.

The amount of grain owned by CCC continued to increase. Prior to 1957, the grain trade, both cooperative and private, had not built enough storage to store the forever increasing carryovers of wheat, corn, sorghum, barley and oats, even though storage rates paid by CCC to storing warehousemen had been increased in 1952, 1954 and 1956.

In 1953, a guaranteed occupancy agreement had also been used as an incentive to have more commercial storage built.

Storage use guarantees were made to commercial firms including cooperatives. Three plans were offered:

* Plan I—CCC would guarantee not to exceed 75 percent occupancy of new commercial storage facilities for three years, at the end of which time the guaranteed occupancy level would drop to 40 percent for the next two years.
* Plan II—CCC would guarantee 60 percent occupancy for five years.
* Plan III—CCC would guarantee 50 percent occupancy for six years.

Over 200 million bushels of commercial space were constructed under this program.

Over 90 million bushels of commercial space had been erected in a somewhat similar program four years earlier.

The last batch of grain bins for storing CCC-owned grain were purchased in 1956. After erection was completed, the total capacity owned by the government totaled 990 million bushels. Even at that time, when storage needs were increasing, a disposition program for outmoded facilities was in place. Most of the bins were sold to farmers; by 1968, the government-owned capacity had been reduced to 380 million bushels.

In 1971, a stepped-up disposition program was activated, and by 1974, the last bins were sold.

Space for storing surplus grain in that period, in the mid- to late 1950s, was so tight that the USDA entered into an agreement with the U.S. Maritime Commission to use a portion of the reserve fleet for emergency grain storage. A total of 384 ships was brought into service. Nearly 90 million bushels of CCC grain were stored within their holds. The vessels were docked at Jones Point, New York; Astoria, Oregon; Olympia, Washington; and in the James River, Virginia. The last vessels were emptied early in the decade of the 1960s.

After becoming part of the Washington scene in 1956, it seemed to me that Secretary Benson was usually on the defensive. He, of course, was dealing with a Democratically controlled Congress.

Like other secretaries who had preceded him, such as Wallace and Brannan, he had jumped far ahead in promoting his own views on agricultural policy, including farm programs and level of price supports. In fact, his beliefs on level of price supports for the basic commodities were not unlike those of Henry Wallace in the 1930s. Both had expressed the view that commodity loans should be available to farmers at disaster-preventing levels.

One need only read the Congressional Record during the Benson era to understand that agricultural issues had become 100 percent political. Hence, the secretary seldom won an all out victory with the Congress. He never had the opportunity to implement his policies to the fullest. It is surprising that he did as well as he did securing what I would describe as disciplined authority in establishing level of loan rates.

The two schools of thought were at work. One school dictated that prices should be made in Washington. The other school dictated to continue to let some semblance of supply and demand operate.

The result was legislation that allowed limited movement in the market but with loan rates at a level that generally established a floor price and in many instances a ceiling with recognition of carrying charges as dictated by market forces.

THE SOIL BANK

In 1956, Secretary Benson requested the Congress to enact legislation to retire agricultural land from production. The program became known as the Soil Bank. The theory being to store productive capacity in the soil by not producing, rather than storing product in bins and warehouses.

As the concept developed within the USDA, earlier proposals were confined to retiring land for 3, 5 or 10 years for an annual payment. Later developments and final legislation authorized two types of programs. One was an annual diversion or land-idling concept known as the Acreage Reserve. During the year 1957, when participation in the Acreage Reserve peaked, 21 million acres were idled.

The second program authorized was a multi-year land retirement concept known as the Conservation Reserve. By mid-July, 1960, farmers had placed 28.6 million acres under contract for a maximum of 10 years.

Two happenings prevented the Soil Bank from being wholly successful in reducing surplus stocks of grain and cotton. One, loan rates were kept sufficiently high to make it financially attractive for producers to "pour on" the production inputs on planted acreage. Two, all manner of improved technology was being applied by more and more farmers; for example, the use of nitrogen fertilizer was going up rapidly.

On the plus side, many years later, one notes across the nation a stand of trees here and there that had been planted on land devoted to the Conservation Reserve.

UNIFORM GRAIN STORAGE AGREEMENT—1960

Grain surplus to requirements is a goal worthy of achievement by most nations.

As was discovered in 1973 through 1975 in the United States, when supplies of grain in the world were relatively tight in relation to annual use, problems created by a surplus indeed appeared to be minor.

Not so in 1960.

After a decade of unprecedented increase in per acre yield in the United States through mass application of improved technology, the nation did not know what to do with still more grain.

The significance of intensive application of known technology is best illustrated in the production of corn—the big tonnage grain in the United States. Early in the decade of the 1950s, the truly progressive corn farmer was attaining per acre yields up to three times the national average. With each passing year another large number of farmers joined the parade by improving their production practices. Production expanded like a tidal wave.

Export markets, particularly for corn, had not yet been developed. Overseas buying power was limited. Domestically, the increasing production simply could not be used—not at the price level established by the Congress.

This was the setting during the last year of the Eisenhower administration.

Too much grain—as yet very limited export markets—a legislated floor price. Price had been made in Washington.

It was also another presidential election year. Outlook for victory by the Democrat nominee looked quite bright. Several senators were actively fighting for the nomination—each one attempting to attract national attention.

Naturally, the agricultural situation was a prime candidate for a campaign issue.

The Congress on many occasions had laid down policy directing the role of Commodity Credit Corporation. Specifically, in 1948, in the act to provide a charter, the body stated:

> The Commodity Credit Corporation shall, to the maximum extent practicable, consistent with the fulfillment of the Corporation's purposes and the effective and efficient conduct of its business, utilize the usual and customary channels, facilities, and arrangements of trade and commerce.

Senator Stuart Symington (D.-Missouri) obviously was well aware of the success enjoyed by Harry Truman, also from Missouri, 12 years earlier in his bid for reelection to the presidency when he blasted the 80th Congress for (supposedly) obstructing construction of facilities by CCC to store grain. Symington took a different approach. He had himself appointed chairman of a sub-committee of the Senate Committee on Agriculture to investigate the Commodity Credit Corporation. His main thrust proved to be one of attacking USDA officials for their relationship with the grain trade. He was probing, largely in the dark, with the hope he would be successful in receiving headlines.

Senator Humphrey (D.-Minnesota), always running for president, was likewise active in matters involving storage of CCC-owned grain.

On the House side, Congressman L. H. Fountain of North Carolina was chairman of the sub-committee, intergovernmental operations of the government operation committee. He and his sub-committee and staff were holding hearings on grain storage and related matters. The sub-committee of appropriations likewise was in the act of compiling more than normal detailed information on the subject.

Assistant Secretary Marvin McLain had asked me, in my new role as associate administrator of CSS since December, 1959, to assume primary responsibility in re-negotiating the Uniform Grain Storage Agreement (UGSA) with the industry and in appearances before the several congressional committees investigating the operations of CCC. The year, 1960, promised to be a busy one.

Volume of grain owned by the government (CCC) was huge. Statistically, the stock situation was about as follows:

* Stored in commercial facilities and owned outright by CCC—2.4 billion bushels of all grains.
* Stored in CCC-owned bins and owned by CCC—700 million bushels.
* Stored in the reserve fleet (liberty ships) and owned by CCC—35 million bushels.
* Stored on farms under the *reseal* program and title, in hands of farmers—300 million bushels.

Finally, in addition to the above 3½ billion bushels being stored for the account of CCC, farmers had placed a substantial volume of their 1959 crop under loan to the government. Title was still in the farmers' hands.

The cost for storing and handling CCC grains under the UGSA in 1960 was to be in excess of $500 million.

This was the setting for that presidential election year.

Historically, the UGSA came into being in 1940. Rates for storing, handling and various other warehousing functions had been changed and/or increased several times. During the decade of the 1950s, negotiations had taken place in 1952, 1954 and 1956. The contract, as the language was made more precise through the years, carefully spelled out the responsibilities of the two parties—the government (CCC) and the storing warehouseman.

Rates under the agreement and in effect at the beginning of 1960 had been established in 1956.

During the latter part of 1959, preliminary meetings had been held between grain division personnel and 18 representatives of the grain trade for the purpose of discussing provisions. It should be noted that the three national grain trade associations selected six members each to represent the industry. The three associations and their respective chief executive officers were:

* National Grain Trade Council, William F. Brooks, President

* National Federation of Grain Co-operatives, Roy F. Hendricksen, Executive Secretary
* Grain and Feed Dealers National (later to become National Grain and Feed Association), Alvin E. Oliver, Executive Vice-President

We, in government, sought during the early meetings some tightening of the language, which when reduced to actual cost to the industry perhaps equated to something around one-half of one cent per bushel for a 12-month period.

This matter of referring to costs to the industry or in turn payment to the industry for storing grain as being so many cents per bushel per year was highly *displeasing*. I knew why, and others should also know. But the rate structure is in terms of a fraction of a cent per bushel per day—per diem rates. Naturally, CCC-owned grain left in a warehouse for 365 consecutive days equated to so many cents per bushel per (that) year.

In describing the per diem rate structure to Congressional committees, I found I was expected to convert the cost to cents per bushel per year, but always with the caveat the grain continue in storage for 365 days. Long after the fact, the matter now sounds simple, but after a discussion of rates with a Congressional committee, I always felt like a bruised player.

As of January, 1960, the industry had placed under contract to CCC under the terms of UGSA about 4 billion bushels of space. In 1952, the volume had been about 1⅕ billion bushels of space.

Also, as of 1952, CCC owned slightly more than 500 million bushels of grain storage capacity. In the years 1953, 1954, 1955 and 1956, nearly 500 million more bushels capacity was built.

Thus, as rates and terms under UGSA became front burner items in early 1960, over 4 billion bushels of commercial capacity was under contract with CCC, and the net *useable* space available to the corporation in government-owned bins totaled something over 800 million bushels.

At that time, as well as in prior years and in later periods—consistent with the Charter Act language (as quoted)—Secretary Benson, chairman of CCC and the board of directors directed the CSS officials in Washington to give commercially owned facilities priority in storing CCC grain as compared to the government-owned bin sites. In turn, the state and county ASCS committees were so directed. This clear-cut policy sounds workable and decisive, but logistics were oftentimes a problem, which is not unusual in the grain business. County committees on many occasions authorized filling bin sites, even though commercial storage capacity might be available in a county at a later time.

In other instances, there was a desire to fill bin sites rather than to utilize commercial space.

During some of the question and answer exchanges in the Congressional halls, some of the legislators criticized USDA for not utilizing government-storage space on a priority basis before storing CCC grain in commercial facilities. Frankly, the provision in the Charter Act mandating a recognition of the usual and customary channels, facilities and arrangement of trade and commerce were being reconsidered.

As some members of Congress claimed, CCC was over-generous in establishing the per diem rate structure for grain storage. I reminded them that the amount paid per bushel for storage *had not*—until after 1956—attracted sufficient capital for building grain storage facilities to keep abreast of requirements. The government had found it necessary to erect some volume of storage to fill the need. To one who believes a profitable rate of return will attract free capital, I knew of no better test of the fairness or soundness of a rate structure.

After 1957, several things were happening; by late 1959, they were quite obvious to us in government.

☆ Cheaper and improved means of maintaining quality of grain had been developed. It was no longer necessary to "run" grain from one bin to another.

☆ Flat storage which costs less on a per bushel basis to construct, as compared to upright storage, had become commonplace.

☆ The grain industry had indeed become innovative in the storing and handling of grain.

☆ Amount of grain being produced and in turn the tonnage owned by CCC had increased dramatically so that the sheer magnitude of volume was instrumental in lowering per bushel or per unit storage costs to many storing warehousemen.

☆ Businessmen not in the grain business and dentists and medical doctors across the Great Plains and the Corn Belt were either entering the grain storage business or making inquiries about the possibility of doing so.

Still another development was unfolding. Annual reports of a few public companies and annual reports of cooperatives to shareholders revealed satisfactory to lucrative returns to owners or lessors of grain storage facilities—as those facilities were filled with CCC grain.

Had improved technology and economy of scale resulted in the *unchanged storage rates* being higher than necessary to satisfactorily house the growing volume of government-owned grain?

The answer: "Most likely!"

What to do?

Seemingly, a customary pattern in arriving at a rate structure under the UGSA had developed since the beginning of the pact in 1938. Traditionally, representatives of the government met with industry spokesmen in developing the several sections of the contract together with a remuneration schedule. After this step an open meeting was held where each and every warehouseman was given the opportunity to express his or her views.

The year 1960 was no exception. A hearing or town hall type meeting was organized for March 30 and 31 in Kansas City. About 1,000 people involved in grain storage attended and about 200 statements were presented and included in the record of the proceedings. At that time the CCC had storage contracts covering about 11,000 warehouses.

Herein lay a dilemma!

Heretofore, as the two parties to the contract got together to hammer out the terms and conditions to be included in the UGSA and a rate structure, both sides had been friendly to an increase in rates.

The situation in 1960 was different! The government insisted on tightening some provisions which equated into some increase in responsibility to the storing warehouseman. Conversely, the government *had* to achieve a rate reduction because:

* Reasons as cited were becoming more self-evident.
* The policy of favoring private industry (in lieu of all-out government involvement), as contained in the Charter Act, was on trial in Congress.
* The taxpaying public was entitled to savings from the application of improved technology in the storing and handling of grain not unlike the per unit cost of production savings being passed on to consumers by farmers.

I knew rates had to be cut—not just a little but in a big way.

Mr. McLain knew it! He, however, did not participate in the give and take with industry in 1960.

It simply was not possible to expect the 18 spokesmen for the grain industry to agree to a cut in rates as we, in CCC, deemed necessary. Certainly, the 1,000 attending the town hall meeting were not in a mood to embrace drastic surgery on the rate structure.

One avenue was left; namely, have the CCC Board of Directors approve a new and lower schedule of rates, include the new schedule in the revised UGSA and offer the pact to the industry for individual consideration.

This take-it-or-leave-it attitude was contrary to the spirit that had been built up between the government and industry in both Democratic and Republican administrations. There was no other option.

McLain asked me to develop a rate schedule for presentation to Secretary Benson and the CCC Board of Directors.

Before doing so, I requested McLain for assurance that the highest level of government would support the new proposed schedule. I simply was not in any mood to have the proverbial rug pulled out from under me—either in relation with Congress or in relation with the grain industry.

Several hours later the positive assurance was relayed to me.

I carried the new suggested UGSA rates to the CCC board meeting. It was a straight per diem schedule of .0037 cents per day for storage of wheat, corn, milo (sorghum) and barley. It was difficult to compare the new proposal with the one then in effect. Giving consideration to language change it did reflect a reduction of about 19 percent. On the basis of stocks then owned by CCC in commercial storage under UGSA, the projected savings to CCC for 365 days were estimated to be $85 million.

Reverberations from this page in the history of the grain price support program and/or the relations between government and the grain industry were both positive and negative. Now, over 20 years later the following impressions still linger:

☆ Government needed the cooperation of the industry and access to storage and handling facilities. Conversely, industry was completely dependent on government for grain to store and in turn for earnings. Government owned most of the carryovers. Because of this, government controlled the whip hand—a rather ugly monopoly if used unfairly.

☆ For more than a decade, because government grain stocks continued to increase, an increasing percentage of those in the grain business were becoming custodians of stocks as contrasted to marketers. Storage rate reductions caused many, both cooperative and private, to take a second look at their respective profit and loss statements and the earnings or lack thereof from specific activities.

As a final note, this chapter on the progression of agricultural development in the political life of our nation, it should be noted that neither the surplus grain situation nor the farm program issues generally were major factors in the presidential outcome in 1960. Analysis of the voting by states and regions in that year indicates that those issues were of minor significance in influencing voters' preference for one presidential candidate as compared to the other.

Storing warehousemen signed the new agreement containing the lower rate structure. In some instances the owners of the facilities felt the pinch of reduced per diem rates—particularly where investment in facilities per bushel cost was abnormally high. The same can be said for farmers who had constructed storage space for storing their grain under reseal. Per diem storage rates for reseal grain had also been reduced. The grain industry, as such, became more oriented towards marketing, a good omen for the future.

So ended another eight years of political debate on agricultural issues and on grain surpluses. It was a relief to pick up the several jackets "friends" had been holding for me in the wings and start a new chapter.

☆☆☆☆☆☆☆☆☆☆☆☆

CHAPTER 2

☆☆☆☆☆☆☆☆☆☆☆☆

Lessening Market Intervention

☆ ☆

A REEXAMINATION OF THE ROLE OF GOVERNMENT

On January 17, 1961, a few days prior to the arrival of the "New Frontier" group at the USDA in Washington on January 20, Secretary Benson held his last press conference as secretary of agriculture.

Secretary Benson held strong feelings on policies having to do with agricultural policy. Rather than describe his feelings, it would be more illuminating and accurate to list his key benchmarks as described by him during the January 17 press conference.

Introducing the benchmarks he said, "The management of our farms and ranches is best left in the hands of farmers and ranchers themselves. Local, state and federal governments can and should provide sound help, but farmers must be free to control their own operations and permit price to play its traditional role in directing production and consumption.

"We have, therefore, tried to move steadily in the direction of more freedom for farmers to farm and toward economically sounder government programs for agriculture based on research, education and the expansion of markets."

Some of the benchmarks follow.

Four-fifths of agriculture is free of government production controls and only five of some 250 commodities produced commercially are still subject to such controls.

☆ ☆ ☆

Fifteen of the 21 commodities under price support are selling at, or above, their support levels. Example: Soybeans, the fifth largest crop in dollar volume, were over 40 cents per bushel above support levels last week.

☆ ☆ ☆

Only 12 commodities are currently in government inventory. Ten items in inventory in 1953 are no longer in government storage.

☆ ☆ ☆

Farmers voted corn free of control in 1958. Under more realistic price supports, corn has been moving into consumption at a rate 9 percent ahead of a year ago.

☆ ☆ ☆

Commodities subject to no price support are currently in a strong position with a favorable outlook.

☆ ☆ ☆

Exports of all farm commodities are at new record highs with $4.8 billion in sales during the 1960 calendar year, making our eight-year total $30.4 billion, of which 68 percent was sold for dollars.

☆ ☆ ☆

Farmers' costs increased 133 percent from 1939 to 1952 and have increased only 4 percent in the past eight years.

☆ ☆ ☆

Farmers have greatly increased their capacity to produce in the past eight years. On substantially the same acreage feed grain production is up 38 percent.

☆ ☆ ☆

The payment-in-kind (PIK) export program has operated to reduce CCC stocks while still utilizing normal trade channels for exports:
  ☆ From the beginning of the program, 1,351,525,000 bushels of wheat moved under PIK through June 30, 1960, with 356,361,000 bushels of wheat moving out of CCC stocks because of PIK payments.

☆ From the beginning of the program, 737,212,000 bushels of feed grains moved under PIK through June 30, 1960, with 70,000,000 bushels of feed grains moving out of CCC stocks because of PIK payments.

The benchmarks as compiled by Benson prior to his relinquishing his position as secretary of agriculture, the position he held for eight years, were publicized for the purpose of supplying an accounting of his stewardship of agriculture during the Eisenhower presidency.

As one reviews his statements, one readily observes that he attached great importance to his accomplishments in lessening the involvement of CCC and/or the federal government in the operation of farms and the commodity markets.

Having been a member of the Benson group for nearly eight years in six different capacities in Washington, D.C., and in St. Paul—and staying on through the transition period which ended during the Washington snow storm January 19, 1961—I realized I had been in government service during a period of great changes in our food and agriculture sector. For example, per acre yields of corn and sorghum—the most important grains for animal feed—had increased about 5 percent per year during the eight-year period.

Perhaps the most significant economic happening for farmers during the period was the stability of production costs—an increase of 4 percent in the eight years—as emphasized by Secretary Benson in his press conference.

As this eight-year period ended and as I noted the benchmarks of accomplishments, it was only natural to ponder on several personal observations as to how well or how poorly we had performed.

I had a feeling then that Benson could have been more flexible in dealing with the Congress. Now, over 20 years later and with much more personal experience with the development of legislation and with agricultural policy issues in Europe, Asia, South America and elsewhere, I am less certain that he should have been more flexible.

Certainly, administration spokesmen—cabinet and sub-cabinet officers—must always be good listeners. There are always new ideas over the horizon. Those in power do not have a corner on original thinking.

Conversely, in our system of government, if the president's spokesman on agricultural policy matters fails to enunciate the limits for expenditure of federal funds as influenced by legislation or proposed new laws, the necessary discipline will simply not be honored. Congress, by its very nature, will not exercise restraint.

Very much to his credit, through the eight years, Benson "took" the criticism from groups in opposition to his views. He was a buffer for President Eisenhower's agricultural policy issues.

Finally, we who worked for him understood well his views on policy matters. If we did not, it was easy to find out.

During the period, there was a further polarization of agricultural interest groups in the two camps favoring more or favoring less government involvement in farm matters. Such divergent views only illustrate the difficulty and ofttime impossibility of arrivng at a consensus.

Before moving on to a discussion of the 1961-1969 period, I am going to describe one legislative change contributing to the Eisenhower-Benson philosophy of retrenchment of government involvement in agriculture.

WHEAT FLOUR AND CORNMEAL DONATIONS

Most presidential candidates during some stage of their campaign for election promise to cut waste in government spending. Without exception this goal proves to be elusive after the candidate becomes president. While there are many reasons the campaign promise is hard to fulfill, there is one over-riding reason wasteful practices in government are hard to correct.

The chief reasons contributing to the difficulty to cut waste are the president's own appointees—cabinet and sub-cabinet officers.

Highly touted commissions and study groups are able to identify areas of waste and areas of duplication, but the president's own appointees have the greatest opportunity to see—firsthand—the day-to-day weaknesses of ongoing authorized activities, or the manner in which those activities are administered. They (the policy level or near policy level appointees) also have the best opportunity to make changes through administrative action or by working with the Congress in securing a change in the law or laws if such is required to effectuate economies.

The subchapter will be an explanation of one change in a law which resulted in substantial dollar savings over a quarter of a century. The change treated businesses involved more fairly; it also resulted in better service to the recipients of the legislation as intended by the Congress.

I refer to a surplus food donation provision, Public Law 85-683, which authorizes the CCC to purchase wheat flour and cornmeal for donation purposes, rather than entering into contracts to have flour and cornmeal milled from grain in the CCC inventory and authorizes CCC to sell an equivalent amount of wheat and corn to offset such purchases of flour and cornmeal. The latter authorization to sell an equivalent amount is not mandatory. This law was approved in August, 1958, by President Eisenhower.

As we compare the expenditure of government funds for flour and cornmeal in that period during the late 1950s to the billions of dollars expended by several other government agenices, most notable of which is defense, this short story may seen inconsequential. This is what makes the description meaningful because most of us understand modest dollar figures, whereas big dollars overwhelm us. The narrative follows:

My first assignment in Washington, D.C., in the two-year period of 1956 through 1957, was as Associate Director and Director of Grain Division in Commodity Stabilization Service (CSS). I observed the division-awarded contracts over a 12-month period to have about 25 million bushels of CCC wheat processed into flour and about 6 million bushels of corn processed into meal for domestic and overseas donations.

The domestic donations were authorized in Section 416 of the Agricultural Act of 1949. The overseas portion was under Title II of the 1954 Agricultural Trade Development and Assistance Act (PL 480).

In a 12-month period, 780 contracts were entered into with 72 flour mills located in 28 states and 35 cornmeal millers located in 17 states.

Distribution of the products was made to domestic donation outlets in all 48 states plus Alaska, Hawaii, Puerto Rico and Guam and to non-profit voluntary welfare agencies at East, Gulf, West Coast and Great Lakes ports for export to needy persons in foreign countries.

The millers retained the by-products, under a competitive bidding procedure. CCC shipped the wheat and corn from storage to the contractor's mills and arranged for delivery of the processed flour and cornmeal from the mills to the recipient agencies. Contracts awarded to millers were made on the basis that delivery of the flour and cornmeal to the delivery point specified by the consignee resulted in the lowest possible cost to CCC.

It was not unusual to receive 100 bids in response to a single bid solicitation.

The evaluation of bids had to include, in addition to comparative price analysis of the cost of milling, the cost of transporting the CCC grain from the multiplicity of storage locations to the mill; the cost of transporting the milled product from the mill to destination points to all utilization points, as mentioned, in such a manner as to best utilize in-transit benefits; and the determination of market value of by-products retained by the contractors (millers).

Dr. Arnold Dahl, an able civil servant, was responsible for administering this program. He and his staff and regional people devoted many man hours to this effort—administrative costs were high.

In consultation with Dr. Dahl and others, we developed the concept that a much better, more efficient method to distribute flour and cornmeal would be to secure legislation authorizing CCC to purchase wheat flour and cornmeal on a competitive f.o.b. consignee delivery point basis.

I formally developed the proposal and discussed it with Assistant Secretary Marvin E. McLain. He agreed, as did Secretary Benson and the bureau of the budget.

In the development stage, I had discussed the matter with a freshman Congressman, Albert Quie (R.-Minnesota). He volunteered to introduce the bill and did so on May 19, 1958.

Senator Edward Thye introduced a similar bill in the Senate also on May 19.

Now for the lighter side.

Political judgment dictated the proposal would be enacted unanimously by the Congress. The proposal made good sense.

Congressman Jennings (D.-Virginia), a majority party member with some seniority, introduced an identical bill. Hearings were scheduled by the House Committee on Agriculture not on the *Quie* bill but on the *Jennings* bill. I was learning the ways of Washington and something about the meaning of the *majority* party.

The committee and the House passed the bill without amendments.

Senator Thye had done his work in the Senate. His bill was also passed without amendment.

President Eisenhower signed it, thereby making it a law August 19, 1958.

This was a small issue, perhaps an irrelevant matter, compared to *big* issues in Washington, but it allowed millions of bushels of wheat to move into consumption without the necessity of its first passing through CCC. The same was true for a smaller amount of corn.

The new law saved hundreds of hours of civil servants' time.

There is a policy concept back of the change in the law which I thought may have been clearly demonstrated at that time. Now, over a quarter of a century later, I am not sure the concept is really understood or if it is, government administrators are inclined to become calloused and oblivious to waste. Certainly, the same can be said for many legislators.

The concept to which I refer is one of "market forces." In discussing this matter with Benson and McLain, they were fully supportive. In fact, subsequent developments lead me to believe one of the major contributions of the Benson era—maybe the chief one impacting commodity prices—was Secretary Benson's belief that forces registered in a market for farm products can more adequately reflect true supply and demand as total use requirements are filled from free market stocks. Producers gain. Those nearby an export outlet or domestic processing plant—over a period of time—receive the advantage of that location as compared to producers farther removed and subject to greater transportation costs.

Further, during that period, I felt progress had been made in developing a better understanding of the total stock concept which encompasses both free and government-owned or controlled stocks. The theory is quite simple. While certain statutory provisions govern disposition of government-owned or controlled stocks, the total volume of any one commodity, be it wheat or corn or something else, includes the total volume—both privately owned and government-owned or controlled.

The point was worth pursuing then and it is today. "Surplus disposal" was an often-used term as donation programs expanded or when PL 480 activity increased. It was not uncommon to be pressured by academia or legislators to program commodities for PL 480 from CCC stocks. The same can be said for the "backers" of barter, which will be discussed in the next chapter. Several exporters and international traders were not free of guilt in being happy with the privilege of raiding CCC-owned stocks—government had performed the function of enmassing stocks into large volumes.

The point is simple.

The tighter the "back door" to CCC stocks is kept closed—the more firmly the front door or the entry to CCC can be maintained.

It costs taxpayers money for title of grain or other commodity to pass to CCC; it costs again when title passes from CCC to a seller or user.

Why let it happen?

The implementation of nonrecourse loan programs, which traditionally are the backbone of non-perishable price support authorities, naturally results in CCC owning stocks in years when production is in excess of annual use.

Disposition programs—domestic and overseas—if limited to free stocks automatically cause the ripple of such movement to be registered in the cash and futures markets. Thus the price signals to producers and users are generated and in some years at least the door into CCC storage can remain closed—hence the inherent saving of a further outlay of funds.

Following the harvest of the 1982 wheat and corn crops, as production was again significantly in excess of disappearance (use), I was once again appalled to learn that several legislators had proposed legislation which if enacted would have resulted in CCC processing government-owned wheat and corn into flour and cornmeal for donation purposes. I am not opposed to the donations—if that is public policy—but why revert back to the wasteful practice of funneling commodities through the front door and out the back door of CCC? There is no good economic reason for such meddling!

The legislative action authorizing the purchase of wheat flour and cornmeal for donation from the open market is only one example of an action designed to lessen government waste and to strengthen free market institutions. The activity only illustrates the desirability of vigilance in weeding out government intervention, when such intervention contributes nothing whatsoever to the creation of wealth nor utility to commodities.

MARKET FORCES OR GOVERNMENT MANDATE (1961 TO 1969)

As I observed Secretary Freeman and his new group take over USDA in January, 1961, the scenario and actions followed a pattern which any reasonably astute farm reporter could have written with precision.

Many old hands from the Production and Marketing Administration (PMA) days under Secretary Brannan of the Truman era were still in USDA and were anxious to reinstate the preeminence of production and marketing controls as envisioned in the 1938 and 1949 laws.

As per script, a crash Feed Grain Act was enacted and approved within nine weeks—March 22, 1961.

Food distribution programs were increased, and a pilot food stamp program was commenced.

Greater publicity attended the overseas food aid programs under PL 480.

So far as possible, and consistent with the projected script, the chief thrust in the Agricultural Act of 1961, which became law in

August, was based on the old PMA philosophy of rewarding compliers and penalizing noncompliers of the farm program provisions.

Twenty-eight months were to elapse before wheat farmers in a referendum were to advise USDA that the old production controls—with teeth—were no longer consistent with the changing farm scene.

The scenario unfolded about as follows:

Early in 1961, as the "new team" dumped an unprecedented volume of CCC corn into the market, for the reason—at least in my opinion—of penalizing noncompliers and thereby attaining a higher percentage of program participation, irritating a great many farmers. The action, of course, devastated the price discovery machinery because CCC made the price. Using an old cliché, the back door and the front door to CCC were thrown wide open.

Three major happenings in the agricultural community had gradually transpired during the decade of the 1950s.

- ☆ "Our farm program," had become the "government program." I alluded to this development in the prior chapter.
- ☆ U.S. agriculture had gradually become a part of the world scene. Overseas markets were now necessary to maintain reasonable farm income. Further, U.S. trading partners and competitors expected U.S. agricultural policy makers to recognize global requirements and disciplines.
- ☆ Improved production practices had operated in a manner further widening the productivity outturn per acre between progressive farmers and those content with the older style farming techniques.

WHEAT PRODUCER REFERENDUM

One little remembered provision in farm program legislation was deleted in the law beginning in 1964—for the wheat to be seeded in the fall of 1963 and the spring of 1964. I refer to the 55-million-acre minimum national wheat acreage allotment. Prior to the Congressional action in 1963, as contained in the 1964 law, the secretary was restricted from reducing the national allotment below 55 million acres. Because of increased yields, the nation simply could not absorb the production from 55 million acres. The surplus was ending up in the hands of CCC and, in some years, in livestock rations.

The major thrust of the Freeman people in having the 55-million-acre allotment permanently killed was to pave the way for the secretary to set individual farm allotments as deemed necessary to control production to the volume required.

Wheat farmers were given the opportunity to decide between two different programs of wheat price supports.

The first choice called for penalties by farmers planting in excess of their respective acreage allotment and provided for issuance of marketing certificates which were based on the quantity of wheat estimated to be used for domestic human consumption and a portion of the volume estimated for export.

The second choice imposed no penalties for overplanting but that wheat grown by producers in compliance with their allotment would be supported at 50 percent of parity.

The first choice was defeated in the referendum in May, 1963, but not without many bitter confrontations out in the country. Those in favor or in opposition were exactly as was to be expected. The AFBF opposed the first choice and the NFU favored it. Farm program enthusiasts generally supported the choice which was defeated.

As I watched the contest at the time, it seemed obvious that producers would oppose tight controls. Again there were several reasons.

☆ Time had elapsed since the "New Deal" days.

☆ Many wheat farmers expected that the Congress and the Kennedy administration (in the event of a defeat of the first system) would support new legislation rather than allow the second choice to become operative. They were correct. A new law passed early in 1964.

☆ There was also an attitude of antagonism in the wheat-producing areas toward government planners and their attempts to oversell a government program.

☆ Finally, wheat farmers—out in the country—had become more globally oriented than the planners on the Potomac. Many of them had been to far-off places and had visions of much more wheat moving into consumption overseas.

While the Cotton-Wheat Act of 1964 was not a direct outgrowth of the negative referendum results, some provisions were designed to put more money in the pockets of wheat producers. The year 1964 was an election year.

The domestic bread tax was born!

Wheat food processors were required to make purchases of certificates to cover all the wheat they handled.

The goal of the certificate program was to increase the financial reward to producers in compliance with acreage allotments and land-diversion programs.

Price supports, as made up of CCC loans and certificates, for the farmers' share of wheat required for domestic consumption (45 percent of a complying farmer's normal production in 1964), were established at $2 per bushel. The balance of the production (55 percent) was supported at $1.30 per bushel.

The wheat certificate program—commonly referred to as the "bread tax"—was in reality an old idea lifted from the Agricultural Adjustment Act (AAA) of 1933—the processing tax invalidated by the Supreme Court in 1936, as mentioned in the previous chapter. It was another instance supporting the thesis that few farm program provisions are really new ideas; they are reruns from former programs.

INCOME DEFICIENCY PAYMENTS

The use of income deficiency payments to maintain some level of income to producers of a few specific commodities is a concept that has spawned great controversy—perhaps more than any other theory.

Several reasons contribute to this ongoing debate between those favoring direct payments versus those who oppose them.

Secretary Brannan, during the Truman administration, promoted the concept of deficiency payments to maintain some level of farm income. His suggestion that direct payments to producers of certain perishable commodities such as pork (hog producers) caused Allan Kline and the AFBF to strike with great force against the idea. The relative strength of the AFBF was high among the nation's farmers— particularly with the hog and other livestock producers.

The Brannan plan combined with the Allan Kline countercharge impacted the attitude of many producers regarding the acceptability of direct U.S. government payments as part of their (producers) gross and net incomes.

Some farmers view the act of applying for deficiency payments as a demeaning experience.

Still other farmers doubt the degree of certainty in receiving deficiency payments over a period of years.

Farmers with larger gross sales fear—with good reason—that limitation of payments per farmer at a shrinking level will result in a very real limitation on economic opportunity.

As years have passed, the negative attitude toward deficiency payments has lessened. I believe, on balance, the nonrecourse loan concept and the uncertainty prevailing, as and if commodities are delivered to CCC in payment of loans, has proven to be more worrisome to producers and the industries servicing farmers and rural communities.

A discussion of the deficiency payment concept seems appropriate as we look at the period of time following the rejection of wheat production and marketing controls "with teeth" in May of 1963. When Secretary Freeman learned that wheat farmers turned their backs on fixed controls he seemed to seek out other avenues to shore up wheat and other grain farmers' incomes. Deficiency payments and their roles received more publicity. Public Law 480 received more emphasis. The bread tax, as already explained, was legislated. Export market development programs moved closer to center stage.

This greater attention to global markets seemed to me to be the signal that high price supports through nonrecourse loans was over. Secretary Freeman, in his public utterances and actions gave that impression. I suspect it was an unpalatable pill to swallow. But he left me with the impression that he had turned to actions other than increasing loan rates to increase and/or maintain farm income.

The voluntary wheat program as provided in the 1964 Cotton-Wheat Act continued in effect with minimum changes through 1970.

The voluntary feed grain program continued. Diversion payments were made as commenced in 1961. Payments were made on the basis of the producer diverting feed grain acreage to soil-conserving crops or practices.

The market price of cotton was supported at 90 percent of estimated world price levels. Special payments were made to cotton farmers for participation in the acreage control program—with special provision for small cotton acreages.

It seemed to me the realization that fiscal restraint as dictated by the Bureau of the Budget and the necessity to observe global food and fiber requirements caused U.S. food and agriculture policy as influenced by USDA to be maintained on "hold" the last five years of the Johnson administration. These same restraints gave birth to the National Advisory Commission on Food and Fiber which will be discussed following consideration of food stamps and the policy to implement an expanded food-aid program.

FOOD STAMPS—A CONCEPT

Making of nutritious food available to low-income people, the unemployed or otherwise unfortunates is a function generally conceived to be within the province of government—at some level.

In some states or communities, a few churches have done an admirable job of taking care "of their own." Most prominent is the example of the Mormons, or otherwise known as the Church of Jesus

Christ of Latter-Day Saints. One of the basic doctrines held by the members of this faith is the dedication to personal and collective responsibility for physical survival—free of assistance from the state. As commendable and effective as this precept is, it encompasses only a minor percentage of the nation's population. Hence, the matter of food distribution or food aid remains an issue of major national significance.

As a full-time farmer and one interested and involved in local political issues, it was abundantly clear to me in the late 1940s and early 1950s that the matter of supplying food to the unfortunate would become a major national agricultural and food issue. Particularly so in our nation which was being called upon to feed the hungry masses in the world and with unused physical productive capacity to do much more.

Lester Anderson, a young county commissioner, in my home of Blue Earth County—certainly no flaming liberal but a progressive thinker—talked this matter of food aid on many occasions. After all, "welfare" was the heaviest cost item in the county budget—in this one of the more wealthy counties in the state of Minnesota and the nation. Anderson favored a national food stamp program, on a trial basis. This was at the time of Mr. Truman's presidency.

I had great sympathy for the recommendation of Commissioner Anderson, who continues in that capacity to this day.

As I observed the domestic food distribution programs as administered by the Eisenhower administration, of which I was a member, I became more disillusioned with the program of distributing food items in surplus and being held in CCC inventory. I am speaking of such items as wheat (wheat flour), corn (cornmeal), dry edible beans, dry skim milk, butter and cheese on occasion and from time to time other more exotic items.

The most fundamental weakness of food distribution being tied to CCC inventories is identical to the principle discussed previously under "Wheat Flour and Cornmeal Donations." The same glaring weakness came into play in the administration of the Feed Emergency Program, whereby coarse grains were supplied, from CCC stocks, at reduced prices to drought stricken livestock producers and feeders.

The very circumvention of normal channels of distribution (wholesalers, retailers and transporters) whereby the function of adding place, time and form utility was taken over by the federal bureaucracy—for a short but unpredictable period of time—was an unconscionable action of bloodletting to our normal enterprising system of economic activity. As I discussed this folly with members of the

Congress—both formally and informally—many agreed but others were callous to the effect of such action.

The ultimate question which I often asked as the opportunity presented itself was "How would you, Mr. Congressman, like to be the proprietor of a retail establishment for the sale of food and/or feed products financed and structured to service a community with basic needs and have the value of your competitively purchased inventory cut in half or made much less valuable—far below the original cost—by emergency and unpredicted action of the federal government?"

Many understood!

Others replied that the benefits to the community and society generally of such crash food and feed distribution programs far outweighed the damage to the normal system of doing business.

You may be sure the number of votes in a given Congressional District affected pro or con was usually more important to many legislators than the long-term wounds inflicted on the food and food distribution and retail system.

The matter of food stamp legislation was discussed by several of us during the Eisenhower-Benson era. The follies of off-again, on-again food distribution programs were well understood. Local governments generally, as intimated earlier, were quite naturally receptive to more dependable and expanded food-aid programs, provided they (the programs) were underwritten by the federal government.

In general this was the setting when President Kennedy and Secretary Freeman assumed power. Simply stated, the stage was set for the implementation of a food stamp program.

We in the Benson team feared the likelihood of a food stamp program being in addition to food distribution schemes. We felt this duplication would likely happen as CCC inventories of some commodities continued far in excess of foreseeable disappearance.

A pilot food stamp program was commenced by the Kennedy-Freeman Administration. The obvious outcome was permanent legislation.

The Food Stamp Act of 1964 was enacted. To carry out the provisions of the act an authorization for expenditure of not in excess of $75 million for the fiscal year ending June 30, 1965, was enacted—with larger amounts for ensuing years. It was to be well along in the Nixon years before every county in the United States qualified for food stamp coupons. States were made responsible for administration of the program.

Over the past 20 years—since the 1964 legislation was enacted—the suggestion that a negative income tax scheme should be legislated as a replacement for food stamps or that money (dollars) from the U.S. Treasury be issued to food stamp recipients rather than food stamp coupons. Without exception, so far as I know, as this concept is discussed, those favoring or opposing such a view admit or believe such dollar assistance would become another so-called entitlement program. In the absence of restrictions as to the items eligible for purchase with food stamps, the utilization of such for non-necessities or other items would simply be unacceptable public policy. I personally believe this to be true whether the judgment is applied to food stamp recipients residing in New York City or in rural Minnesota.

The advent of food stamp legislation was a foregone conclusion. Democrats more often than not claim credit for the program coming into being. Quite often a number of Republicans maintain expenditure in the billion-dollar-a-month level is excessive, wasteful and fraught with fraud. Investigations give some credence to this charge. Further, as level of unemployment has decreased, federal expenditure for food stamps has not lessened to the extent judgment would dictate.

From the policy view, I maintain food stamp legislation and the magnitude of the program would have been very similar, regardless of the political party in control of the executive branch. Food stamp legislation was inevitable in the nation's political process. Both political parties have a history of supporting farm legislation designed to enhance farm income. Political judgment mandates that a reasonably free society insists the lower end of the income spectrum be recognized with financial favors as an offset to income enhancing legislation for a few (farmers).

Those who have maintained that food stamps will be in addition to food distribution to the needy of CCC-owned stocks of selected food items—such as dairy products—have a sound logical argument.

As CCC-owned or -controlled inventories of agricultural commodities dwindled or were non-existent, food aid was confined generally to the issuance of food stamps. But as CCC again acquired stocks via the price support programs, public clamor caused government administrators to again authorize donations of surplus dairy products to the states for distribution to needy people. As an observer, this action seemed inevitable to me. Of course, the dairy price support legislation was at fault for causing the accumulation of CCC stocks to transpire.

Once again, this happening is a classic example of opening the back door of CCC which automatically creates the draft thereby opening the front door to the same government entity. Food stamps are simply utilized to purchase food items—other than dairy products—in this illustration.

The consequence?

Distribution of government-owned (CCC) dairy products tends to reduce the volume moving through normal markets and thereby once again upsetting the normal channels of trade and contributing to the cost of the dairy products price support programs by further opening both the back door and the front door to CCC. This tends to nullify the basic intent of food stamp legislation.

NATIONAL ADVISORY COMMISSION ON FOOD AND FIBER

In the Washington cocktail circuit, there is one item always tailor-made for jokes—the matter of national advisory committees.

In reality, there are generally three reasons for a president and the Congress to assign a problem to an appointed commission for study and development of recommendations. In some instances, all three reasons may apply, in others, one or more may apply. The three reasons seem to fall as follows:

* A commission study postpones the need for definitive political action.
* Recommendations and / or findings of a commission diffuses the blame for politically unpopular laws or regulations.
* A commission's recommendations may be utilized to develop policy changes or to rewrite laws.

President Lyndon Johnson, January, 1966, charged the newly appointed members of the National Advisory Commission on Food and Fiber:

> . . . I am asking you as a Commission to make a penetrating and long-range appraisal of our agricultural and related foreign trade policies in terms of the national interest, the welfare of our rural Americans, the well-being of our farmers, the needs of our workers, and the interest of our consumers.
>
> I am asking you as a Commission to construct a thorough and searching study of the effects of our agricultural policies on the performance of our economy and on our foreign relations.
>
> I am asking you as a Commission to prepare a report which will serve as a guide and focus for future decisions and policies in the vast and diverse complex of food and fiber.

I was not at that time, nor to this day, privy to the rationale establishing the commission, but as an observer, I thought the timing for a study of government involvement in matters involving agriculture was indeed timely.

As the report stated, the evolution of U.S. agriculture had been a dramatic happening. Productivity had risen at an unprecedented rate. Real demand for farm products had not kept pace with increased production. PL 480 served as a foreign market development tool. And the significance of exports continued to be of increasing importance to the entire agricultural sector.

The submission of the findings of the commission to the president, July, 1967, near the end of the Johnson-Freeman era, came during a period which allowed ample time for agricultural policy students to absorb the appraisal and recommendations before major legislative changes were to be debated.

During my two appearances before members of the commission, it was quite apparent that individual commission members were not in agreement on many issues or proposed recommendations. This had to be expected because the very need for a commission highlighted the variation in views on how best to deal with dynamic forces buffeting farmers and the industry groups servicing the entire sector.

Commission members agreed: ". . . too many resources are available for farm production—which results in agriculture's capacity to oversupply its markets at prices which cover costs and return profits to many producers."

Members also agreed: ". . . on several important commodities, program price supports have been maintained at levels substantially above competition with other commodities and foreign production. . . . It also has held a price umbrella over world market prices, encouraging foreign producers to expand."

Perhaps the major recommendation of the commission for transition was "U.S. farm policy should be directed toward establishing a fully market-oriented agricultural economy as quickly as possible. . . ."

And for capitalizing on the global opportunity the report stated that "U.S. farm production should take full advantage of the rising demand for food and fiber around the world, and exploit the comparative advantages in the production of food and fiber commodities."

Did the recommendations of the commission have an impact on U.S. agricultural policy?

Yes!

The extent of impact cannot be accurately gauged but I was given the privilege or the dubious honor of shepherding the Agriculture Act of 1970 through the Congress—about three years after the public release of the recommendations of the Food and Fiber Commission. One factual incident best describes the significance of the commission's recommendations on my thinking or at least as that thinking was assessed by a not so friendly Washington lobbyist.

Keep in mind that the commission came into being and completed its assigned task under a Democratic president.

I was a presidential appointee in a Republican administration.

During the period in which I was negotiating and working with the Congress in developing the Act of 1970, I agreed to meet with several Washington-based representatives of as many farm organization and commodity groups. The volatile, impolite and outspoken representative of the National Farmers Organization (NFO) accused me of utilizing the commission report (which was on my desk) as my bible. I informed the gentleman that I would prefer his not confusing the commission with the message conveyed in my bible—but that I did recommend the commission report as *night time reading* for the agency heads reporting to me.

It is sufficient to say the findings and recommendations of the commission impressed me. I can also say with certainty that those recommendations have withstood the test of time.

FOOD AND AGRICULTURE ORGANIZATION
(FAO), ROME, 1969

The Food and Agriculture Organization (FAO), the agricultural development agency of the United Nations, came into being in 1943. The mission as developed at that time has been:

* Raising levels of nutrition and standards of living of the peoples under their respective jurisdictions.
* Securing improvement in the efficiency of production and distribution of all food and agricultural products.
* Bettering the condition of rural populations and thus contributing toward an expanding world economy and ensuing humanity's freedom from hunger.

In simple terms, "FAO was established for the purpose of overcoming world hunger."

I was the U.S. government representative to the 15th FAO Conference in Rome in mid-November, 1969. I had returned to USDA in January, 1969, as assistant secretary responsible for international affairs and commodity programs. A more complete explanation of my return to government under President Nixon and Secretary Clifford Hardin is contained in the next subchapter.

☆ *The U.S. delegation to FAO, Rome, 1969. Left to right: Congressman de la Garza, Texas; Deputy U.S. Assistant Secretary of Agriculture Andy Mair; Palmby; Congressman Ed Jones, Tennessee; and Congresswoman Catherine May Bedell, Washington.*

Secretary Hardin was unable to attend the conference in Rome at that time; I was, therefore, named to present the U.S. position.

I was not wildly enthusiastic about representing my government at this 15th conference because I had misgivings regarding the trend of programs being financed and administered by FAO in 1969. Equally important to me was the prevailing attitude within FAO which, in my judgment, was off-course from the mission of the organization.

In the eight years prior to my returning to USDA in 1969 I had headed the U.S. Feed Grains Council. The council was actively engaged in promoting improved livestock husbandry in at least a score of countries in Asia, Europe and South America. I had been dealing almost exclusively with commercial and academic interests in as many countries. We were not engaged in basic research. We were involved in the promotion and dissemination of proven and practical technical animal industry production and distribution practices. Our goal was to promote more efficient systems and thereby demonstrate the financial reward inherent to enterprisers. The total program was dynamic and it was working.

While the thrust and goal of the U.S. Feed Grains Council was not comparable to that of FAO, I had learned through hands-on experience the positive as well as the negative aspects of programs aimed at improving a nation's agricultural productivity. The matter of attitude—or as some may say, positive thinking—was and still remains of primary importance.

I was not enthused with the attitudes expressed at the Rome conference in that November, 1969, by other country delegates, particularly those spokesmen from the developing countries. To more clearly explain my negative assessment it would be well to share background.

Prior to the November conference, FAO policy makers had completed a planning document entitled, "Indicative World Plan." Such planning by an international organization must, of necessity, represent a great amount of compromise. This plan was not an exception to this tradition. The envisioned thrust as detailed in the plan emphasized sharing the abundance of the world at the expense of fulfilling the mission as contained in the preamble.

Several examples of wrong direction thrusts deserve mention.

* The plan left the impression the "green revolution" had gone far in winning the war against hunger. Several country delegates seemed satisfied with this assessment.
* The plan paid little heed to the generally accepted necessity for further family planning—so necessary to lessen vulnerability of food-short countries to starvation.
* A cornerstone of the plan's trade strategy was the assumption that the developed countries (the United States) should substantially curtail their inputs to agriculture in order to accommodate the export availabilities of the less-developed countries. More than a few country delegates chose this plan recommendation as the chief theme in their respective presentations. On behalf of the United States, I expressed serious reservations on this point. I stated that the world needs the output of the areas—wherever they are—that can produce the most efficiently. And only in this way can adequate supplies of food and fiber be made available to increasing populations.
* International commodity arrangements or other programs for organizing markets also figured in the plan's trade strategy. I also took exception to this recommendation even though a majority of delegates enthusiastically supported the item. I

shared the U.S. view that instead of freeing up trade in the world such arrangements brought rigidities to marketing. Agreements are unlikely to be viable when prices are determined largely by governments that may have mutually inconsistent objectives.

☆ The plan did recognize a few positive aspects of the world food situation. It stated, "It is the market demand in relation to supply that determines whether prices will rise—causing a food crisis with greatest hardship among the lower income strata in the urban areas . . ." This was an accurate and timely observation.

☆ Further, in relation to world commerce, the plan urged a reduction in protectionism. This sound recommendation, if put into practice, would give relative comparative advantage a chance to function.

I left the FAO Conference with a heavy heart.

I was the *only* country delegate reemphasizing the *one* and *only* mission of FAO.

A large lopsided majority of country delegates supported the hidden thrust of the plan.

> Let us concern ourselves with more equitable distribution
> of that which is grown in the world at the expense of emphasis
> on production technology and efficiencies.

World developments were such within four years when food shortages did threaten. And when—consistent with the language in the plan—market demand in relation to supply did cause prices to rise.

Now, years later, the most important and most meaningful statement in the plan, in my judgment, was that simple recognition of economic truth—which was hardly recognized at that FAO Conference. Unfortunately, the price for veering away from the true mission proved to be costly indeed.

The most significant lesson on agriculture learned in this closing period of the decade of the 1960s has now become quite clear; that is, economic realism is still at work in the matter of food production and distribution.

Several developing countries in 1969 seemed more concerned about dividing plentiful supplies than focusing on their own respective developmental policies. Threatened world shortages did cause countries such as India—and others—to reexamine level of incentives to producers or lack thereof. Policy changes were made. As one would expect, the response from farmers and those servicing farmers was positive.

Now, after the fact, it is clear; the glaring weaknesses of the social planners became evident, and market forces did work to bring forth a greater abundance of food.

AGRICULTURAL ACT OF 1970

As stated throughout this book, the federal government, including the Congress, has for over 50 years been deeply involved in passing laws designed to intervene in the marketing as well as in the production and distribution of farm products. Because of this, anyone with a desire to really impact agricultural policy must at sometime participate directly in government. The cynics call the process of moving in and out of government as the revolving door. Maybe that descriptive phrase is as good as any other. In my opinion, the strength of the U.S. representative government system is dependent upon constant infusion of talent at the policy level.

From time to time office seekers emphasize the desirability of utilizing "dirt farmers" in the top positions in USDA. This is understandable because a large percentage of legislation enacted by each successive Congress in one way or another is farm income-oriented.

On the other hand—with all due respect to one moving to Washington, D.C., into a top USDA policy position directly from his or her farm—the person involved learns quickly of the complicated problems other than production-oriented issues confronting USDA policy makers. I know, because I was one of those during the Eisenhower-Benson era who did move into the Washington, D.C., arena directly from my farm.

During the eight years of the Kennedy and Johnson administration, I continued on in Washington, D.C., as head of the U.S. Feed Grains Council. My activities during those years and the role of the council will be described in a later chapter. During my years with the council, if indeed I needed a refresher course, I learned that not just 4 or 5 percent of our labor force is engaged in agriculture. (This is the percentage most often mentioned.) Factually, over 20 percent of the nation's labor force is involved in the production, processing, transporting, wholesaling, retailing—or in one way or another—servicing our nation's dynamic agricultural sector.

From time to time, it is almost a national pastime for one group or another to drive propaganda wedges between the various interest groups in the agricultural or food chain. The basic reason for such sensationalism is ignorance, short-run political goals or downright justification for existence of those perpetrating less than scholarly factual information. My work overseas quickly demonstrated to me that this phenomenon is not confined to the United States.

I know the agricultural enterprise as a whole in our total economy or in any other nation's total scheme of things is no stronger than its weakest link. Herein lies the weakness of the communist overall agricultural policy. Central planning simply does not lend itself to keeping the entire production, processing and distribution chain intact.

The matter of the many and diverse interest groups being involved in our nation's agriculture is only introduced at this time because some appreciation of the complexity of the sector is helpful as a major legislative initiative is about to be discussed.

I first met Clifford M. Hardin in Lincoln, Nebraska, where he was Chancellor of the University of Nebraska. Early in December, 1968, he was selected as Mr. Nixon's Secretary of Agriculture designate.

As Dr. Hardin discussed the possibility of my returning to USDA in the new Nixon administration, he gave me the opportunity to describe my specific interests and wishes for agricultural policy changes. I had given this subject considerable thought for several years. I recommended that he assign the agency responsible for farm programs (ASCS) along with the international agency (FAS) under the policy guidance of one assistant secretary. Since my arrival in Washington, D.C., 12 years earlier, I had observed the constant conflict between domestic farm programs and policies involving other nations and our own export and import policies.

Dr. Hardin agreed. The new job, Assistant Secretary for International Affairs and Commodity Programs, was born.

Further, we discussed in length the possibility or probability of the new Nixon administration moving in the direction of normalizing trade in farm products with the Soviet Union, People's Republic of China and other socialist countries.

Second, and of primary importance to the subject discussed in this subchapter, I expressed the hope that the new administration would achieve in new legislation a legal suspension of marketing quotas for wheat and cotton. Dr. Hardin made no commitment regarding his attitude on this rather delicate matter. He did give me a good hearing and that was satisfactory to me at that time.

After returning to USDA with Dr. Hardin in January, 1969, we spent several months debating farm program provisions preparatory to developing a policy for the Nixon administration. The then farm program legislation was set to expire December 31, 1970.

Both the House and the Senate were under the control of the Democrats.

Dr. Hardin advised both committees on agriculture in the House and the Senate that there would not be a Hardin program such as the Freeman, Benson and Brannan plans of his three latest predecessors as secretary of agriculture. He further advised that he did not consider himself to be the sole architect of farm policy.

Now, years later, political judgment dictates that the Congress would probably not have enacted any Hardin plan, had there been one. We did, as time passed, develop alternatives which provided the basis for the Agricultural Act of 1970.

A novel approach designed to increase communication between members of the House Committee on Agriculture and Dr. Hardin and the few of us working on legislation was born. Over a period of seven months a total of 27 informal evening discussion meetings were held. Some of the chief discussion items included parity and how it was mathematically derived, imports, exports, foreign markets, commodity agreements, domestic wheat and cotton programs, feed grain programs and Public Law 480.

In many ways the informal discussion meetings were helpful but time consuming for committee members as well as for us in the USDA. My personal calendar shows I made over 120 trips to Congressional meetings including the 27 evening sessions. Many of the smaller sessions were one-on-one discussions or with sub-committee members on specific portions of the legislative package. Twenty-two months from the date President Nixon was inaugurated were to have elapsed before enactment of the legislative package.

Each revision of farm legislation and the nuances involved in enactment contributes to humorous activities as well as frayed feelings. The 1970 act was no exception. The time elapsed from beginning of incubation to birth must have established a record. Hours of time expended by committee members was quite unbelievable.

Several milestone happenings are worth noting.

* Wheat and cotton marketing quota authorities were suspended.
* The extension of PL 480 authority contained language removing the prohibition against trade with the Soviet Union and China, if the president determines it to be in the national interest.
* A producer-payment limitation on a graduated scale was included.

* A "set-aside" approach was included, as a provision for program participation in grain and cotton programs.
* Low level price support provisions were included along with deficiency payments, the specific per bushel or unit amount constituted the beginning of the target-price concept. It should be noted the term "target price" was not mentioned. It was in subsequent legislation.

As usual with farm legislation, the law was really written in conference. Because of the diversity in views on some sections, a few of the conferees became quite bitter. While this is not unusual, the intensity of commitment to some pet provisions on the part of a few of the Senators resulted in bitter exchanges between conferees.

Suspension of cotton marketing quotas was particularly galling to Senator Ellender, Chairman of the Senate Committee. He had nurtured the cotton program during his entire career in the Senate. He was voted down by Senators Holland and Eastland, which had to be a bitter pill. In recognition of Senator Ellender's stature, I will say that he was most respectful and gracious to me following this episode.

The Hardin approach worked. The law never became known as the Hardin program. No one organization really confessed to liking the program. Farmers did. They liked the freedom to plant concept. They liked the freedom to substitute specific crops without losing program benefits.

Somewhat surprisingly, following passage of the act was the absence of producer criticism with the suspension of the wheat and cotton marketing quota authorities. It was obvious that farmers would prefer flexibility to do their own planning. They were ahead of their elected legislators.

Did the administration make friends with the new law?

Yes, out in the country, but not with the heads of general farm organizations nor with commodity interest groups.

The AFBF did not like the deficiency payment provisions—at least not publicly.

The NFU objected to the low loan rates.

The Grange just said, no!

The National Farmers Organization expressed displeasure with about every provision.

From a personal standpoint I was pleased with the new law. Of course, the act carried some excess baggage, but such was the result of compromise.

The success or lack of success a sub-cabinet officer realizes in developing legislation through working with the Congress is greatly

☆ *Palmby; William J. Kuhfuss, president of AFBF; and Roger Fleming, executive vice-president of AFBF, 1971.*

influenced by understandable policy guidelines as agreed to by the President and the White House staff. I am sure the same principle applies to a member of the cabinet. As the Agricultural Act of 1970 was being developed and as the painstaking negotiations with members of the committees continued, I felt comfortable with authorities delegated to me. I understood the limits acceptable to the President. There were good reasons for my confidence because the cast of players was informed and in accord.

In October, 1969, after the weekly meetings with Chairman Poage, Page Belcher and members of the House Committee on Agriculture had already commenced, Secretary Hardin arranged a meeting with President Nixon in the cabinet room on matters having to do with agricultural legislation. In addition to President Nixon and Secretary Hardin, the other two participants were Bryce Harlow, counsellor to the President and myself. The Friday afternoon meeting extended for nearly two hours. We discussed every important feature of the chief provisions to be incorporated in the new farm bill. During this session, it was abundantly clear to me that the four participants in this detailed exchange were on the same wave length. Further, I left the meeting convinced that President Nixon, while very positive in wanting new legislation, did not expect the new law to be more costly than the one due to expire December, 1970.

Would he veto legislation with a higher price tag?

I thought so; he inferred as much! That was satisfactory to me! I had never believed that more expenditures for farm programs were better for agriculture (including farmers) or the nation.

One other meeting which also took place in the cabinet room in the spring of 1970 proved to be of inestimable worth in convincing House members of the determination of President Nixon in containing the cost of the farm program. The meeting had been requested by Page Belcher, ranking minority member of the committee on agriculture.

Belcher believed in seniority; he expected the Republicans on the committee to take directions from him. He did the negotiating with Chairman Poage. Under this type of discipline, several of them were restless and wanted an opportunity to talk with President Nixon firsthand on the subject of farm legislation.

The most notable exchange was introduced by Congressman Kleppe, North Dakota. Kleppe asked the President about what the maximum annual estimated cost to the government he would approve. The answer was clear and firm: $3.1 billion annually—the then present annual expenditure for the farm program. This was the same figure Hardin, Belcher and I had been using. But coming directly from the President, the dollar figure took on added meaning.

Incidentally, the Act of 1970 cost about that much in 1971 and somewhat more in 1972 and much less the following year.

In working with the Congress on this complicated and costly legislation, I again gained an insight on how our "system" works. It was a reaffirmation of my earlier impressions gained during the Eisenhower period. I again learned that federal government spending can only be disciplined by the president and his designees.

Members of Congress have accomplished the art of voting costly benefits of every conceivable type for their constituents and supporters. I mention supporters because such may not even live or operate within the confines of a given legislator's state or district. While the Congress has given lip service to budgetary controls the representative system as we know must be disciplined by the chief executive officer. If the president does not do so, it will not be accomplished.

Consistent with this logic, I have observed instances when prestigious legislators have voted for and spoken eloquently in favor of costly farm program provisions and in off-the-record comments expressed the wish that the president would have the fortitude to not allow the provision to become law. Such is our "system"!

While I have referred to the Senate, most of the painstaking development had proceeded on the House side. Two members were key to its progress.

First, Chairman Poage of Texas devoted an endless amount of time and effort and on some provisions not necessarily to his liking.

Second, Page Belcher, ranking minority member from Oklahoma, who really had zero agricultural interests in his district, performed yeoman service in forcing through language consistent with agreed-to estimated budgetary outlays for the life of the act. He was a pillar of immovable strength.

The chief policy feature of the 1970 Act and one foreign policy and foreign trade aspect was discussed during the evening sessions. To my knowledge, it has not received publicity since that time. It deserves mention and explanation.

That significant feature is the provision providing for deficiency payments to meet a minimum national average producer *return* for wheat, cotton and feed grains. In this case and in some years—return to be made up of price received at the marketplace plus a deficiency payment if the national average price (from the marketplace) received by producers for the specific commodity during the first five months of the marketing year would be less than the statutory (target) price.

This was not a new concept. The prior administration under Secretary Freeman had embraced legislation providing for deficiency payments. It was of more than passing interest that a Republican administration endorsed such a policy. This policy was the quoted reason for the AFBF not supporting the legislation. The alternative traditionally had been higher loan rates which acted as a deterrent to utilization or consumption. And to more rigid production controls. This was the problem Secretary Benson fought through the decade of the 1950s. Stated simply, the low loan rate authority matched with a deficiency payment provision was a more market-oriented policy. Further, it was interpreted to be more friendly to consumers or in descriptive words, disliked by many producers; it could be labeled as a low food price policy. That was the main reason many labor- or consumer-oriented legislators voted for the act. In fact, it was a competitive price approach.

The low loan rate policy was conducive to expanding overseas markets; it was designed to encourage utilization. It was tailor-made for an ever-widening circle of global consumers, eager to express their wants and desires in the U.S. marketplace.

The significance of this policy and the interest of EEC officials with the attitude of the Nixon administration regarding this key policy issue did receive a fair amount of thought and discussion—more as an aside than in straight question and answer sessions.

An impression molded during my feed grains council years led me to believe several European agricultural leaders were hoping and expecting the Nixon administration to not embrace the deficiency payment concept. I believed they hoped the Republicans would opt for more producer price protection through higher price support rates. Such a policy would be closer to the EC policy.

During a conference with the four agency heads reporting to me—following enactment of the new law—this matter was discussed. There was common agreement—a continuation of a direct payment concept in the United States, matched with low loan rates, would continue to be in direct contrast to the forever increasing intervention, target and threshold price scheme in European Common Agricultural Policy (CAP). We all agreed the schism would likely widen in the future. It did!

★★★★★★★★★★★★★

CHAPTER 3

★★★★★★★★★★★★★

Striving Toward a
Global Market

☆ ☆

AGRICULTURAL TRADE DEVELOPMENT AND ASSISTANCE ACT

Two actions having lasting impact on agricultural policy were commenced during the 1950s. Both happenings involved the continent of Europe. One was the result of U.S. Congressional action and the other took place in Europe.

First, I refer to passage of the Agricultural Trade Development and Assistance Act, Public Law 480. The second historical development was the signing of the Treaty of Rome formalizing the customs union, European Economic Community (EC or EEC). The EEC and the Common Agricultural Policy (CAP) will be discussed in a later chapter.

Several pressures on the Congress culminated in the writing and passage of Public Law 480 in 1954. Now long after the fact, it would be well to remember that our immediate past relations with the continent of Europe at that time—following World War II—contributed to enactment of the new act.

U.S. farmers, particularly wheat producers, had become accustomed to supplying vast amounts of wheat and wheat flour to war-ravaged nations. Wheat output in the United States increased over 25 percent during the war years. All of the increase went overseas to feed hungry people. Many legislators referred to recipient countries as "our market."

In a true sense of the word, war-ravaged nations did not really fall into the category of being a market. The then temporarily destitute countries were recipients of donated wheat, flour and other food items from the U.S. larder.

During the early 1950s, one by one the countries of Europe were rebuilding their agricultural production. As this happened the United States again found itself carrying stocks of grain in excess to real demand at home and abroad. This situation, coupled with stated altruistic goals, contributed to the novel authority contained in the new Title I of the Agricultural Trade Development and Assistance Act.

Title I authorized the President of the United States to ". . . negotiate and carry out agreements with friendly countries to provide for the sale of agricultural commodities for dollars on credit terms or for *foreign currencies.*"

It was this latter authority which attracted the attention and support of legislators from wheat-producing states. Many nations in Europe and Asia at that time were woefully short of dollars and hard foreign exchange. They had plenty of their own currencies, which were being freely printed. The rationale: "Sell our wheat or flour or other farm products for local currencies and in turn authorize the recipient nation authority to invest the proceeds in developmental projects within the country."

This approach appealed to many lawmakers. The new law had its positive aspects. It resulted in a continuation of exports to nations unable to pay dollars. It helped hold down wheat surpluses within the United States, and over a few years' span resulted in the overseas movement of a substantial volume of cotton. And as the authority was continued, a growing volume of vegetable oil, corn, sorghum, nonedible fat, tobacco and other commodities were supplied under the country-to-country agreements.

The Congress did specify the executive branch: ". . . to further the use of private enterprise to the maximum" in carrying out the intent of the law. This was a significant policy because the very nature of the authority mandated U.S. officials to negotiate the terms and conditions contained in each agreement with friendly recipient nations. The necessity to negotiate government agreements or terms of sale—had it not been for the policy declaration of Congress—could easily have resulted in government-to-government trading. With few exceptions the actual selling under Title I, within the framework of the government-to-government agreements, has been done by the private trade.

Because of the uniqueness of the Title I authority and the magnitude of food assistance rendered to recipient nations that are lacking the economic ability to trade hard currency for food, the trends in evolving policies regarding the program are worthy of discussion.

It must be recognized that the economic and humanitarian aid rendered under Title I has been tremendous—in the early years of the program (1954 to the mid-1960s)—by the selling of commodities for local currencies and in the following years on long-term dollar sales at concessional rates of interest. Many political leaders in the United States claim political credit for having been responsible for developing the concept. The number of those assisting is so voluminous and so impressive that the naming of specific people is fraught with risk. PL 480 is best described as a foreign aid program and as a sales development scheme tailor-made for U.S. agriculture at a time when the need for food and clothing assistance was rampant in the world—and in a period of unprecedented development of technical agriculture in the United States.

Worth repeating is the observation that political leaders and much of the populace are content to bask in the sunshine of the nation's generosity in this government-financed program of food sharing. It is well to realize the concept of selling surplus food on concessional terms has also been convenient for the United States. How better could a nation dispose of merchandise not wanted or needed at home?

One other goal of Title I as contained in the original authority was the provision for export market promotion. Greater analysis and explanation of this activity is contained later in this chapter.

A part of the early framers of Title I looked upon the program as surplus disposal. A smaller number of supporters believed the authority would assist in building long-term dollar export markets. Both of these groups cherished the idea that surplus disposal and market expansion would increase farm income. A still smaller support group visualized Title I, Public Law 480, as having diplomatic value—a foreign policy tool.

As we examine the decision-making process in determining which specific countries should be offered agreements (benefits), the dollar magnitude of each, the commodity makeup, and agreed-to use of local currency funds, I volunteer my judgment of power polarization since inception of the program in 1954.

An analysis of political strength or lack thereof in administering a program as complicated as Title I over a 30-year period must reflect judgment. On the other hand, the role of Title I in effectuating U.S. foreign policy is quite clear.

In such an analysis, one must remember that Title I, PL 480 program activities are financed by Commodity Credit Corporation. The Secretary of Agriculture is the chairman of CCC. Further, the act states that only commodities declared to be in surplus by CCC are eligible for financing under the Title.

At the outset this would seem to place USDA in the driver's seat because the appropriation of funds is within the jurisdiction of the sub-committees for appropriation of the House and Senate for agriculture. Second, the commodity availability or commodity mix responsibility rests with USDA.

The hypothesis that USDA is the agency responsible for administering the activity is in theory only. Public Law 480 has continued to be a function delegated to USDA because of expediency. How better to finance a program designed to gain foreign policy objectives than through USDA!

Regularly, less wise officials in the Department of State and the Agency for International Development (State / AID) attempt to have PL 480 assigned to the Foreign Policy Agency, but agricultural interests have prevailed in opposing such transfer.

If the program were shifted to State/AID, I predict the annual dollar limitations would be halved or quartered immediately by Congress.

While commodity availability for programming lies within the jurisdiction of USDA, this little matter is relatively pro forma in nature.

If one were to construct a line graph illustrating relative political potency in the administration of Title I, PL 480 since inception, it would be drawn as follows:

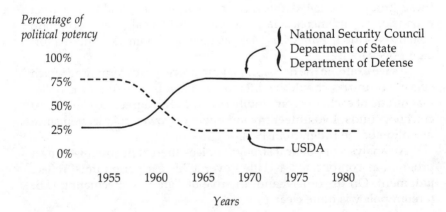

During the last years of the Eisenhower period PL 480 was labeled, "Food for Peace." Much goodwill had been gained through Title I and the dependable Title II food donations.

Somewhat ironically, and concurrently with our deeper military involvement in Vietnam, the percentage of proceeds of local currency approved within recipient countries for local defense purposes increased dramatically. This trend hardly seemed consistent with the title, "Food for Peace." George McGovern was the White House Food for Peace coordinator in that turn-around period. This trend in policy further illustrates the declining political potency of USDA.

In reality, Title I for the past 20 years has been a foreign policy tool. At times the promise of a Title I agreement to a sovereign nation or the hope of such a prize has been a reward for good behavior in the judgment of State or National Security Council (NSC). This type of diplomacy seemed to me to be particularly noticeable during the reign of Henry Kissinger as Secretary of State. Observing such diplomacy dished out or denied in a rewarding or punishing manner illustrates the economic importance of American agriculture. During the short period (1972 through 1975) when world grain stocks were somewhat tight in relation to need, the productivity of the U.S. agricultural system as compared to the communist agricultural system should increase the flow of adrenalin in any U.S. Secretary of State. It is difficult to imagine a king of olden years toting a more sought-after prize than a cargo of U.S. milling wheat.

PL 480 IN ITS FOURTH DECADE

Title I, with few modifications, survived three decades because of three basic reasons.

 * The ability and habit of U.S. agriculture to produce greatly in excess of domestic requirements and overseas willingness and/or ability to buy has not really changed over the 30-year period, except for limited periods, most notable of which were the years 1972 through 1975 when world grain and oilseed supplies were tight.
 * The need for food aid assistance continues to a long list of friendly countries. The intensity of the need naturally varies from year to year or from season to season.
 * Our nation's superiority in food production and distribution has traditionally been the most effective "ace" held by those responsible for accomplishing foreign policy goals.

While having diverse interests and goals, this combination of agricultural producers—and those who service them—and our diplomatic service working in tandem make a potent political entity.

In the early stages of the fourth decade of PL 480, many foreign policy enthusiasts are again touting the benefits of expanded Title I activity and expenditure—as do several agricultural interest groups. On the surface, a recommendation of this nature has many positive ramifications. Conversely, warning flags of concern must also be examined.

On the positive side, an expanded food aid program capitalizes on the greatest strength of the U.S. economy—namely, the nation's agriculture. Approaching this positive thought from the standpoint of an adversary—can anyone imagine the manner in which the Soviet Union would flex its diplomatic muscle should that nation possess our productive superiority in agriculture?

I can!

Another argument supporting greater PL 480 expenditure is the presumably lower cost to the U.S. Treasury as compared to paying farmers not to produce certain commodities or to pay for storage of surpluses. This is a viewpoint rather eloquently stated by those favoring this policy. Such a script in actual practice is not simple and is fraught with a certain amount of terror.

From the standpoint of a budgetary outlay saving, the thought process takes for granted that commodities moving overseas on concessional terms under PL 480 represent an additional market—additional to dollar sales or projected dollar sales.

This oftentimes is not true. The files are loaded with examples of Title I sales for local currencies or on the basis of long-term subsidized credit. These sales are not necessarily additional. It will always be thus as diplomatic and/or military goals are uppermost in determination of destination (recipient countries).

Herein lies a real conflict between foreign policy goals and Yankee salesmanship aimed at capturing the biggest bang for the buck—with several years in mind.

As an example of this conflict, let us assume that the authorization to expend $1 billion on Title I for a 12-month period is being allocated to recipient countries and by commodity mix.

Let us further assume (hypothetically) it is the professional opinion of USDA that the greatest benefit to U.S. agriculture—both in short term and in future years—could be achieved through programming a few hundred million dollars of soybean oil or other U.S. vegetable oils to an Asian country. And in this hypothetical situation the recipient

Asian country is eager to participate. In this example, the additional soybean meal or other oilseed meals generated in the United States as a consequence of the stepped-up processing to meet the increased oil shipments could readily be marketed for dollars. The global use market for soybean meal is far from being saturated—particularly at a price. Carrying this example a bit farther in the minds of some agricultural specialists, the larger agricultural family benefits—meaning soybean producers, processors and specific business groups servicing the entire industry.

In sharp contrast to this hypothetical example is a situation where the Defense and State departments in order to achieve agreement of a foreign government—shall we say in the European-African Theatre—for the continual privilege of air-base use by our armed forces consents to program corn and wheat against a $70 million Title I agreement. It may be argued that the transaction represents additional corn and wheat sales—over and above the volume that would have been sold for dollars—without a Title I. In fact, such a finding is a requirement according to the language and intent of PL 480. True additionality in such an instance is most difficult to document or to prove otherwise.

There is absolutely no doubt in my mind that the greater the influence of U.S. foreign policy goals on specific destination of commodities under PL 480, the weaker the substantiation for additionality becomes.

This trend as represented by forces other than U.S. trade expansion goals is thus one of the causes for concern as and if PL 480 is further expanded and more heavily influenced by State, Defense and the National Security Council (NSC).

One other worry inherent with an increased allocation of food aid to foreign countries is the possible impact of such on the recipient country's own agriculture. The matter can be explained quite simply.

Almost without exception, we who have involved ourselves with the problems of food shortages in the world agree on one thing. If a developing country—almost without exception—is to improve the diets (both quantity and quality) of its people, that country must develop its own agriculture. For example, India discovered this in the mid-1960s. I referred to this in the previous chapter as the matter was handled by FAO.

Of course, there are exceptions to what a nation can produce because of climate, weather, land area and other physical characteristics. That is why we believe in foreign trade.

On the other hand, there have been instances where a food aid recipient nation has become too dependent on an allocation of Title I from the United States. Again, India offers a good example, when in the early 1960s huge amounts of PL 480 wheat were being imported and became a disincentive to Indian wheat and rice producers. The nation, because of too little emphasis on its own grain production, came perilously close to disaster.

As a wrap-up of an assessment of PL 480 and as a judgment on the merits of expanding the program, I have two observations. One is historical, the other is projective.

After three decades, PL 480 is still a popular law because it has been generally well administered. As one would expect there have been exceptions.

For instance, in the early years of PL 480, from 1955 to about 1958, the United States may have been a bit over-zealous in selling wheat under the Title I authority to several developing nations. Canada felt our new market development sales program (PL 480) was cutting into its normal cash export sales. A structured system of consultation between representatives of the two nations was put into place. In fact, an expanded system of consultation among several export competing nations resulted. The outcome was a more sophisticated appreciation of global markets and a more meaningful recognition of additionality.

I have already referred to foreign policy and defense goals in some instances over-riding the true goal of PL 480.

Looking to the future for a proper niche of PL 480 in our bag of tools to disseminate foreign aid—and it is foreign aid—I still rate the positive impact to our nation from PL 480 expenditure far ahead of other foreign economic aid programs.

Further, I believe the program can be maintained and probably expanded into the future. I believe thus because:

  ☆ An expansion of PL 480 would be built on the most successful economic enterprise in our nation—agriculture.
  ☆ Longer term agreements, with proper safeguards and contingent upon annual appropriation of funds, are feasible for commodities—a higher percentage of which should be value-added items such as the soybean and/or vegetable oil example.
  ☆ The executive branch of our government can through proper discipline contain the over-zealous foreign policy achievers by insisting not only the written goals of PL 480 be respected but also the intent of the Congress. In reality, the accomplishment of this greater discipline would actually represent a reversal of policy as it has developed in the executive branch over the last three decades. This policy change on emphasis of PL 480 is not

what many State / AID career people have in mind but is necessary for the survival of the law as it has been intended.

Does this mean the foreign policy goals of our nation as determined by the president should not impact or influence PL 480 activities?

Not at all!

In fact, I believe those goals can be better attained by administering the PL 480 legislation in a manner that respects long-term foreign policy goals—with much less weight given to short-term objectives.

THE BARTER PROGRAM

Title III of the Agricultural Trade Development and Assistance Act (Public Law 480) authorizes CCC . . . to the maximum extent practical, barter or exchange agricultural commodities owned by CCC for various items as follows:

* Strategic or other materials which the United States does not domestically produce its requirements and which entail a risk of loss through deterioration.
* Materials, goods or equipment required in connection with foreign economic and military aid and assistance programs.
* Materials or equipment required in substantial quantities for offshore construction programs . . . in cooperation with other government agencies.

The act wisely contains two caveats which limit the use of the authority. The Secretary of Agriculture shall ". . . take reasonable precautions to safeguard usual marketings of the United States and to assure that barters or exchanges under this authority will not unduly disrupt world prices of agricultural commodities or replace cash sales for dollars."

The barter and stockpiling division in CSS administered the barter program; the division was staffed with capable civil servants. Activity reached its peak in 1958 to 1959. Most commodities owned by CCC were eligible for acceptable barter transactions, but grains and cotton were most frequently sought.

During this period, when CCC owned a cumbersome surplus of agricultural commodities, a strange phenomenon was developing. The dollar value of hard items in the strategic reserve and supplemental stockpile totaled over $8 billion—about the same as the total of agricultural commodities owned by CCC.

Pressure on USDA in 1958 and early 1959 to do more and more bartering seemed to come from many corners. Several members of the

Congress expressed unusually great interest in pushing specific proposals. The Secretary of the Interior looked upon the program as a vehicle to strengthen or as a minimum to support prices of several metals.

Somewhat as an aside, but as a lesson learned through frustration, I discovered that proponents of barter or barter-type transactions are most aggressive when:

☆ Dollars or other hard currency are scarce in a given country.

☆ World demand for a particular metal is static or depressed.

☆ Volume of agricultural commodities owned by the U.S. government (CCC) is in excess of foreseeable demand.

The House committee on agriculture held hearings in 1959 on proposed legislation, which if enacted would have mandated CCC to barter agricultural commodities at a rate in excess of $300 million annually.

The proposal was not enacted by the Congress.

I was the government witness.

We in the executive branch had simply run out of an acceptable list of items to further stockpile. Further, it was increasingly difficult to satisfy ourselves that in accepting some barter offers we might actually be replacing dollar sales. We also sympathized with friendly competing nations like Canada as their officials maintained that some of the barter transactions were disruptive to the world grain market. They had a substantive argument.

It must be explained that barter as conceived by this Title was not a simple transaction such as swapping CCC cotton for South Africa's industrial diamonds and for shipment of the cotton to South Africa.

The typical barter transaction is best illustrated by a swap of CCC wheat for bauxite from Jamaica and the wheat sold and used in a third country and the bauxite to the U.S. supplemental stockpile. The General Services Administration (GSA) (the custodian of the supplemental stockpile) paid cash to CCC with funds derived through the regular appropriation procedure. The barter contractor had received CCC wheat for the bauxite delivered to GSA. The contractor, usually through another party, sold the wheat to an acceptable third country, received cash and paid Jamaica for the bauxite.

The most logical question is: Why was such a complicated transaction attractive to contractors? The answer is likewise complicated but real. It deserves explanation.

In order for government officials to satisfy the additionality requirement, all countries buying U.S. agricultural commodities and countries that may conceivably buy, at some price, were classified on the basis of the history of their buying (importing) U.S. farm commodities.

* Those placed in A category were dependable buyers.
* Those placed in B category were occasional buyers.
* Those placed in C category had a history of buying very limited or zero amounts of U.S. agricultural commodities.

The country classification on buying history and financial capability to pay in dollars was reviewed regularly.

Sales of grain, cotton or other CCC-owned commodities to A category nations were hardly ever approved. Limiting or restricting barter sales to A countries was necessary to insure against replacing dollar sales. It was not uncommon for a country, upon review, to be reclassified as an A country from the B category or from the C grouping to B.

There were, of course, instances when the farm commodities did go to the country originating the hard goods. One such was a transaction of CCC wheat to India for manganese and ferro manganese. Several firms in 1960 participated in this $40 million swap. I considered that transaction as one demonstrating additionality and one definitely not disruptive to world markets.

A company or merchant handling metals generally did not merchandise farm commodities. Likewise, exporters of farm commodities did not deal directly in metals and minerals destined for the stockpile. A new type of activity came into being. A barter contractor, upon being awarded a contract acceptance with USDA to supply a mineral or metal acceptable for stockpiling at a price satisfactory to GSA, received payment in a CCC agricultural commodity such as wheat. Oftentimes, the primary contractor was neither equipped nor able to merchandise the wheat overseas. This resulted in a free market clearinghouse activity. Traditional grain exporters in this example, if they so chose, would pay for the "right" to attain an amount of government-owned wheat for sale to an overseas destination acceptable to CCC. Typically, the "right" changed hands at a discount of 1 to 5 percent. The grain exporter's selling price for the wheat to the foreign entity was also less than the traditional free market quotation for identical merchandise. The discounted price feature is what upset friendly competing nations, particularly if proof of additionality was weak.

Why was this type of complicated buying and selling system attractive to numerous entities involved in international trade?

Two reasons, really!

One, CCC transferred title to the government-owned grain or other commodity on basis of a letter of credit being posted. Whereas delivery of the hard items by the contractor to GSA may be several months into the future. From the standpoint of CCC, this practice made sense. Delivery to the contractor stopped further cost of storage to CCC—even though reimbursement from GSA may be sometime in the future.

The second reason is more difficult to explain but is perhaps best illustrated as follows.

If one assumes the world is utilizing x volume of bauxite (as an example), the price is y and originating countries were prepared to fill an order to purchase at y price. As demand for stockpiling became real, it always seemed logical to me that the additional amount could be supplied at a lower price. It is not unlike being able to sell a given production from a mine at a price. But if an outlet for 25 percent additional production presents itself, the per unit cost of producing the additional amount is likely to be lower—by spreading the overhead over a larger total output.

Leastwise, these two reasons satisfied my judgment on the glaring weakness of CCC being engaged along with GSA and other government agencies in a complicated bartering activity.

I was never comfortable with all the facets of the CCC barter program; even though for the eight years of the Eisenhower-Benson administration, the barter program accounted for nearly $2 billion of agricultural exports—about 9 percent of the total.

Some pluses, as well as negatives, emanated from the exhaustive studies of barter program activities. First, the negative.

Some contractors became over-zealous and falsified destination of some commodities. At that time, the country of Austria was determined by USDA officials to be an acceptable destination for feed grains attained from CCC for export under the barter program. The U.S. government rationale was quite simple. There was no record of Austria having been a meaningful importer of U.S. feed grains. Austria was classified as a C category country. That destination for feed grains satisfied the additionality requirement.

Long after the fact, investigations proved that the volume of feed grains under the barter program supplied to barter contractors for destination Austria was considerably greater than imports of feed grains into Austria from the United States.

Legal action was taken and penalties were imposed but such international chicanery leaves much to be desired.

On the positive side, numerous international merchandisers of unquestionably high repute and motives honed their marketing skills. They learned to compete for business and to more thoroughly examine the globe for buyers—particularly at a price. Such is the art of salesmanship.

Philosophically, and from within government sessions, one wise statement has stayed with me. In one of the worry sessions when it appeared barter transactions may have become disruptive to U.S. cash transactions and those of our competitors—Preston Richards, deputy administrator, CSS, deathly ill at the time, stated that "Barter should have died when the Dutch traded trinkets with the Indians for wampum and the island of Manhattan."

One final note on the barter authority as it refers to commodities owned by the government needs mentioning.

To the extent that government-owned stocks are used to supply an overseas demand and replace goods which may have originated from the free market, every free holder of stocks—whether a producer or a merchandiser—is shortchanged. The marketplace price discovery institutions never reflect that specific transaction or usage.

Maybe this *one* reason was why I rejoiced when we defeated the forces mandating that a fixed volume of goods move through CCC hands for purposes as defined in Title III (Barter). It was another victory for those who believe a more equitable price is discovered as the full impact of world business is felt in the cash and futures markets.

One final observation should be shared. Barter of goods or services for commodities or items may deserve a niche in the world of commerce. But leave CCC out of it! If our government, because of reasons of national security, foreign aid or any other acceptable goal, chooses to stockpile items, so be it. Buy the goods at competitive prices for spot or future delivery.

If subsequent statutes mandate paying for stockpile items with U.S. farm commodities, the exercise can take place without involving CCC. It can be done through normal channels of trade and commerce. If it is in the best interest of the nation to funnel most exports and domestic sales through normal channels, and I believe it is, then there is a still stronger reason for directing all such movement in that manner. The price discovery system reacts more responsively as all transactions take place competitively in the market and delivery is made from free stocks of farm commodities.

THE ROLE OF PRICE IN EXPORT
MARKET DEVELOPMENT

During the last half of the decade of the 1950s—in the Benson era—stocks of grain sorghum owned by CCC had become particularly cumbersome. Several developments contributed to this problem.

Producers had rather quickly switched to planting improved hybrid varieties. Heretofore the old open pollinated varieties were low yielding and were grown almost entirely on dry land, without the advantage of irrigation. Production from the old varieties often lacked palatability and uniformity. The new hybrids resulted in a much improved feed ingredient. The *new* sorghum was high in energy, low in fiber and uniform in quality and was high yielding.

In fact, students of agricultural development in the United States often refer to the rapidity of acceptance of high-yielding hybrid sorghum seed as a classic example of the U.S. farmer's ability and readiness to adopt improved production practices in any farming enterprise.

The improved sorghum seed combined with increased irrigation in states such as Texas and Kansas resulted in surpluses much in excess of demand. Most of the increased carryovers were owned by CCC as a consequence of the price support program.

Reflecting on developments during that period of the late 1950s, it is well to remember that commercial cattle feeding had not really become a factor in that area of the nation. That came later.

We who were responsible for administering the CCC price support program and as mandated by the CCC Charter Act as well as urging by the Congress offered government-owned grain including sorghum at what was interpreted to be competitive prices for restricted uses—meaning export.

In 1956, CCC stopped offering government-owned wheat for export and implemented an export subsidy program. The activity became known as the payment-in-kind (PIK) program because the subsidy, the level of which was announced daily, was paid in kind with CCC-owned wheat.

A PIK export subsidy program for coarse grains (corn, sorghum, barley, oats and rye) was commenced in 1958. Similar programs were also activated for cotton and rice.

The rationale for adopting an export subsidy program as an alternative to CCC making its stocks available for export at competitive prices was simple and straightforward.

The program was designed to at least partially shut the front door, or the entry, to CCC and to force more grain into export from the open market. On the other hand, the relatively small volume of CCC grain required for the export subsidy did allow CCC some latitude to dispose of stocks and thereby provide some flexibility in handling the government-owned inventory.

The PIK grain export program did throw more burden to assemble grain back to the private sector. This resulted in greater variation of prices offered to country grain dealers and producers.

Not everyone engaged in buying and selling grain for export was happy. A few liked and had grown accustomed to the government assembling huge stocks of grain and making such available in large lots. In sum, the action reflected a retrenchment of the hand of government. Some call it less intervention in the marketplace.

The manner in which CCC offered stocks of grain and cotton for export in the late 1950s is important in a discussion of export market promotion because overseas buyers were being courted. Statutory minimum price for CCC-owned commodities applied to sales for domestic consumption and/or use. Conversely, CCC was mandated to make stocks available for export at competitive world prices. World grain prices, at that time, were interpreted by U.S. officials to be somewhat lower than U.S. domestic prices. The CCC price support program effectively established a floor price in the United States somewhat higher than the price level at which grain and cotton was changing hands in world markets.

At times, during this period, on a seasonal basis, the United States was the only meaningful seller of sorghum, oats or even corn.

The sorghum export price was held at 18 to 22 percent below that of corn. The price was thus maintained by direct sales of CCC stocks for restricted (export) use or later through subsidy in PIK. This relatively low price did begin to attract attention among feed manufacturers in Japan.

Hideo Tokoro, agricultural attaché, Embassy of Japan, in Washington, D.C., familiarized himself with the U.S. sorghum situation at that time. He encouraged the Livestock Bureau of the Ministry of Agriculture, Forestry and Fisheries (MAFF), Tokyo to promote increased imports of the feed ingredient.

By the early 1960s, sorghum had found a sizeable niche in layer (layer hens) rations in Japan. That country was rather quickly to become the largest market in the world for sorghum (outside of the United States).

I have referred to this period when the sorghum export price reflected large subsidies as the "green stamp" promotional program of CCC.

On the other side of the globe and for a few years our sorghum was also attractive to feed compounders in the United Kingdom, but for rather different reasons. The British liked broilers with white skins—less yellow pigment than we prefer in the United States.

Sorghum was a natural high-energy grain for such broilers, because a high percentage of yellow corn in their rations contributed to heavier pigmentation. Because of this, their compounders liked sorghum or wheat, particularly when the price was "right."

We did not hold a meaningful market for sorghum in Britain, but events there were to be due to other political and economic developments.

GOVERNMENT AND INDUSTRY COOPERATING IN EXPORT MARKET DEVELOPMENT

The U.S. Feed Grains Council (USFGC), an association organized in 1960 for the sole function of promoting exports of U.S. feed grains—and later other feed ingredients—was first headquartered in Amarillo, Texas. D. G. "Bill" Nelson, executive secretary, was the first chief executive officer.

During the closing months of 1960, the Board of Directors of USFGC was deciding to move the headquarters of the council to Washington, D.C. This just happened to coincide with the end of the Eisenhower administration and the beginning of the Kennedy-Johnson years.

As suggested by Secretary Benson, I stayed on as associate administrator of CSS during the transition period. I emptied my desk and left government service January 19, 1961. I enjoyed the period from early November, 1960, and until leaving USDA at the end of the Republican administration. I enjoyed briefing some of the staff selected by Governor Orville Freeman, who had been designated Secretary of Agriculture by President-elect Kennedy.

I found the transition educational, and hopefully our work was helpful to the Freeman transition team. Mr. Benson requested us to be as helpful as possible, and we were. Perhaps with premature confidence, but with very little personal doubt, I wanted to participate in turning over the reigns of government—as long as the electorate had made a decision—because I fully expected to be back in taking over the reigns of USDA at a later date on behalf of another and future administration.

Several weeks after my departure from USDA, I was offered the position of Executive Vice-President of the U.S. Feed Grains Council. I agreed to head this new organization and to move the headquarters to Washington, D.C.

The new organization was practically without funds and consisted of seven members. The members were diverse in their specific interests but unified in their belief that a growing world market for U.S. feed grains was more than imagination. The seven members were:

* American Seed Trade Association
* National Corn Growers Association
* Cargill, Inc.
* North American Export Grain Association
* Continental Grain Company
* Farmers Grain Dealers, Des Moines
* Grain Sorghum Producers Association

During my first session with representatives of the seven groups and/or companies, I was of the opinion the seven had at least that many individual ideas on how an export market development organization should be operated. And at least seven views on priority of goals. All of the executives had had experience internationally and most were actively engaged in overseas activities and enterprises.

My own observations of other commodity groups had caused me to believe constructive projects could be rather quickly put together, but that it would be well to utilize a so-called rifle approach as compared to a many-faceted shotgun blast.

During the five years I had been in Washington, D.C.—up to that moment—I had become quite well acquainted with the activities of a few groups working with the Foreign Agricultural Service (FAS) of USDA.

Truthfully, the USFGC would never have been organized had it not been for funds being available for allocation for export market development work—on a matching basis—by FAS. Title I, Public Law 480 mandated a portion of the local currency proceeds acquired from foreign countries be convertable to hard currency for export market development activities.

Some commodity groups in existence when PL 480 was enacted in 1954 were already engaged in export market development activities utilizing their own funds or were prepared to cooperate with USDA in the then newly authorized promotional endeavor.

Three such examples of commodity interest groups at that time were National Cotton Council, American Soybean Association and Western Wheat Associates. There were others with various degrees of experience and expertise.

It is well to remember that there were no textbooks known to me on the subject of organizing and administering export market development programs. Each organization had its own idea on how to proceed in increasing exports.

Worthy of note is also the action taken by the Congress in 1954 in strengthening the hand of the Secretary of Agriculture through the agricultural attachés stationed overseas. The Congress mandated the attaché service to encourage and promote the marketing of agricultural products of the United States. The agricultural attachés in 1954 became the representatives of the Secretary of Agriculture and USDA—for program purposes. Each one was assigned to a specific embassy and continued on as a member of the U.S. ambassador's staff in that respective foreign country.

This added function assigned to the attaché service combined with additional funding for allocation to industry groups was designed to increase the positive impact of USDA and private sector commodity interest groups in marketing U.S. farm products overseas. Hence, the phrase, "cooperative export market development" became a common cliché.

As I observed other interest groups and the manner in which they operated to accomplish their respective goals, I discovered they were employing a diversity of techniques.

For example, the cotton people emphasized the advantage of cotton in ladies' clothes and men's shirts. They publicized "Miss Cotton" and featured the young lady in many foreign countries. The National Cotton Council had had many years of experience in such promotional activities.

Western Wheat Associates (WWA), rather early in the period, featured modern bread baking in Japan. The WWA utilized a number of buses in such demonstrations throughout Japan.

The American Soybean Association in Japan in the early years featured the desirability of utilizing more U.S. soybeans in several soybean-based food products.

I discovered rather quickly that if the USFGC was to be of any service to its members or to the nation, a thrust of its own would need to be developed. The number one question which any rational person should pose was "Who or what utilizes corn, sorghum, other coarse grains or other feed ingredients?"

The answer was quite simple; it was then and remains so today— the hen, the sow, the cow and their offspring.

It was obvious that animals cannot determine whether they are going to eat more or less grain or be allowed to multiply. Humans decide that for them.

This was all very simple to me but not so with many people with whom it was necessary to work.

One school of thought expressed by persuasive people was to work with importers and convince them that U.S. grain was a better buy!

Still another block of supporters urged me to work towards influencing government policies having to do with terms of entry for our grain—or with our own U.S. officials in influencing U.S. government export aid programs.

Still another tangent mentioned by several which had blind alley overtones, in my opinion, was the matter of grade standards for corn and other coarse grains. I did not want to become involved with the fine tuning of the parameters of the factors determining a specific grade. It would have been time consuming and far removed from the animals *using* our grains. One of the major appeals to me in my heading the USFGC during these early years was the thought that I would again be rather closely involved in animal agriculture. My formal training had been in animal industry.

One humorous observation regarding the rapidly expanding membership of USFGC brings pleasant thoughts. I observed shock on the faces of some, and on occasion a bit of chagrin, as new members participated in their first meeting of the council when time would be devoted to a constructive discussion on the state of the art of animal production in a specific country. But the concept caught on. I believe the thrust of the council in those years was correct, and I know the council impacted the positive use of feed grains in a long list of nations.

As often happens in a dissertation on U.S. export market promotion for farm products, the country of Japan comes in for maximum discussion. In the case of feed grains, the country offers a classical example of changing eating habits and the impact of such on U.S. agriculture.

Before explaining a country's program—in this case, Japan—it is necessary to establish a principle which I believe to be true.

The principle is that "Corn from the United States is no better than corn from Thailand or Argentina." Corn of each origination may have unique characteristics which may cause it to be favored slightly by a user for a specific purpose. So be it. Basically, however, the chief way to increase the export of U.S. corn is to enlarge the world market. In this instance, both Thailand and Argentina are friendly competitive producers and exporters. They also want to increase their exports. Of the three exporting nations in this specific discussion only the United States is capable of shipping corn, literally every day of the year. Because of the diverse regions producing corn in the United States, a specific vessel of corn, largely because of logistics, may contain portions from several states, or regions within the states—and the production from more than one crop year. Because of this blending, the nation does have an advantage in being able to service a market every day of the year. No other corn exporting nation is endowed with such capability. From this standpoint, the United States has a natural advantage in servicing an overseas user of corn. Generally, though, the decision of a buyer to import from a specific origination, when all other factors are considered equal, is decided on the basis of price.

Thus it was established with the members of the council that the way to increase U.S. corn and sorghum exports, as well as other feed ingredients, was to expand the production of poultry and livestock. This concept gave more or less concern to several of the career people in the Foreign Agricultural Service. Inherent in the minds of several was the thought that our U.S. grade standards should be restudied or that we should develop techniques to extol the advantages of U.S. corn, sorghum or other ingredients.

Now, over 20 years later, the "total uses" approach sounds better than ever—as being in the best interest of the United States, and in this example, the country of Japan.

Japan offered great opportunity as a growth market for U.S. feed grains in that year of 1961. The nation had imported less than 1 million tons of corn and sorghum from the U.S. in 1960. Our improved hybrid sorghum was not yet well known to that nation's feed manufacturers. The importation of both grains was subject to quota and currency allocations by the Japanese government. Japan's layer and broiler rations were high in fiber because of the inclusion of rice bran. These rations were low in energy; they were sufficiently high in protein but not well balanced; some amino acids, such as lysine, were much too low to secure maximum feeding efficiency. The fledgling swine industry of Japan was nourished on mixed feed consisting of "odds and ends" of domestic ingredients. As a consequence, the amount of feed required to produce a pound of pork was unsatisfactorily high.

The Japanese government officially encouraged its people to increase their daily intake of eggs, poultry, pork and dairy products. It was to develop that over the eight years in which I headed the USFGC and during the 12 lengthy visits I made to the country I was given the privilege of meeting with three consecutive prime ministers. During each of the three visits we only discussed the developmental progress of Japan's livestock and poultry industry. What a favorable environment for expanding the use of feed grains and other ingredients!

In a free society, the encouragement of government to increase per capita consumption of animal products does not in itself accomplish the goal. People must *desire* to buy a greater amount of eggs, poultry, meat and dairy products. Herein lies a problem. People who

☆ *Mr. Kawada, president of Japan Feed Manufacturers, Washington, D.C., and Palmby, 1970.*

for centuries had been nourished on rice and fish could not be expected to automatically change their eating and buying habits.

Japanese feed manufacturers, specific livestock interest groups, retailers and grain importers were all prepared—at the encouragement of the Japanese government—to work with the USFGC in developing projects designed to expand and enlarge the livestock and poultry industry.

The Japan Feed Council came into being for the purpose of encouraging Japanese animal agriculture and to work cooperatively with the USFGC in working toward that end.

The founders of the Japan Feed Council were men of stature. Many should be named but three immediately come to mind as follows:

- ☆ Mr. Kawada, president of Japan Feed Manufacturers
- ☆ Mr. Emori, senior officer of Mitsubishi and president of the Grain Importers Association
- ☆ Mr. Mihashi, president of Zenkoren, the giant supply cooperative—later to become Zenno

☆ *Palmby and the president of Zenkoren, Mr. Mihashi, in Washington, D.C., 1969.*

☆ *Signing the Market Development Agreement with the Japan Feed Council, 1961, in Tokyo.*

MADE IN WASHINGTON ☆ 74

A leading member of the Japan Parliament, and on occasions head of several ministries, including the Ministry of Agriculture and Forestry, Mr. Kono was a political power encouraging Japanese agriculture, especially animal enterprises. Mr. Kono, a rural faction leader within his political party, never endeared himself to the U.S. diplomatic service. There were several reasons for this cool relationship, none of which are of significance to the subject matter at hand.

Let it be recognized that Mr. Kono did, almost single-handedly on behalf of the Japanese government, free-up the importation of sorghum early in 1963. Sometime earlier corn had been allowed to enter Japan for feed use—free of duty and free of quota restriction and also free of the currency allocation requirement. Would that wheat for food use could have been accorded such liberal trade treatment, but that is another story discussed later.

Within this favorable environment provided by the government of Japan and industry leaders, the USFGC opened an office in Tokyo and prepared to undertake market development projects.

Without exception, Japanese animal agriculture leaders stressed the need to expand the real demand for animal products within the country. It was necessary, in their opinion, to encourage increased consumption. They further maintained, with sound logic, that animal agriculture could only be expanded at a rate commensurate with consumers' willingness to buy more of the end products—eggs, broilers, pork and dairy products.

It quickly became apparent that eggs offered the most immediate growth opportunities. The reasons were obvious.

Home refrigeration in the early 1960s in Japan was largely nonexistent; eggs could be kept for several days without a refrigerator. Cooking facilities were limited; eggs are easily prepared with minimum heat and facilities—and in a variety of ways. The Japanese liked eggs but per capita consumption was very low—80 per year compared to 290 in the United States.

Our market studies indicated Japanese homemakers purchased most of their eggs for home consumption from mom and pop–type retail stores. Eggs were displayed in bulk bins, sold by the piece and carried home in paper sacks. Breakage enroute was quite high, averaging about 10 percent. Through an unscientific survey, we determined plastic egg cartons would be welcomed by retailers and homemakers alike. Project number one had been born.

Working jointly with the Japan Feed Council and in financial tandem with retailers, we distributed plastic egg cartons by the millions throughout major population centers across Japan. Upon return

☆ *Far East feed manufacturing representatives arriving at Des Moines airport for Nutrition and Feeding Short Course at Iowa State University, Ames, 1968.*

trips to that country it was always a thrill to see Japanese ladies entering mom and pop stores returning empty egg cartons and exiting a few minutes later with a full carton of eggs. It worked. (About 20 years later, in the early 1980s, the per capita consumption of eggs in Japan was equal to that of the United States.)

Major project number two was a joint undertaking of commuter train advertising of eggs. Commuter train use by the Japanese is legendary. Pictures and art work displayed in those ads were seen by millions almost instantaneously. Department of health support for this program was of inestimable benefit. As one would expect, not all of a country's population believe more eggs in the diet may be beneficial. But with a goal to increase protein intake their health department officials were strongly in favor and made known their positive recommendations.

From the beginning of 1961, we worked closely with the private and cooperative feed manufacturers. As the market for compounded feed within Japan expanded, the group requested normal supplier-to-buyer type information. We did two things to service this request.

We organized short courses on feed formulation for the Japanese in the United States. The first such training program was held at Oklahoma State University at Stillwater. Another was held at Iowa State University at Ames. Each session was about two weeks long. Over 80 junior executive type people from Japan participated in these two programs. Most of the participants were responsible for formulation of rations for their respective companies back in Japan—or were about to be responsible for decisions regarding ingredient mix.

The goal of the young feed formulators was consistent with the thrust of the USFGC. We believed the lowest cost ration per pound of gain for livestock and poultry production in Japan would lead to increased sales of U.S. corn and sorghum. On the other hand, the commercial feed manufacturer representatives desired to manufacture feed leading to lower feed conversion rates.

In addition to our continuing work on feed formulation, the council through the years sponsored several major animal nutrition type seminars in Japan. Most of these were held in the American Trade Center in Tokyo.

Perhaps the most significant such event held in the American Trade Center took place in March, 1966. It carried on for 12 days. During that period seven specialists from the United States presented papers and responded to questions. A like number of leaders from Japan made similar contributions. Subject matter included feed formulation, animal nutrition, feed sales techniques, animal health, the role of the integrator, poultry breeding and end-product promotion.

This seminar was noteworthy because it marked the fifth anniversary of the USFGC in Japan. During this period the sales of U.S. corn and sorghum to Japan had more than quadrupled. Globally, the sales of the two grains from the United States for that year were to reach nearly 25 million metric tons (close to 1 billion bushels). This compared to 10 million tons in 1960.

G. Robert "Bob" Peterson was Far East director for the USFGC during that interesting period. It was the period during which egg production had been modernized, swine husbandry had been greatly expanded and the broiler industry had been established.

Bob Peterson did an article at that time entitled "Japan Broilers—One Year Later. (April 1, 1966, to March 31, 1967.)" He wrote in part as follows:

During the period since we held the U.S. Feed Exhibit and Seminar in March of 1966, there has been an intensive build-up in several important areas of the broiler production industry that almost guarantees a further rapid growth in numbers of broilers to be produced in Japan.

Included in this intensive build-up which foreshadows sharply larger broiler numbers are, (1) capital investments in modern processing facilities that will require stepped up supplies of live birds to operate at profitable levels, (2) importation of grandparent stock of several major American broiler breeds including the capital investment in breeding farms, organization, and facilities by Arbor Acres-Mitsui, Cobb International-C. Itoh, DeKalb-Toshoku, and others, and (3) varying degrees of capital investment, supported by integration type arrangements with broiler producers and poultry meat distributions, by several large feed manufacturers and trading companies. The exact nature and extent of these investments and arrangements are difficult to determine, but in total they are quite significant.

Peterson went on to say:

Again the U.S. Feed Grains Council.in cooperation with the Japan Feed Council, and its broiler industry members, are finalizing a major project to attempt to increase the per capita consumption of broiler meat.

The major obstacles to greatly increased use of chicken meat are, (1) the fact that only 10% of all Japanese households eat meat every day, (2) most Japanese menus relegate meat, including chicken meat, to side-dish status, and therefore most chicken meat is purchased in small lots in the form of small boneless slices where the superior quality of properly fed broilers cannot be judged, and (3) because of the inefficiency of distribution in general and the high cost of handling poultry meat to support point (2) above, the spread between farm prices and retail prices is about 68% of the retail price on the basis of boned chicken meat in 100 gram lots, and this retail price does not fluctuate much regardless of the price movement up or down at the farm level. (Sources [1] MAF Study of November 1966 and [3] A Study of the Market Structure for Poultry Meat in Japan, by Coral, Inc., Japan, 1966)

With this situation to deal with, we have adopted the strategy of promoting purchases of whole broilers, cutting them up at home, and cooking with bone in. This is a combination educational and promotional project involving lectures, cutting and cooking demonstrations, sampling, special discount sales, use of point-of-sale materials such as posters, and widespread distribution of recipe folders which also contain pictures of each stage of cutting up a chicken. The idea is to quickly increase the amount of chicken that can move into consumption with the same expenditure of yen, while attracting additional consumers to add some of their food money to the yen spent for chicken meat.

In summary, the article contained the following observations:

This period stands out as the real "birth year" of Japan's broiler industry. After two or three years of intensive investigation, detailed planning, careful negotiation, and exploratory operations (the "gestation" period in livestock terminology), the Japanese broiler industry really exploded in 1966. Amongst the significant developments:

(1) Broiler feed tonnage jumped from 452,459 metric tons in the year ending March 31, 1966 to 703,418 metric tons in the year ending March 31, 1967. This was a growth of more than 55% in one year and reflected more than the 16% growth in numbers of broiler chickens fed from 128,000 million to 148,000 million. It also reflected the fact that late in 1965 and during 1966 most leading Japanese feed manufacturers added a modern broiler finisher to their product line for the first time. During this period, a new class of high energy feeds was introduced in Japan and a new market for U.S. feed grains was established.

(2) Chicken meat production in Japan increased about 20% with the total rising from 204,000 metric tons in the year ending March 31, 1966 to 240,000 metric tons in the year ending March 31, 1967.

(3) During this year, the tonnage of chickens fed for meat exceeded the tonnage from old hens and culls for the first time. The proportion of chickens fed for meat went up sharply from 43.7% in 1965 to 57.3% in 1966. At the same time, the proportion of chickens fed for meat supplied by layer cockerels dropped sharply from 13.2% in 1965 to 7.3% in 1966.

(4) Per capita consumption of poultry meat went up about 50% from 4.5 grams per day in 1965 to 6.8 grams in 1966. This rise in consumption in terms of pounds per year per person amounts to an increase from 3.62 lb. in 1965 to 5.40 lb. in 1966. Also 1966 was the first year that poultry meat consumption in Japan exceeded beef consumption.

(5) This year witnessed the first large scale production of American broiler breeders from grandparent stock raised in Japan.

All of these developments are milestones in the expansion of markets for U.S. feed grains. The information and encouragement provided by the U.S. Feed Grains Council based on projects such as the broiler feeding trials of 1964 and the U.S. Feed Trade Exhibit and Seminar of March 9-18, 1966, with its emphasis on up-to-date information on the genetics, nutrition, production, and marketing of broilers, undoubtedly contributed to the birth of this dynamic industry in Japan.

It should be noted that the introduction of American broiler meat to the trend-setting hotel, restaurant, and department store trades by the Institute of American Poultry Industries in 1963, 1964, and 1965 helped to develop a taste amongst the Japanese for high quality broiler meat and thereby helped prepare the way for the birth of the Japanese broiler industry in 1966.

This classic example of increased use of feed ingredients based on imported grain is a tribute to the many people involved in the application of improved technology to improve the diet of millions.

Jumping over the span of time to the present as compared to 1966, U.S. corn and sorghum sales to Japan again quadrupled. We now look upon that country as a dependable buyer of over 15 million tons of the two grains annually from the United States. The solid base for increased use was predicated on building a dependable market for eggs, broilers, pork and dairy products.

From a personal standpoint, my close relationship with industry leaders and government officials in that country proved to be of great assistance to me later as a government official seeking improved terms of entry for U.S. farm products, other than feed grains.

The early years of market development work for feed grains in Japan also had a near bon-fire impact in other dynamic nations in the Orient. Agricultural enterprisers and investors in Korea and Taiwan were well aware of the expanding poultry and livestock industries in Japan. They observed the importance of high energy grains (corn and sorghum) and quality protein (soybean meal) in the feed formulas. With minimum encouragement, they set annual growth records in importation and use of these excellent ingredients from the United States.

☆ ☆ ☆

During the early years of the USFGC, the board of directors and membership were primarily interested in Western Europe as a market for corn, sorghum and other feed grains—and naturally so. Citizens of our relatively young country have largely descended from Britain or the Continent. Further, U.S. farm products, in varying degrees, had been flowing toward that area of the world for decades and in some

☆ *European staff conference, U.S. Feed Grains Council, Rome. Clockwise: Maywald, Rotterdam; Jean, FAS/USDA, Washington, D.C.; Comben, London; Biseo, Rome; Golberg, Rome; Palmby, Washington, D.C.; Graziani, Rome; Rivera, Madrid; Lykiardopulo, Athens; and Schoel, Hamburg.*

instances such as tobacco and cotton for generations. During and following World War II, Europeans, because of the devastation on the continent, were heavily dependent on our grain and other food stuff.

It was thus only natural that the supporters of the USFGC should first look to Europe.

Opportunity or prospect for market development by the council in Europe was in direct contrast to that which existed in the Orient. Eating habits and tastes in Europe were identical to our own. Level of sophistication in livestock and poultry feeding and management varied from being comparable to that which existed in our own country to little better than primitive in *some* regions in countries such as Italy, Spain, Greece and Portugal. Even in those more isolated areas technical information was attainable but tradition in livestock feeding practices was deeply ingrained. Capital resources were often very limited.

Upon reflection, the pattern followed by the USFGC, in cooperation with the Foreign Agricultural Service and the agricultural attachés in each European country, was predicated on servicing the users of U.S. corn, sorghum and other feed ingredients.

Charles Gidney from Texas, stationed in Rome, was European director. He was with the USFGC when I had assumed my new role with the organization. Gidney had hired an Italian citizen, Dr. Romano Graziani. Early on, we designated Graziani as director for Italy. He continues with the council—now 25 years later—and in a broader capacity.

Graziani possessed an almost missionary dedication to improve the livestock industry in his country. His accomplishments are many. He continually developed projects designed for the betterment of livestock production. Italy presented a fertile environment for improvement because of the original six founding member countries of the European Economic Community (EEC). The livestock sector in Italy rated sixth in level of sophistication in relation to the Netherlands, West Germany, Belgium, France and Luxembourg. Because of this lower level of developmental status—particularly in southern Italy—Graziani, second to no one, urged the agricultural interests in Italy be granted a longer period of time in which to comply with EC harmonized grain price levels. As a consequence, Italy in 1964 was granted an extension of four years in which to fully comply. This was later extended. This subject of EC harmonized grain prices will be discussed in greater detail in a later chapter.

The USFGC in Italy under Graziani impacted several specific modernization developments among which were:

* Growth and importance of 3P Clubs (not unlike the 4H Club movement in the United States).
* Slat floor cattle feeding operations, particularly in the Po River valley (preceded development of similar type feeding in some regions of the United States).
* Expansion of year-round fresh pork availability (through market development with livestock butchers).

The beginning country director in the United Kingdom was one who proved to be another true professional, Norman Comben, D.V.M. In this period of the early 1960s, there was not a great amount of impetus within the United Kingdom for talks with leaders of the six EC countries leading to membership in the European Community. The agricultural policies within the United Kingdom were quite different than those which were developing within the EC.

Following World War II and until the early 1960s, Britain had followed a rather open agricultural trade policy. The country was heavily dependent on overseas sources of hard wheat for flour milling and corn for distilling and animal feed and, of course, soybeans. Compared to Continental Europe, the British had generally stuck to a low food price policy. West Germany, for example, prior to the formation of EC had utilized a skimming-charge technique on imported grain to protect a high domestic grain price policy.

☆ *H. E. "Mike" Sanford, Roy Hendricksen and Fred Maywald in 1963.*

Comben in the United Kingdom was an accepted part of the professional agricultural business corps in his country. Within this type of environment, he, on behalf of the USFGC carved out a niche of acceptability with the feed compounders and the community of academia.

In West Germany the first country director was Egon Schoel, Ph.D. He was an animal nutritionist as was his successor, Klaus Werner, Ph.D.

As in Britain and Italy the project work in West Germany was aimed at the users of corn, sorghum and other feed ingredients.

Procedures for conducting feeding trials, publicizing the results and follow-up were formalized but conducted in a manner best suited to the mores and customs within each country.

One other activity of the USFGC in Europe, underway when I joined the organization—but of lasting impact—was the contact work being done by Harold "Mike" Sanford from Portland, Oregon, a retired Vice-President of Continental Grain Company. Sanford was posted in Rotterdam. He served the council for four years in Europe as a marketing specialist—a modest title for a prestigious gentleman.

Fred Maywald, the outgoing elected president of the USFGC in the summer of 1964 succeeded Mike Sanford. Maywald had just retired as manager of the grain department of the Farmers Grain Dealers Association of Iowa.

Sanford and Maywald brought dignity and prestige to the USFGC in Europe. They became still better known in trade circles and with

U.S. government representatives stationed in Brussels, home of the EC.

A snapshot overview of the work performed by USFGC in European countries other than the EC would not be complete without limited reference to project work in at least two other countries—Spain and Greece.

Allen Golberg, a native of North Dakota, had been named European director in the spring of 1964. His presence in Europe made it possible to speed up activities in more countries. Darwin Stolte joined Golberg in Rome two years later.

Animal industry development work in Spain and Greece proved particularly interesting. We were staffed to undertake more projects and to publicize the results in a timely manner. During the decade of the 1960s these two countries were vastly different in many ways, but similar in one regard. Each was and is a great opportunity for local entrepreneurs to not only produce more animal products to fulfill the demand of tourists but also improve the quality of lamb and poultry.

We undertook lamb grain feeding demonstrations in Spain. It was a logical promotional type project. A small amount of grain and protein concentrates fed to lambs prior to weaning and immediately afterwards improved the quality of the lamb carcasses and greatly added to the weight of edible meat.

One modest activity in Greece continues to impress me many years later. The USFGC participated in feeding demonstrations, largely with poultry at the American Farm School at Thessalonica. The school was under the leadership of Bruce Lansdale, an American trained at Cornell University. Dr. Lansdale, one of the finest "products" ever exported by the U.S., believed in practical training for rural youths interested in increasing their knowledge of technical agriculture. He and the American Farm School have had a most favorable impact on small farmers in Greece—and many not so small.

In September, 1968, the annual membership meeting of the USFGC was held in Williamsburg, Virginia. Most of the overseas staff was in attendance. This ninth annual meeting proved to be the high point in my years as head of the council. As a group we had worked toward common goals, and I felt the organization was being well served by competent dedicated professionals. From the standpoint of commerce, feed grain exports from the United States in the eight-year period had increased from less than 1 million tons per month (10 per year) to about 2½ million tons (30 per year). Not for one moment did we in the USFGC take all the credit for this phenomenal increase in global use, but we were riding the right wave. Consumers in the more

☆ *U.S. Feed Grains staff, Williamsburg, Virginia, 1968. Left to right, back row: Graziani, Rome; Werner, Hamburg; Campbell, London; Stolte, Rome; Fondahn, Washington, D.C.; Dyke, Washington, D.C.; second row: Golberg, Rome; Amavisca, Madrid; Vlastaris, Athens; Palmby, Washington, D.C.; Peterson, Tokyo; Minagawa, Tokyo; front row: Kallen, Rotterdam.*

affluent countries were registering their desires in the food markets in their respective countries. They were prepared and able to pay the price for more meat, poultry, eggs and in some instances, dairy products.

This matter of price, however, was one subject that was causing clouds to appear on the horizon!

Ray Ioanes, administrator of the Foreign Agricultural Service, should be credited above anyone else in maintaining sanity and judgment in allocating government funds for market development work by commodity groups, of which the USFGC was one. He insisted on fiscal accountability and professional performance. Consistent with this expectation, Hubert Dyke, vice-president of the council with responsibility for administration, performed well.

Ioanes, on several occasions had predicted that future increases in export of farm products could become harder to attain or that such exports could even slip backwards. He, too, was watching developments in Europe, and most likely recognized one school of thought within the United States, which gave emphasis to securing higher fixed prices for commodities moving overseas.

Darwin Stolte, livestock development specialist for the USFGC in Europe at that time, presented a paper on "Interchangeability of Feed Ingredients in EC Feed Formulas as Influenced by Price."

Stolte concluded that three basic areas of interchangeability were taking place within the EC: "(1) EC produced cereals, namely, wheat and barley; (2) oilseed and cereal by-product ingredients as energy sources; and (3) corn silage in substitution of a portion of cereal utilization as an economical system of beef production." He concluded, "All three are propagated by the CAP-EC cereals pricing policy and emphasize the impact that the community program has had—and will have—on the U.S. feed grains market."

In his paper, Stolte listed 28 ingredients commonly used as substitutes for grains in the Netherlands. As I review the list, it is obvious to me that he overlooked several more.

The Stolte paper reflected precisely what needed to be recognized by producers and marketers of feed grains in the United States—and all other servicing groups in the feed grains chain.

One other address at the Williamsburg conference recognizing the relative grain and ingredient price issue and a major U.S. trade policy issue attracted my attention.

It was the remarks given by Erwin E. Kelm, president, Cargill, Inc.

Kelm stated that "U.S. trade policy has in no way (as of September, 1968) improved our prospects for tapping the markets of Eastern Europe."

It should be noted that the USFGC involved itself with neither the U.S. agricultural legislation nor the farm program provisions. Membership by 1968 was broad. In addition to the earlier groups of producers, seedsmen and marketers, the family had grown to encompass chemical and fertilizer companies, rail and barge interests, bankers, brokers and several associations. The integrated organization maintained harmony by sticking to the common objective of maximizing exports.

Following the Williamsburg conference and with the council's program thrust firmly in gear, I was concerned about three agricultural and/or trade policy matters, none of which as chief executive officer of the council I could do anything about, or at best—very little.

The issues troubling me were:

* The continued isolation of the Common Agriculture Policy (CAP) of the EC from the rest of the world.
* The lack of access to the markets for grains in centrally controlled economy countries.
* The rather fragile appreciation in rural America of the necessity to be price competitive with other grain and feed ingredient suppliers.

The three concerns illustrate why private sector commodity groups must work together with government policy-makers and administrators if maximum progress is to be attained in an activity such as trade expansion.

Attaining legal access to foreign markets can only be accomplished by governments. Private groups can only urge or encourage governments to act.

Discussions of another country's internal policies finally is a task for diplomats.

Legislative development and the policy thrust of such legislation is the function of government officials.

Now, 15 years after ending my 8 years as head of a market development organization, several observations come to mind. During the eight years, traveling to many countries and to points within the United States had become a way of life.

During the eight years, I estimated I had visited over 150 farms in more than 20 countries. We had conducted feeding trials and/or demonstrations on many of the farms.

I observed farmers in every country taking pride in their work. They want to be respected. They, almost invariably, have an emotional feeling for what they are doing.

On a broader front relating the United States to other countries, I gained an impression that prime farm land in the United States—in relation to land of a lower level of productivity—was certainly not over-priced. Secondly, I observed that generally our most beautiful home-sites on lakes, streams—those with a view of natural beauty—were under-priced in relation to those in the older countries. Thirdly, it seemed to me that intercity cooperative- and condominium-type apartments in our largest cities as compared to comparable-size foreign cities would experience an upward movement in price. These general observations had little to do with market development work, except as the wants and desires of people are registered through buying and selling.

A key question must be asked about the contribution of private commodity groups in the United States in working with the Foreign Agricultural Service of USDA in promoting the exports of U.S. farm products. Has the system been constructive and worthy of support since its general inception about 30 years ago?

I can speak with authority on the eight years in which I had hands-on experience with the U.S. Feed Grains Council. We accomplished two major objectives.

One, we accelerated the use of grain for feed in several countries. As a consequence, the United States did expand the export of grains and other ingredients faster than would have happened had the acceleration not been encouraged and stimulated. Citizens in the importing country improved their diets more rapidly because of the greater availability of animal proteins. Are these happenings desirable? In my mind they are. Others may think otherwise.

Two, the USFGC had what I choose to call a back-sell effect. In the eight years with the USFGC, I estimate that I devoted nearly 40 percent of my time in working with the board of directors and members of the council. I deemed it to be my responsibility in performing my assignment to write information bulletins and to accept speaking engagements. The function is really one of communication and education. The theme is simple: "If we want to export; we must also import!" Then also it was constantly necessary to remind supporters that an expanded export market will not be *the answer* to all the worries facing U.S. farmers. It is part of the answer, provided the simple economic truth of being price-competitive continues to be understood and appreciated.

It is the back-sell function which is the most important role of most commodity groups. Apparently, it is a never-ending chore and necessary to our maintaining a reasonably liberal trade policy.

The back-sell role and the attendant communication and education function is not a very glamorous task but a required activity of the vested interest groups.

New entrants engaged in market development work must constantly be reminded that encouraging and working toward increased foreign trade is more complicated than the hosting of lunches and dinners.

The increase in producer check-off laws has led to substantially more producer money available for export market promotion and for specific commodity research. In some instances one must be impressed with the broad license taken by some state groups and even some national groups in claiming credit for the entire volume of a specific commodity exported each year. Too much of such unwarranted bragging only contributes to loss of credibility.

I have believed that each contributing business endeavor, be it producing, merchandising, transporting or servicing by supplying supporting goods such as fertilizers and chemicals, takes unto itself a degree of risk which must over a period of time be rewarded and at all times be heard. On the other hand, we who have worked in market promotion did not carry any day-by-day monetary risk.

What is the message? Each and every group contributing to the utility of a commodity, be it form, place or time utility, is entitled to share in the rewards of increased marketings.

Finally, it is my belief that the expenditure of public funds in overseas market development activities for U.S. farm products has resulted in a favorable return on a modest investment. I hope the effort is continued. From the standpoint of government officials with responsibility for fund allocation to industry groups, dynamic and imaginative projects and activities must be expected.

I mention imaginative market development projects because that is the heart of the concept that government and industry cooperate in this endeavor.

If one believes that the growth in utilization of farm products is most likely to occur in the developing countries, as I do, it is obvious where the future emphasis should be. The "AID" countries of former years are the most rapidly expanding commercial markets of today.

☆☆☆☆☆☆☆☆☆☆☆

CHAPTER 4

☆☆☆☆☆☆☆☆☆☆☆

Enlarging the Trading World—Access to More Markets

☆ ☆

When Mr. Nixon became president in January, 1969, about 30 percent of the world's population was restricted from purchasing U.S. produced farm products competitively, even though U.S. farmers were being paid to limit production, and several commodities were in surplus to our domestic requirements and to the needs of our overseas trading partners.

There really was no valid reason for such buying restriction, except that a mistake had been made by the late President Kennedy. People not eligible to buy our farm products competitively were citizens of the People's Republic of China and the Soviet Union and Eastern Europe, with the exception of Yugoslavia, Rumania and Poland.

A great amount of discussion on trade policy issues had taken place since the early 1950s. Feelings were strong on the pros and cons of the United States doing business with the communist countries. Few people by the late 1960s were neutral on the issue.

To arrive at my own feeling on the matter of our country opening its grain, oilseed, cotton and other commodity markets to the so-called centrally planned economies, I had done a great amount of soul searching and study. First, it was necessary to reconstruct attitudes of past and present leaders. I developed my own rationale for favoring global trade. To not engage in commerce was ignoring the desirability for continued dialogue between peoples under conflicting political systems. It seemed to me that the buying and selling of food and farm products was one activity that could contribute to some better understanding between people living under diverse political systems. Such discussion is ahead of the story. First, I wish to reconstruct some of the happenings.

In a letter to Premier Krushchev on July 14, 1958, President Eisenhower responded to an earlier letter from him, wherein he (Krushchev) proposed a considerable increase in United States-Soviet trade.

President Eisenhower was positive, constructive and forthcoming. Among other things he wrote:

> Americans believe that the economic welfare of each contributes to the economic welfare of all. Therefore they cannot but welcome the emphasis you place in your letter on striving to expand the supply of consumers goods and housing available to the Soviet people. Our people have done a great deal in recent years to promote higher standards of living through expanded trade with many countries. They would like to trade with the Soviet Union as well, for the same purpose.
>
> As you know, United States export and import trade is carried on by individual firms and not under governmental auspices. There is no need, therefore, to formalize relations between United States firms and Soviet trade organizations. Soviet trade organizations are free right now, without any need for special action by the United States Government, to develop a larger volume of trade with firms in this country. They may not be taking advantage of all available possibilities. In recent years, United States firms have bought far more from Soviet trade organizations than the latter have purchased from the United States. Furthermore, many of the more important Soviet trade items mentioned in your letter are accorded duty-free entry into the United States. Thus, the situation favors the expansion of Soviet purchases in this country. While the extension of long-term credits for Soviet purchases in the United States would raise complex legal and political questions, the normal commercial credit terms presently available to Soviet

trade organizations permit the further expansion of trade between our two countries.

Following this period of some economic thaw between the United States and the Soviet Union, several unfortunate political developments took place, among which was the U-2 incident, the coming to power of Castro in Cuba and the Cuban missile crisis.

There were far more reasons for the United States to think negatively about increasing trade with the Soviets than to think positively. And that is precisely what happened until 1963, when political events were in a less inflamed condition. In addition, the Soviet Union produced a small most distressing wheat crop. Grain bins in the United States were bulging with wheat, corn and other grains.

President Kennedy decided to allow the Soviets to buy U.S. wheat, and he directed USDA to see to it that the grain was priced competitively with wheat of other origins. A statement, identified as the President's statement, was distributed to members of Congress by the Department of State. It follows:

President's Statement
On the Sale of Wheat to the U.S.S.R.
and Eastern European Countries

The Soviet Union and various Eastern European countries have expressed a willingness to buy from our private grain dealers at the regular world price several million tons of surplus American wheat or wheat flour for shipment during the next several months. They may also wish to purchase from us surplus feed grains and other agricultural commodities.

After consultation with the National Security Council, and informing the appropriate leaders of the Congress, I have concluded that such sales by private dealers for American dollars or gold, either cash on delivery or normal commercial terms, should not be prohibited by the Government. The Commodity Credit Corporation in the Department of Agriculture will sell to our private grain traders the amount necessary to replace the grain used to fulfill these requirements, and the Department of Commerce will grant export licenses for their delivery to and use in the Soviet Union and Eastern Europe only.

An added feature is the provision that the wheat we sell to the Soviet Union will be carried in available American ships, supplemented by ships of other countries as required. Arrangements will also be made by the Department of Commerce to prevent any single American dealer from receiving an excessive share of these sales.

No action by the Congress is required, but a special report on the matter will be sent to both Houses.

Basically, the Soviet Union will be treated like any other cash customer in the world market who is willing and able to strike a bargain with private American merchants. While this wheat, like all wheat sold abroad, will be sold at the world price, which is the only way it could be sold, there is in such transactions no subsidy to the foreign purchaser; only a savings to the American taxpayer on wheat the Government has already purchased and stored at the higher domestic price which is maintained to assist our farmers.

This transaction has obvious benefit for the United States. The sale of four million metric tons of wheat, for example, for an estimated $250 million, and additional sums from the use of American shipping, will benefit our balance of payments and gold reserves by that amount and substantially strengthen the economic outlook for those employed in producing, transporting, handling and loading farm products.

Wheat, moreover, is our number one farm surplus today, to the extent of about one billion unsold bushels. The sale of around 150 million bushels of wheat would be worth over $200 million to the American taxpayer in reduced budget expenditures. Our country has always responded to requests for food from governments of people who needed it, so long as we were certain that the people would actually get it and know where it came from.

The Russian people will know they are receiving American wheat. The United States has never had a policy against selling consumer goods, including agricultural commodities, to the Soviet Union and Eastern Europe. On the contrary, we have been doing exactly that for a number of years, and to the extent that their limited supplies of gold, dollars and foreign exchange must be used for food, they cannot be used to purchase military or other equipment.

Our allies have long been engaged in extensive sales of wheat and other farm products to the Communist bloc, and, in fact, it would be foolish to halt the sales of wheat when other countries can buy wheat from us today and then sell this flour to the Communists. In recent weeks Australia and NATO allies have agreed to sell 10 million to 15 million tons of wheat and wheat flour to the Communist bloc.

This transaction advertises to the world as nothing else could the success of free American agriculture. It demonstrates our willingness to relieve food shortages, to reduce tensions, and to improve relations with all countries, and it shows that peaceful agreements with the United States which serve the interest of both sides are a far more worthwhile course than a course of isolation and hostility.

For this Government to tell our grain traders that they cannot accept these offers, on the other hand, would accomplish little or nothing. The Soviets would continue to buy wheat and flour elsewhere, including wheat flour, from those nations which buy our wheat. Moreover, having for many years sold them farm products which are not in surplus, it would make no sense to refuse to sell those products on which we must otherwise pay the cost of storage. In short, this particular decision with respect to sales to the Soviet Union, which is not inconsistent with many smaller transactions over a long period of time, does not represent a new Soviet-American trade policy. That must await the settlement of many matters. But it does represent one more hopeful sign that a more peaceful world is both possible and beneficial to us all.

10-10-63   Office of Public Service
                                  Bureau of Public Affairs
                                  Department of State
                                  Washington, D.C.

When President Kennedy announced that U.S. wheat would be available to the Soviet Union at subsidized prices, no one was really surprised. Rumors had been circulating for several days that such announcement was imminent. What was a surprise was the contingency which became known as the "hooker"—the cargo-preference provision whereby up to 50 percent of the wheat sold by exporting firms to the Soviets would be required to be transported on American flag vessels, the cost of which was greater than that of foreign flag vessels. In fact, the "hooker" would prevent any sales from actually taking place unless or until the U.S. government found a way to pick up the tab for the greater cost of ocean transportation.

I wondered at the time of the announcement whether or not USDA officials had been aware of the "hooker" provision.

In reality, the sales announcement reflected action rightfully described as "Now you have it; now you do not!"

In the President's statement released by the Department of State, reference was made to 4 million tons (about 150 million bushels) as an example of the sale. This total figure apparently reflected the administration's estimate of the volume to be purchased by the Soviets.

The announcement also established another new and unusual policy with the provision that "Arrangements will also be made by the

Department of Commerce to prevent any single American dealer from receiving an excessive share of these sales."

The implementing regulation read:

> Each U.S. exporter participating in the export of wheat and wheat flour to Country Group Y destinations is limited to a maximum of 25 percent of the total quantity expected to be purchased in the United States. License applications which meet all of the requirements for approval will be processed promptly if there is sufficient evidence that the 25 percent participation rule is met.

The 4 million tons mentioned as an example in the President's statement was obviously the target figure utilized by the commerce department as the first export license was issued to Continental Grain Company for export of 1 million tons of wheat to the Soviet Union (25 percent of 4 million).

A few weeks later Cargill, Inc., announced the firm had sold 700,000 tons of U.S. wheat to the Soviets.

USDA officials had found a way to pay for the additional cost of shipping part of the wheat in American flag vessels. They paid the shipping cost differential by paying more export subsidy on durum wheat. At that time durum wheat was exported sporadically. Durum was not a front-burner commodity in the trading world. Level of export subsidy for durum was established by USDA through a bid procedure. The bidding procedure provided a framework for the seller to make subsidy offers at a level which could provide sufficient revenue to cover the higher costs of shipping a part of the wheat destined to Soviet ports on American flag vessels.

The subsidy paid by USDA for the export of most of the 550,000 tons of durum was 13 cents per bushel higher than the amount paid two weeks earlier for the export of durum to non-Soviet destinations (73 cents per bushel vs. 60 cents). A small amount of the durum in the Soviet sale for shipment from the Atlantic in that spring of 1964 was subsidized 84 cents per bushel.

The balance of the transactions—1,150,000 tons—consisted of hard winter and western white wheat and was subsidized at the rate of 60 to 64 cents per bushel.

Apparently, the subsidy paid per bushel for the 62 million bushels involved in the total transaction averaged about 66 cents.

Whereas it was thought the total movement would be 4,000,000 tons, sales stopped at 1,700,000. I suspect it will never be known whether or not purchasing of U.S. wheat by the Soviets would have continued had it not been for the shipping provision controversy.

Likewise, it can be said with certainty the shipping provision, "hooker," prevented any further export of U.S. wheat and other grains to the Soviet Union during the balance of the Johnson administration and for nearly the first three years of the Nixon era.

Was the use of the CCC borrowing authority to subsidize American flag vessels engaged in commercial exports for dollars illegal? Probably not. But the issue will be discussed again later in this chapter.

CZECHOSLOVAKIA—A NATION IN FERMENT, 1966

In the spring of 1966, in my capacity as executive vice-president of U.S. Feed Grains Council, I organized a feed utilization study trip to Czechoslovakia. That country had been importing a record volume of sorghum, corn and barley from the United States—over 500,000 tons in an eight-month period.

The Czechoslovakian ambassador to the United States in Washington, D.C., urged such a trip and promised the full cooperation of his government in Prague.

James Forster, production manager, De Kalb Agricultural Association and president of the USFGC, accompanied me. Joining us from Europe were Allen Golberg, European director, Rome, and Robert Ramsay, Continental Grain Company, Paris.

In most ways this was just another typical assignment, but with one difference. Czechoslovakia, at that time, was dreaming of improving economic ties to the West.

The impressions gained during that one-week trip convinced me that the urge to improve living standards was indeed great in this centrally controlled economy. Expectations of the people were almost at a feverish pitch.

Government officials in Prague were most helpful, as had been expected. We interviewed agricultural policy officials and visited several state farms and the Xaveros integrated broiler operation.

Over 90 percent of the agricultural land in Czechoslovakia is socialized—about one-third in state farms and two-thirds in cooperative units. The prevailing attitude among the workers on the state farms we visited lacked enthusiasm. This was my first visit to a government owned and operated farm in a communist nation. In subsequent years, as I visited several such enterprises in as many socialized countries, I discovered the morale and attitude always to be the same.

If I were required to describe the unenthusiastic feeling and to give the reason I would choose the words "Lack of dignity and respect!"

Conversely, as I have now lived my last three years during this decade of the 1980s in rural America, again becoming acquainted with farmers and those who service them, I am convinced that the perquisites and the possibilities to enjoy such, lends dignity and pride to our farmers, who are entrepreneurs in their own right. I am speaking of such things as good roads, modern transportation, schools, churches, freedom of the press, freedom to organize and many others.

Even minor decisions having to do with planting, harvesting and livestock feeding on the Czech farms were made by those "up the line." How demoralizing to personalities!

The Xaveros broiler operation servicing Prague was a showplace and was operated by technically qualified people. But, in a way, it too was quite sad. The breeding stock lacked in uniformity and conformation. The manager said, "What I would give for some male breeding stock from the United States."

The ration contained 40 percent imported corn, 15 percent locally produced wheat and 8 percent soybean meal. The chief nutritionist would have preferred a higher percentage of soybean meal but additional high-protein ingredients as available were being incorporated into the mix. The balance of the ration consisted of indigenous ingredients.

One trade impediment practiced by the United States at that time made no sense whatsoever in the minds of Czechoslovakians; it was known as the part-cargo requirement. The import of corn and sorghum by Czechoslovakia was averaging about 60,000 tons per month and could only be shipped after a validated license had been issued by the U.S. Department of Commerce. After this the commodities were subject to the part-cargo provision, an impediment against which regulations had never been published by the U.S. government. The restriction was invoked and administered by word of mouth from commerce department officials.

The restriction required that a full cargo of grain shipped from a U.S. port be partially discharged at some port in the free world prior to making the second and final port of call—usually Gdynia or Gdańsk (Poland), in that Czechoslovakia is a landlocked nation. The first partial discharge was usually accomplished at Hamburg or

Bremen. The requirement mandating two discharge ports represented an additional cost to the Czechoslovakians of about $1.50 per ton (nearly 4 cents per bushel).

As an aside, I understand well the need for an export administration law but I never could receive a meaningful explanation of the word-of-mouth part-cargo trade impediment as applied, at that time, against sales to bloc countries. It was a classic example of intervention in the marketplace.

From a policy standpoint, the central planning structure in Czechoslovakia and the impact of such on the efficiency of the agricultural economy left much to be desired. Food stores seemed reasonably well stocked but variety and eye appeal were lacking. Drabness prevailed.

One could not help thinking that if both Czechoslovakia and the United States were part of an open world, both countries would have much to gain. The Czechoslovakians, by nature, are skilled artisans being forced to use their human and physical resources in the manufacture of heavy equipment and bulk goods. What a waste of great talent! The planet suffers from the loss.

RUMANIA, AN EAGER PRODUCER OF PORK AND POULTRY, 1969

President Nixon visited Rumania on August 2 and 3, 1969. He was the first American president to visit a communist satellite country.

Sometime after the President's return, Secretary Hardin requested me to travel to Bucharest for the purpose of offering a CCC credit line to Rumania. If the Rumanians would agree to the terms and the line established, Rumania would be eligible to purchase selected U.S. farm products on short-term credit. Several crops in Rumania had been damaged by adverse weather in late summer and fall.

Following a short appearance in Rome at the FAO conference, I traveled to Bucharest on November 19, and remained in Rumania for three days. During that time, I was given a whirlwind tour of Rumania's agriculture and was shown several livestock enterprises, all of which were state owned and operated.

As expected, the poultry and hog operations in Rumania were similar to those in Czechoslovakia. The units were huge in size and much more lavish than a competitive economic system can support.

★ *Palmby in Rumania, 1969. The fourth man from the left is Dan McCarthy, Economic Section, American Embassy, Bucharest.*

On the other hand, the general health of the animals in the units I saw was excellent.

Both the swine and the poultry rations were formulated with the help of computers, and the Rumanians were incorporating the lowest-cost ingredients with the goal of attaining maximum feeding efficiencies. They were short on soybean meal and other high-protein ingredients. Because of a tight supply situation, they also found it necessary to incorporate less corn than they would have preferred. Some barley and low-quality wheat were being substituted.

Up to that time, I had never made the acquaintance of feed formulation technicians more eager to secure choice feed ingredients. Being on location in Rumania caused me once again to more fully appreciate the quality and abundance of high-protein feed ingredients available to U.S. compounders—not to mention the availability of corn, sorghum and other grains in our country.

A credit line of about $20 million was extended to the Rumanians. Subsequently, it was increased. They purchased feed grains and several other commodities, including alfalfa seed. The inclement weather had devastated quality seed output.

There were two aspects of this short trip to Rumania that intrigued me.

Number one, it was common knowledge that Secretary General Ceausescu of Rumania, a fiercely independent chief of state, had good relations with the People's Republic of China as well as with North Vietnam. To this day, no one has drawn pictures for me of the significance of our President wanting to show friendship to Rumania. My own judgment dictated that our agricultural abundance just might be a concrete and positive force for improving relations between our two countries. And without further cost to us, because the credit line as established was non-concessional in nature.

Number two, we in USDA were working on guidelines for new farm legislation as discussion items with the Congress. It was still too early to predict with certainty the exact direction those guidelines would take us in developing a new farm program. I was confident that improved access to the growing market for commodities in the Eastern bloc countries would be compatible with our market-oriented policies.

My impressions of the potential demand in Czechoslovakia and now the feverish grasping for better livestock and poultry rations in Rumania naturally caused my pulse beat to increase.

NORMALIZING EXPORT SALES OF U.S. FARM PRODUCTS TO SOCIALIST COUNTRIES, JUNE, 1971

The first major policy decision made by Dr. Hardin after he became secretary of agriculture in January, 1969, was the soybean loan level (price support) for the 1969 crop. For 16 years prior to his becoming secretary, he had been Chancellor of the University of Nebraska. He was not experienced in the administration of farm programs. I detected his uneasiness in making a major decision on the level of price support for the great U.S. "miracle crop," soybeans.

Many people and groups presented views and recommendations on the soybean price support level which had been $2.50 per bushel for the years 1966, 1967 and 1968. The loan rate had been increased 25 cents per bushel in the Congressional election year of 1966 and had been maintained at that level.

The results of the higher loan level for the three-year period (1966 through 1968) offered a classroom example of government intervention stifling the growth of an industry.

In the few years prior to 1966, utilization (domestic and foreign) of U.S. soybeans had increased at a rate of about 8 percent annually.

During the three years, 1966 through 1968, the total utilization remained almost static.

The carryout of old crop beans at the end of the crop year, August 31, 1967, had increased to 91 million bushels, a large portion of which was owned or controlled by CCC. By August 31, 1968, the carryout was 167 million bushels and with a continuation of the $2.50 loan level the carryout by August 31, 1969, was projected to be 331 million and 581 million one year hence (August 31, 1970).

I suspect Dr. Hardin conferred with many other interested people, which was highly pleasing to me because I was recommending lowering the loan rate to $2.25 per bushel. I knew the action would draw sparks from some producers and one or more farm organizations, such as the National Farmers Union. Regardless of this, I wanted the soybean industry to again become a growth industry based on market forces.

After considerable discussion within USDA policy circles, the loan rate of $2.25 per bushel for the 1969 crop was announced.

Immediately following this announcement, I contacted members of the House committee on agriculture and presented the reasons for the action. A few agreed. Several said they would await judgment. Others were not sympathetic with the action.

(To complete this story, the outcome must be noted. In the marketing year ending August 31, 1969, the value of U.S. soybeans "disappeared" was $2.3 billion. Two years later in the marketing year ending August 31, 1971, the value was $3.6 billion. A rise of more than half in two years and an increase in farm earnings of $1.3 billion for the year from the marketplace.)

The retrenchment of government in influencing soybean prices is mentioned in this subchapter because the action was one of the most significant made by USDA during the Nixon years. I felt it set the pattern for recognition of market forces in arriving at provisions for government farm programs. I also felt it may encourage more people within the administration to appreciate the significance of greater U.S. access to more foreign markets. My impressions three years earlier of the "pent-up" demand for U.S. farm products in Czechoslovakia inspired me. At that time I had not been in the USSR nor in any other East European countries other than Czechoslovakia, but I suspected that all East Europeans including the Soviets hungered for more meat, poultry, eggs, and "California type farm commodities."

In fact, as the Agricultural Act of 1970 took shape, it was quite apparent that several members of the House and Senate committees on agriculture were building a record of holding the policy people in the Nixon administration responsible for building a larger export market for farm products. Failure to do so was creating a straw man for blame if exports did not increase.

I was also concerned about the possibility of program cost to the government if we did not succeed in improving access to foreign markets on as many fronts as possible.

Almost from the first day of my returning to government in January, 1969, I was satisfied with the reception I received from Secretary Hardin and the appropriate people at the White House. I regularly contacted John Whitaker on the White House staff, and he also routinely contacted me. Always, I kept Hardin fully informed and constantly received guidance from him.

As mentioned earlier in this chapter, no meaningful sales of U.S. farm products had been made to the Soviet Union since 1963. The USSR, together with bloc countries and the People's Republic of China, was—through various unilateral actions by past U.S. presidents—barred from buying our farm commodities on a competitive price basis. In addition to the several shipping impediments contained in President Kennedy's executive order in 1963, the President Truman embargo on trade with China was still national policy.

I was comfortable in seeking support of my colleagues in the departments of State, Treasury and Commerce because I could see no conflict with the President's goals. Hardin agreed. We simply wanted the issue to receive policy consideration. Or, stated in another way, I thought it was an issue worthy of consideration.

I had urged the Food and Fiber Commission under President Johnson (1966 to 1967) to recommend normalization of trade in farm commodities between the United States and the socialist countries. Others had also made the same recommendation.

The commission stated in its report that "The Nation [U.S.] has a great deal to gain through a liberalization of world trade in agricultural commodities."

The commission further stated that "We urge the elimination of the 50 percent U.S. flag vessel and part-cargo requirements as applied to commercial trade. We concur in the recommendation that steps be taken to permit U.S. shipping firms to operate at rates competitive with those offered by foreign companies."

In the summer of 1967, I applied to the USSR Embassy in Washington for a visa for travel to the Soviet Union. I was still with the U.S. Feed Grains Council at that time but a few USDA economists had invited me under the Cultural Exchange Agreement to accompany them on an exploratory trip. The visit did not materialize because the proposed appointments and travel within the Soviet Union as arranged by Intourist were simply not worthwhile. The official Soviet travel agency wanted us to spend most of the time with research institutions. This was of very little interest to me. I wanted to observe the state of the art of livestock and poultry production.

We withdrew our application for visas.

In preparation for this trip I had informed myself on the annual production of total grains (including wheat) in the Soviet Union and the net foreign trade for each year commencing with July 1, 1961. I particularly mention wheat because I had read in many publications that wheat was an important feed ingredient in that country. Even the best publications on Soviet agriculture were not very illuminating.

Incidentally, in my years with the council, I always consented to be interviewed by staff from the Central Intelligence Agency (CIA) after my numerous overseas trips—and they made frequent requests. I doubt whether information or observations shared with them were of any great help to their pool of intelligence or knowledge. Conversely, I don't remember learning anything from them on agriculture or trade that I had not already read in the papers or observed firsthand myself. But the CIA was a U.S. federal agency.

This pattern of being interviewed by the CIA continued on sporadically after I joined the Nixon administration as an assistant secretary of agriculture.

Almost from the first day after my return to government I continued to "stir the pot" in encouraging policy consideration of the several impediments then in force discouraging or preventing the export of our farm products to the socialist countries.

As I recall, the first informal discussion I had on this matter—outside of visits with Secretary Hardin and others in USDA—was in the Executive Office Building. National Security Council (NSC) had agreed to hear my pitch. The subject was of such little importance to NSC staff that I do not remember of any other department or agency being represented at the meeting.

I carried statistics on Soviet grain production and trade with me to that discussion. Ironically, the interest of NSC was so limited I never took the time to lift the figures from my brief case.

Now long after the fact, the grain production and trade figures seem more interesting than at that time.

The figures I carried with me to that short informal meeting in early 1969 follow:

USSR PRODUCTION AND NET TRADE FOR TOTAL GRAINS AND WHEAT BY CROP YEAR

(in Million Metric Tons)

	Total Grains		Wheat	
	Production	Net Trade	Production	Net Trade
1961-62	130.8	−6.5	66.5	−4.8
1962-63	140.2	−6.4	70.8	−5.2
1963-64	107.5	+6.1	49.7	+7.0
1964-65	152.1	−1.9	74.4	0.0
1965-66	121.1	+4.5	59.7	+5.9
1966-67	171.2	−1.8	100.5	−1.3
1967-68	147.9	−4.3	77.4	−3.8

The grain production and disappearance figures as well as their net trade in grain should lead most anyone to observe that the Soviets had not encouraged importation of grain. The Kremlin generally seemed to follow a policy of "making do." On the other hand, limited information appearing from time to time in *The New York Times* and occasionally elsewhere led me to believe the diets of the Soviets were terribly short on meat, poultry and eggs. Then, too, they (the Soviets) from time to time arranged to buy sizeable tonnage of broilers and pork carcasses from Western Europe.

E. Fred Bergsten (later to become an assistant secretary of the Treasury in the Carter administration) on the staff of NSC was the person with whom I met on this first discussion involving the 50 percent American flag shipping provision for grain sales to the Soviet Union. Mr. Bergsten said his advice from "up the river," meaning Langley, Virginia (CIA headquarters), was that the Soviet Union in any 12-month period would not expend more than $50 million for U.S. farm products. With this observation on the table the meeting ended almost before it began.

I was not unduly disappointed with this "put down"—only determined to muster support from other quarters.

Secretary Hardin and I discussed this matter from time to time through the balance of 1969 and on into the following year. He also was keeping the issue alive with some of his counterparts. Then a positive attitude was formulated. A sub-cabinet level working party was established to develop projections on level of trade activity which may take place should the President take actions normalizing economic relations between the U.S. and the People's Republic of China and the other communist countries. I mention China first because the working group, chaired by Ambassador Winthrop Brown devoted most of the meeting time on a discussion of the outlook for trade with China. As I participated in several meetings of this group, I thought the Department of State was the logical choice to head the exercise. Treasury and Commerce indicated enthusiasm for the possibility of more trade. Defense and CIA were negative.

Early in 1971, it was quite apparent that the NSC (Henry Kissinger), State, Treasury, Commerce and Agriculture—each for different reasons was generally on the wagon favoring normalization. CIA consistently stated elimination of shipping provision impediments with the Soviet Union would not result in any meaningful volume of U.S. grain sales.

As the ball toward presidential action continued to roll, there were days when I thought the normalization action may only apply to China and not include the USSR and the bloc countries. At that time I did not know why all the fervor from the NSC was primarily pitched toward China. Of course, I was soon to find out. The great penchant for secrecy emanating from NSC was something to behold.

We in USDA, because of Ray Ioanes and others in the Foreign Agricultural Service, had done our work well in projecting the flow of trade in U.S. farm products to China in the event the embargo were to be lifted and the shipping impediments rescinded. Early on, it was estimated that China would probably be a meaningful "price" buyer of U.S. wheat. This would mean a larger market for our soft red wheat and on occasion ordinary hard or maybe some of the soft white in our Pacific Northwest (PNW). We further advised cotton sales could be large but would undoubtedly be related to the willingness of the United States to import fabrics and garments. Vegetable oil sales may also be a possibility along with coarse grains in some years. (Our guesses proved to be accurate.)

Projecting level of farm commodity sales to the USSR proved to be more difficult. There were several reasons for our worries about what might happen if the President should move forward with actions leading to trade normalization.

Two years had elapsed since I had prepared USSR grain production and trade tables. Results for the latest two years were:

	Total Grains		Wheat	
	Production	Net Trade	Production	Net Trade
1968-69	169.5	−5.5	93.4	−5.6
1969-70	162.4	−5.5	79.9	−5.3

A few of the participants in the working party continued to remind me that if the President should remove the impediments and no sales transpire it would prove to be most embarrassing to him and his administration. Under such a scenario organized labor would be alienated and there would be no off-setting pluses. I readily understood this political risk but I also felt the chances for an increase in livestock and poultry production based on imported grains was a worthwhile risk.

On the other hand, the Agricultural Act of 1970 had now become law. The goal of the legislation was to boost farm income but at the same time supply food in abundance to consumers—a tight wire trick under known circumstances. The new law had a much greater chance of success with our having access to as many markets as possible. Then, too, Ioanes and the attaché service were well informed on the food riots of 1970 in Poland. We were not well informed on uprisings in some areas of the Soviet Union. In the back of my own mind was the thought that if the Czechoslovakians and the Rumanians want more meat, poultry and eggs then certainly the Soviets must also be restless.

The CIA did not buy this reasoning!

I did not find concurrence with this thought in the academic community. There seemed to be a common thread running through the statements on this matter emanating from the Ivy League schools, University of Chicago and others—all very similar to the Langley, Virginia, expression that the Soviet Union simply would not expend any meaningful amount of hard foreign exchange for agricultural commodities from the United States. This nearly identical pronouncement gave me cause for concern, because the unanimity of expression emanating from CIA and much of academia seemed like a well worn record—maybe a broken one.

In April, 1971, President Nixon announced the termination of the embargo on trade between the United States and the People's Republic of China.

During this period of fast breaking foreign policy decisions, I was once again impressed with the relative unimportance of agriculture, as a sector, in our total economy, as world diplomatic and military decisions were being considered. Our domestic food production capability was and is to this day simply taken for granted by those responsible for foreign relations of our country. Much more so than is the case in Japan, European and the communist countries. There are two reasons for this, in my opinion.

One, the U.S. agricultural sector because of many positive reasons has always been dependable in supplying the food requirements of the nation with very little price fluctuation, and two, the United States has no choice but to lead in the world of diplomacy, and in so doing, those in responsible positions oftentimes fail to understand basic domestic economics. (This troublesome phenomenon will be illustrated later.)

On June 10, 1971—about eight weeks after terminating the trade embargo between China and the United States—President Nixon rescinded the shipping provision and other impediments as contained in the Kennedy executive order of 1963. As a result of this action, the communist countries were enabled to purchase U.S. farm products free of the validated licensing requirement.

Without any assurance whatsoever from the countries so affected, one could not predict that his action would lead to any great increase in the export of U.S. agricultural commodities.

The most important benefit to the East European countries was (after the June 10 action) access to our commodities without the necessity of acquiring a validated license. The part-cargo requirement impediment was also rescinded. Regular communications between U.S. merchandisers and foreign trading entities in these countries were well established. Flow of pertinent commodity information originating in countries like East Germany, Hungary and Czechoslovakia was quite good. Thus the level of purchasing could be projected with reasonable accuracy by USDA, U.S. exporters and any other interested person or associations.

The People's Republic of China was largely an unknown. Anyone could guess the potential demand for grain and cotton from the United States. To quantify that into *real* demand was quite a different story. Both public and private groups believed China would move slowly.

The Soviet Union was more difficult. At that time, in mid-1971, the only information available to USDA (including myself) regarding the outlook for U.S. sales to the Soviet Union was the knowledge of that country's historical export and import activity. In the four crop years commencing July 1, 1966, the Soviets had been a net exporter of all grains at the *annual* average rate of 4.275 million metric tons (170 million bushels of corn equivalent or about 157 million bushels of wheat). Further, in 1970 (crop year 1970-1971) the Soviet Union had produced a record grain crop of 186.8 million metric tons, nearly 100 of which was wheat, (second only to the record wheat crop of 100.5 million tons in 1966). One more piece of information available was the fact that in no one year had the Soviet Union been a net importer of more than 6.1 million tons of grain and that was in crop year 1963-1964 when the country had produced only 107.5 million tons of all grains.

Seasoned analysts of Soviet agriculture in USDA believed the Soviets would *only* be net importer of grain under one or more types of situations.

☆ Extreme Soviet grain crop production would shortfall (and then more likely to cause the Soviets to be importers if two such years should be back-to-back).

☆ Import for building reserves (and such a policy likely would be related to commitments to satellite countries).

☆ A change in centrally planned policy whereby the agricultural sector would be expected to continue a dependable increase in production of animal products regardless of availability of domestic grain and other feed ingredients.

The number one reason as listed above could be projected with some degree of accuracy. The second one could be guessed with some assurance of perfection by flow of information from several sources. The third situation would require knowledge of Soviet decision-making procedure, at the highest level—an unknown bit of knowledge in the United States. (This weakness in our intelligence gathering system would prove to be embarrassing to the United States.)

Following the June, 1971, removal of trade impediments and through the balance of the year the sales of grain and soybean meal to the bloc countries continued about as before but with some noticeable increase to East Germany—nothing unusual or spectacular!

Exporters of U.S. tobacco, cotton, grain and oilseeds were, with various degrees of priority, attempting to establish themselves with the appropriate Foreign Trade Organization (FTO) in China—after three decades of isolation.

Along in August and September, 1971, a few grain exporters stopped by my office and shared their concern that if they (the exporters) should be successful in making a U.S. grain sale to the Soviets, would the U.S. dock workers work the vessels. Thomas W. Gleason, president of the International Longshoremen's Association (ILA) had made noises to the contrary. George Meany, president of AFL-CIO made no secret of his unhappiness with President Nixon for revoking the 50 percent flag shipping provision, even though the 50 percent stipulation had resulted in zero work for his members for over seven years. The Kennedy executive order on shipping resulted in no more U.S. grain sales to the Soviet Union after February, 1964.

Now that the President had acted in the affirmative on the long-standing impediment, I felt obligated to encourage my counterparts in the other government agencies—Commerce and Labor as well as White House staff—to encourage further action that may be helpful to the U.S. business community (exporters and shippers) in making sales and deliveries to the Soviets.

In the meantime, and since the beginning of the Nixon adminstration, the Commerce Department and certainly a few of the White House staff had become increasingly interested in securing results as a consequence of the President's action. After all, the matter of seeking cooperation of labor was not within the province of agriculture. During this period I kept in close contact with John Whitaker.

As I had expected, Andrew Gibson, assistant secretary of Commerce responsible for maritime affairs, came to my office and visited with me on the possibility of expending CCC funds under some grain export subsidy scheme—as had been done in 1964 to implement the Kennedy wheat sale—as a disguised method to subsidize American flag vessels. I was prepared for this suggestion and had had a long discussion of the matter with Hardin. I shared my view that while such expenditure *may* be legal it would establish a most unwise precedent and be a needless expenditure of CCC funds (I had discussed the feasibility of such expenditure with General Counsel, Ed Shulman, USDA. I do not believe he prepared a written opinion but he took a dim view of developing a legal justification for expending CCC funds to cover the additional cost of transporting commercially sold commodities in American flag vessels).

I was uneasy about the possibility of someone higher up in the hierarchy approving (other than in USDA) the use of CCC funds to subsidize a portion of the cost of ocean transportation of farm products to the socialist countries. I emphatically stated to Whitaker that I would not attempt to justify any such expenditure before Congressional committees. Interestingly, this issue died before it became a real option. I was not, and to this day am not, opposed to the federal government assisting the maritime fleet but it is an issue that should be debated and decided on its own merits.

Along in October, 1971, because of many American businessmen contacting more and more government officials in several departments, the question of solving the shipping problem was receiving more attention. More top government officials were taking an interest.

President Nixon had established the Council on International Economic Policy (CIEP) early in the year 1971. Peter Peterson was named director. By summer and fall he involved himself in the shipping matter as did Secretary of Commerce Stans. These two officials along with Hardin, presidential assistant Peter Flanigan and Colson (special counsel to the President) were all helping to bring the matter to a workable conclusion.

Colson and Gibson and maybe others met with the several labor leaders in as many unions and secured their cooperation in allowing competitive flag vessels from third countries to be serviced and loaded at U.S. ports. Cooperation was attained largely on the basis of "business in the future." The administration did agree to negotiate a maritime agreement with the Soviet Union—in the following year (1972).

Concurrently, with the meetings within government circles on shipping, grain exporters were talking to Cliff Pulvermacher (administrator of Export Marketing Service) on the availability of CCC-owned barley for sale to the Soviet Union. This gave me some concern because the United States was harvesting a record corn crop, and free market prices were depressed. The Soviet interest in U.S. grain as expressed by exporters for feed purposes was not a surprise. On the other hand, we favored the export of corn and sorghum from the free market. An increase in export of grain from free stocks would have an earlier and more favorable impact on farm prices than sales of grain from CCC.

As the exporters discussed this matter of specific grains with Pulvermacher, and on occasion with me, there was a common thread developing. The private sector merchandisers were telling us the Soviets were prepared to purchase corn immediately but they (the Soviets) also wanted U.S. barley at competitive prices. As Pulvermacher and I discussed this between ourselves and then in staff meetings which included Ioanes and Worthington (associate administrator, FAS), Kenneth Frick and Carroll Brunthaver (administrator and associate administrator of ASCS) we recognized barley production in the Soviet Union and in the satellite countries may have been somewhat disappointing in 1971.

(Somewhat later it did develop that the 1971 coarse grain crop [largely barley] in the Soviet Union was about 4.7 million tons less than the year before but the second largest ever produced.)

I also believed that the Soviet state farm managers responsible for big livestock operations were a bit reluctant to incorporate (too quickly) a higher percentage of corn in rations. The Soviet Union was not a major corn feeding nation. While livestock feeders in the United States look upon corn as the prize feed ingredient, less sophisticated feeders, because of tradition and experience or lack thereof, are generally hesitant to incorporate *too* high a percentage of the low-fiber, high-energy grain (corn) in livestock rations.

After considerable discussion with the agency heads, it was decided to recommend CCC offering barley and oats for restricted use (export to approved destination) at or above competitive world prices.

Exporters were telling us they could sell free corn to Exporthkleb, the Soviet Foreign Trade Organization (FTO), provided they (the exporters) could also offer some barley at world prices. The United States had become a residual and seasonal exporter of barley because domestic prices were generally above world prices. On the other hand, the volume of barley owned by CCC was not as large in relation to domestic requirements as was oats. A portion of the oats in the hands of CCC represented a storage investment greater than the original loan (procurement price) level. We, therefore, were anxious to dispose of oats and thereby save CCC further outlay of funds for storage. We countered the exporters' requests. We would consider offering barley but only on the condition that at least one-half the barley tonnage be matched with a purchase of oats from CCC at or above the world price.

Finally, to pave the way for sales of feed grains by U.S. exporters to Exporthkleb, it was decided to prepare a public announcement for release by the CCC regional office at Kansas City, routinely announcing CCC barley and oats for sale for restricted use to specific destination on a bid basis, on a specific date, with CCC reserving the right to accept or reject.

The Kansas City announcement mandated that for each ton of barley and/or oats purchased from CCC and shipped to acceptable destinations, the exporter would be required to sell and ship at least 2 tons of corn from the free market. This provision was changed prior to accepting offers to a one-to-one provision—1 ton of corn to 1 ton of oats and/or barley. The change was made because of work stoppages and threatened work stoppages at Gulf ports.

(As a wrap-up of this first feed grain sale to the Soviet Union and in spite of concern on operations at the ports, the difficulty experienced by CCC in delivering barley to the exporters, approximately 3 million tons of U.S. grain were sold and delivered to the Soviet Union—about 1.9 million tons of corn and a little more than 1 million tons of oats and barley.)

At the time of the November 5, 1971, Kansas City announcement, I was participating in a meeting of the Organization for Economic Cooperation and Development (OECD) agricultural task force in Paris. The Kansas City announcement had not been released until the loose ends involving possible difficulties with labor were resolved to the satisfaction of the officials working on the matter. John Whitaker had kept me informed.

CIEP Director Peterson made the public announcement of the action on Capitol Hill. J. Phil Campbell, undersecretary of agriculture, represented USDA at the public briefing.

The *Washington Post* called the happening a "significant policy shift."

As I was returning to Washington, D.C., from Paris on November 6, the day after the announcement made by Peterson, I reconstructed in my own mind the number of meetings I had attended within the government culminating in a reasonable degree of unanimity on the policy changes.

The unwieldy forces of government—each interest group for varying reasons—had finally banded together to agree on one move regarding the export of agricultural commodities to the socialist countries.

We, in agriculture, wanted the policy change to round out our overall market-oriented policy. The global market access, in my opinion, would work toward increasing net farm income and thereby lower the cost of government farm income assistance.

Commerce and other business interests favored the normalization action on the premise that "increased business is in the best interest of our nation."

NSC embraced the action because sales of farm commodities to the Soviets fit in well with the grand design of detente. In fact, the President had announced in October, 1971, that he would be going to Moscow for a summit meeting in the spring of 1972. All presidential appointees in the Nixon administration were gravely concerned about the lingering and disastrous situation in Vietnam. There were times, however, when I felt we were being used rather than being brought into the fold of a trusted "team." The secretive attitude of NSC contributed to this feeling of discouragement.

On that November 6, I gave thought to the Kansas City announcement itself. If I had had my preference I would not have been in favor of offering CCC barley and oats for export. I would have preferred all of the new "movement" coming from the market (free stocks). I was also convinced that by sticking to such an attitude and policy the feed grain sales would have been delayed, the extent of which was an unknown. My experience through two administrations in government had taught me that timing is of the utmost importance. The various forces in government had come to common agreement, and the sooner we in USDA and the private sector could show positive action through the culmination of a sale, the greater the credibility of the new harmony. Consistent with this philosophy, I did make some notes on my return trip in preparation for an appearance before the House committee on agriculture or the appropriate sub-committees. I had informed committee leaders that I would be ready—at their pleasure—to testify on the entire development, which was of great interest to their constituents.

Some producer groups including the Great Plains Wheat, Inc., expressed displeasure with the leadership of the House committee on agriculture for scheduling hearings on the sale of feed grains to the Soviet Union. They (the producer groups) expressed concern that public hearings in the United States may discourage additional business. I did not share this feeling. I welcomed the announcement of a hearing scheduled for December 8, before the sub-committee on livestock and grains and the sub-committee on department operations. I thought the hearing provided an opportunity for us to explain the steps taken by the administration to put the matter together.

The two respective chairmen were Graham Purcell (D.-Texas) and de la Garza (D.-Texas). (Mr. de la Garza became chairman of the committee on agriculture in 1981.)

As I had expected, chief questions centered on the matter of CCC offering barley and oats for export at a lower price than for domestic use, the uncertainty of U.S. corn shipments because of threatened work stoppages and the philosophical decision to do more business with the communists.

On balance, the hearing was an evenhanded affair. The exchange between members of the sub-committee did provide anyone interested the opportunity to learn more about attitudes of Congressmen regarding the moves to normalize trading relations between the United States and the socialist countries.

Shortly after the Kansas City announcement on November 5, Secretary Hardin resigned as secretary of agriculture and within a few days thereafter Earl Butz was nominated to the post by President Nixon.

I had known Dr. Butz for nearly 20 years, much longer than I had known Hardin.

I was distressed for two reasons to see Hardin leave.

First, the two of us had become well acquainted. During the long period of working on the 1970 agricultural legislation, we had spent a great amount of time together. I had become accustomed to his style of operating. I fear most of us are more or less creatures of habit.

Second, the goals I had hoped to achieve during the first term of the Nixon administration seemed to have been accomplished. Hardin and I had agreed on these goals which was very much to my satisfaction.

SUMMARY

The bold decision to open the U.S. farm commodity markets to more than 30 percent of the population of the world which heretofore had not been allowed to buy such commodities on a competitive basis is worthy of summary enunciation.

What was the significance of such action?

From the standpoint of one interested in national and global agricultural and trade policy, it meant a giant step forward in contributing to a more open trading environment. Further, the action laid the foundation for an increase in farm income in the United States. The action gave the Agricultural Act of 1970 a much greater likelihood of being more workable, because the law was designed to allow a higher percentage of farm income to be derived from the marketplace rather than from CCC (price support).

Removing the trade impediments offered the potential for increased jobs and a greater return to labor through the entire marketing and transportation chain.

Finally, the action demonstrated to the world the superiority of our relatively free enterprise agricultural system compared to central planning in the Soviet Union.

☆☆☆☆☆☆☆☆☆☆☆

CHAPTER 5

☆☆☆☆☆☆☆☆☆☆☆

Growing Pains: U.S. Agriculture in a Global Economic Environment

☆ ☆

WHEAT AND CORN SALES, SOVIET UNION, 1972

On December 9, 1971, Soviet Union Minister of Agriculture Vladimir Matskevich called on Secretary of Agriculture Earl Butz. Butz had been sworn in as secretary a few hours earlier.

The Matskevich trip was in response to an invitation issued by Hardin just prior to his resigning his cabinet position.

Matskevich was also invited to the Oval Office for a meeting with President Nixon and Henry Kissinger. In his book covering his first four years in the White House, Kissinger describes the conversations between President Nixon and Matskevich. The subject, according to Kissinger, was the India–West Pakistan crisis.

As minister of agriculture in the Soviet Union, Matskevich was responsible for production of food and other farm products in his country. He had no responsibility for importing or exporting agricultural commodities. That was and is the responsibility of Exporthkleb in the Ministry of Foreign Trade.

Matskevich was gregarious, folksy and somewhat disarming. He was enthusiastic about wanting to increase production of meat, poultry, eggs and dairy products. He mentioned several times his desire for more corn and protein in animal rations. In his talkative manner he made it clear that he did not consider himself or his ministry as having responsibility for importing feed ingredients nor other farm products. While in the United States, he met with several representatives of as many agricultural business interest groups.

Now, years later, it seems to me his appointments within the United States throughout several of our agricultural regions reflected more of his own personal curiosity as compared to gathering information on technical agriculture developments.

President Nixon had been in office nearly three years. The changing attitude on the matter of doing business with the Soviets had come nearly full circle. During the Matskevich visit I reflected on my first session nearly 30 months earlier with E. Fred Bergsten of NSC on presidential consideration to remove trade impediments. During that early period in the Nixon years it was most difficult to receive an "open" ear on normalizing trade with the communists. This closed mind attitude was a carryover. For example, some of the utterances of President Johnson led me to believe that he thought the 1963/1964 wheat sale was a foreign policy mistake.

The extreme hard-liners in and out of government still believed it was possible to starve the communists into submission or at least into a change of their system. World developments had eroded this attitude but one other philosophy held by many at that time and up to this very moment dictated the theory that the United States did the Soviets a favor by selling grain to them.

In a structured debate it is comparatively easy to come down on either side of this issue, namely, "Who gains from a transaction in world commerce?"

To my satisfaction, both sides to a trade must either have something to gain or at least think they have something to gain from the transaction or no trade will transpire.

For example, the isolationist policy followed by the United States in the late 1920s and early 1930s contributed greatly to the severity of the Great Depression. Everyone living through that period has memories of personal economic sacrifice. As years have passed my own recollections cause me to question some of the policies of our national government at that time. I disagree with the view that during a recession or depression the populace is best served by turning inward. The depression mandated my applying for and accepting for three years a

National Youth Administration (NYA) job at the University of Minnesota. This was the WPA for college students. The young lady I was to marry was also an NYA student at the University of Minnesota. We were pleased to have the government-made jobs but at the same time understood that the economic policy of our nation of shrinking away from the world was a negative response to realism.

Later on, the economic boycott of the United States against Cuba did not cause the Castro government to crumble.

Perhaps the most impressive muscle flexing of all times—the Vietnam experience—ended with the United States demonstrating to the world that even with the use of near limitless military resources under the command of civilian restraints, our country cannot win by going it alone.

And so by December, 1971, many Nixon appointees were practically standing in line lauding the breakthrough in trade with the Soviet Union. Secretary of Commerce Stans, who had a history of favoring more trade, visited the Soviet Union. He was familiar with the export financing program administered by CCC known as the General Sales Manager-4 (GSM-4) program. This was a non-concessional credit scheme whereby certain agricultural commodity export sales to approved destination could be financed for up to three years at a rate of interest at least as high as the cost of money to CCC. Upon the return of Mr. Stans, he apparently informed the NSC, Butz and others that the Soviets may be receptive to conversations on GSM-4.

It is to be remembered that Rumania was granted a line of CCC credit (GSM-4) as discussed in Chapter 4. It seemed to me establishing a line of CCC credit for a nation for purposes of encouraging the nation to import our farm products carried some degree of prestige or sophistication for the recipient country. In the case of Rumania such a friendly gesture pleased the NSC and apparently was consistent with the broader Nixon foreign policy goal of the United States warming up to China with some help from Rumania and Pakistan.

In discussions with Butz on the background of the 1971 U.S. feed grain sale by exporters to the Soviet Union, I described the tedious steps taken within the administration leading to trade normalization in farm products to the socialist countries. I again reviewed the volume of grain imported and exported historically by that country. By that time in early 1972, USDA statistics for the decade of the 1960s were complete. Those figures showed the Soviet Union as having exported net about 20 million more tons of grain (approximately 750 million bushels of corn and/or wheat net exports for the decade) than they had imported—even with consideration for their disastrous crop of only

107.5 million tons in 1963-1964. With this sober statistic before us, the logical question from the new secretary was a good one.

"What makes you think they [the Soviets] may be interested in buying any meaningful amount of grain?"

Incidentally, he, too, was already aware of the negative view of the CIA regarding the likelihood of the Soviets becoming a regular buyer of U.S. grain.

My answer, which was one of optimism, was based entirely on the growth of livestock and poultry feeding in virtually every country importing grain in volume from the United States. We, of course, reviewed the increased use of grain and high-protein feed ingredients in Czechoslovakia, Rumania and East Germany. I had never visited the Soviet Union; because of my not having been there I could not speak with hands-on knowledge of the Soviet livestock industry.

Soon after Butz became secretary, we had an informal discussion on a matter not unrelated to the United States offering a CCC credit line to the Soviet Union. He came to my office and talked about the organization and lines of authority within USDA. He was specifically interested in why two seemingly different agencies, namely the Foreign Agricultural Service (FAS) and the Agricultural Stabilization and Conservation Service (ASCS), had been placed by Hardin under one assistant secretary—in this case me—as well as the same assistant secretary being president of Commodity Credit Corporation.

I stated that prior to my returning to government in 1969, I had requested these two functions be combined under me as an assistant secretary. My rationale was simple. In the United States where agricultural exports are so vital to the nation's economy and to the economic health of the agricultural sector, export promotion and overseas market development must be correlated as closely as possible with domestic farm programs. I know of no better way to accomplish this than to have those government employees responsible for these activities under one sub-cabinet officer. I described to Butz how, several times in the past when the functions were not under one sub-cabinet official, those responsible for domestic price support programs screamed for higher domestic supports while at the same time those government servants with responsibility for maximizing exports encouraged greater export subsidies for the same commodities. This, in my opinion, was an example of irresponsible government.

I am not sure whether Butz agreed with me; I do know he did not change the organizational reporting lines.

(It is interesting to note that both Secretary Bergland under President Carter and Secretary Block under President Reagan maintained these same reporting lines in USDA. But in both administrations the sub-cabinet officer in this position was not in the forefront in working with the Congress in developing farm program legislation. As a consequence, unfortunate and costly provisions were included in the omnibus farm legislation. In the Carter administration, the cost of production concept became a part of the basic formula determining level of target prices for specific commodities. This not only proved costly but in many cases acted as a reward to deplete scarce water resources. It certainly was not in the public interest. The Reagan administration, even though the Congress was blamed, allowed the support prices (loans) and target prices to be established at too high a level. As a consequence, the 1981 law acted as an incentive to farmers in other nations such as Canada, Australia and Argentina to increase their production and grab a higher percentage of the world market. And in the United States caused several commodity groups to plead for export subsidies. It was this very contradiction in policy—high loan rates matched with export subsidies that my concept of USDA reporting lines was designed to contain.)

In further briefing Butz on the U.S. grain situation and outlook and as such may relate to the possibility of GSM-4 credits being offered to the Soviets, I requested FAS and ASCS to prepare summary statements. The statements as presented to Butz follow:

U.S. GRAIN SITUATION AND OUTLOOK

Production and Exports

Wheat

The record 1971 *wheat* crop of 1.6 billion bushels pushed supplies to the highest level since 1962/63. Decreased disappearance, due mainly to strike reduced exports (575 million bushels this year compared to 739 million last year), is causing ending stocks to increase to near the billion bushel level. The outlook for the 1972 crop is for production of 1,561 million bushels. Despite the forecast for improved exports (650 million bushels in 1972/73), ending stocks are expected to increase to almost 1.1 billion bushels on June 30, 1973.

Feedgrains

The *current* situation is dominated by large supplies because of record corn, sorghum and barley crops. Exports during the current marketing year are projected at about 19.2 million tons, up about 500,000 tons from last year due almost entirely to increased shipments to USSR/Eastern Europe, since exports to the other main markets (Western Europe and Japan) are down. Ending stocks are projected to increase to 50 million tons compared to 30 million at the end of last year.

Outlook

Feedgrain production in 1972 is currently forecast at 170 million metric tons compared to the record 186 million harvested in 1971. Exports are forecast to increase about a million tons and domestic use is projected to increase around 4 million tons. Ending stocks are 48.5 million tons compared to 50 million at the end of the current season.

I also summarized the Soviet statistics. The Soviets in the crop year ending July 1, 1972, harvested 181.2 million tons of grain, second only to the year before when they had harvested a record 186.8 million tons. The FAS people advised heavy feedstuffs imports may need to be permitted if they (the Soviets) continued to follow a policy of encouraging meat production at their present expansion rate of 4 percent annually.

It was also recognized that our farm program payments were hitting record levels because of U.S. grain production in excess of our domestic requirements and export demand. A larger export outlet would be welcome news to farmers as well as to the Office of Management and Budget (OMB).

In mid-February, 1972, Kissinger sent the following memo to three cabinet officers—State, Agriculture and Commerce as follows:

> The Department of Agriculture in cooperation with other interested agencies should take the lead in developing for the President's consideration a position and a negotiating scenario for handling the issue of grain sales to the USSR. This should include a recommendation on how the private transactions of the U.S. grain sales would be related to Government actions including the United States opening a CCC credit line and a Soviet commitment to draw on it. In cooperation with the Department of State, Agriculture should explore with the USSR the time and modalities of beginning such negotiations as soon as possible. This should be submitted to the President by no later than February 28.

After preliminary discussion with Butz, I reviewed the contents of the Kissinger directive with the heads of the three agencies—FAS, ASCS and Export Marketing Service (EMS). During this review, Ioanes suggested an interagency group within USDA be established as an ad hoc working party to develop the scenario. Upon receiving the concurrence of Butz a group of three was named as follows: Cliff Pulvermacher, administrator, Export Marketing Service, Claude Coffman, deputy general counsel, and Donald Novotny, grain division, FAS.

In reality, I was quite pleased with the Kissinger directive because the objective was clear. In my language, we were directed to write a suggested plan of action utilizing the provisions of GSM-4 (CCC credit) and with the goal of securing a Soviet commitment to utilize the credit.

Another factor contributed to the clarity of this assignment. GSM-4 was an ongoing program. Regulations and procedures were printed in pamphlet form. Further, the reference to the CCC credit program—at least in my understanding—ruled out any further thought, at that time, of tying grain sales to the United States purchase of natural gas. As a matter of clarification, there had been rumblings, originating in Commerce, regarding the desirability of relating gas to grain. I was uneasy about the possibility of gas imports being tied to grain sales because the administration had not solidified a policy position on liquefied natural gas purchases from the Soviet Union. I visualized the policy uncertainties as an obstacle that would hold up any further grain sales indefinitely. And finally, I understood the directive to convey the message that the manner of selling grain—if in fact further sales should materialize—would be no different than the method our industry was utilizing to service all other export demand.

There had been one other happening during that period which caused me and others in the administration concern on the agricultural domestic policy front. We had harvested a record corn crop in the fall of 1971. Prices were low. In fact, during the Senate confirmation hearings for Earl Butz as secretary designate in early December, he said corn prices were too low. Consistent with this view and after he became secretary, he utilized the CCC Charter Act Authority as enacted in 1948 which authorizes the secretary—among other things—to stabilize certain farm prices. He purchased corn on the open market for the account of CCC. The action did have some positive impact on corn prices, particularly in regions suffering price depression.

Any reasonably keen observer of the Washington scene could predict still another chapter in the agricultural and/or political policy script. Senator George McGovern (D.-South Dakota), a member of the Senate Committee on Agriculture, introduced legislation to increase the price support (loan) rates for grain by amending the Agricultural Act of 1970. He was seeking the Democratic nomination for president and was courting the farm vote.

This type of proposed legislation is a classic example of how Congress seemingly cannot or at least often does not discipline itself in expending public funds. As I have stated and inferred several times throughout this book, the very existence of CCC causes reckless spending by both the Congress and the executive branch. Reimbursement to CCC "via" the appropriation process is simply after the fact. Witness the Butz expenditure to purchase corn.

But, of course, the proposed McGovern amendment would have been much more costly, and if enacted, would have further eroded fiscal management of overall federal expenditure. Further and most meaningful to me, the provisions of the wheat and feed grain programs for 1972, which had been agreed to by OMB were designed to reduce carryovers slightly. I had discussed these provisions with the leadership of the Senate committee on agriculture as well as the House committee.

The White House staff and OMB wanted the McGovern proposal defeated in committee, because if it were to receive a favorable committee vote and reach the floor of the Senate, it would undoubtedly receive a favorable vote by that body.

It was agreed within the administration that I would appear before the committee on January 26 when the issue was to be considered. I worked with Tom Korologos, deputy assistant to President Nixon. Korologos and I kept in close contact during the weekend before the bill was to be considered. In fact, my weekend was spent on the telephone, talking to supporters of wavering Senators on both sides of the aisle.

As I left my office on the morning of January 26 to go to the Senate, Korologos was pessimistic. He figured, at best, the vote would be 7 to 7. There were 14 Senators on the committee. If it should end in a tie and if Chairman Talmadge sided with McGovern, one of the dissenters could likely be talked into supporting the measure.

I assured Korologos the vote would be 10 to 4 in opposition. I was not wholly confident because the chairman had not made any commitment to me nor had I asked him to do so. On the other hand two Republicans, Young of North Dakota and Curtis of Nebraska, said they were going to support the measure and they did.

Consistent with the wishes of the chairman, I did not present formal testimony on the price support proposal. I only took part in the discussion, which was pleasing to me but not so pleasing with McGovern.

The chairman asked for a vote on three different provisions of the proposal and finally on the complete bill. On all four questions the vote was 10 to 4 in opposition.

This vote of the Senate committee further highlighted the importance of increasing grain exports to improve farm income. This attitude was mentioned several times by the members of the committee during the two-hour discussion of the McGovern proposal.

The ad hoc group consisting of Pulvermacher, Coffman and Novotny prepared a suggested negotiating scenario; I approved it and Butz sent it to the President prior to the deadline of February 28.

The scenario as proposed was built around offering the Soviets a CCC credit line for export financing of privately owned grain stocks under the ongoing provisions as contained in GSM-4. In exchange, the Soviet Union would commit itself to buy agreed quantities of U.S. grain for shipment within specified periods.

The suggested scenario further stated that if agreement can be reached with the Soviet Union, agriculture proposes to formalize the agreement in a memorandum of understanding.

Following the transmittal of the suggested scenario by Butz to the President, he and I talked very little about the next step because there seemed little more to discuss until or unless State and NSC through official channels would arrive at hard dates for a meeting with the Soviets. I advised the three members of the ad hoc group that they should be prepared to accompany me to Moscow for a meeting—if in fact that should be the decision.

Personally, I was becoming somewhat uneasy—not unlike the way Pulvermacher certainly felt many times when he could not get approval from all the government agencies involved in the terms of a PL 480 agreement with a foreign government.

I knew many agencies outside of agriculture were interested and involved with the plan to offer the USSR a GSM-4 program. Rightfully so, because many matters outside of discussing grain were involved. Nevertheless, the possibility of a first trip to Moscow with less than full knowledge of the desired full objective was leaving me feel a bit empty.

Over the weekend on Saturday, March 12, I had been away from my home on personal errands, but late afternoon, Andy Mair, deputy assistant secretary, phoned and said Butz had been trying to contact me. Mair conveyed the message that he (Butz) had been requested by Kissinger to go to Moscow for the purpose of upgrading the mission. I mentioned to Mair that the proposed trip to the Soviet Union was now developing into an entourage. In reality the purpose of traveling to that country was to discuss the GSM-4 Program and to secure a commitment that the credit line would be utilized.

The following week in conversations with Butz, Mair and the ad hoc group, we all agreed that copies of the GSM-4 regulations should be transmitted to the American Embassy in Moscow with a directive that the regulations be delivered to the appropriate people in the Soviet Ministry of Foreign Trade. This was precisely what I had done over two years earlier with the Rumanians.

I had another reason for wanting the regulations in the hands of the Soviets. First, they were public documents and could be readily attained by most anyone. Second, I thought it well to establish the fact early on that from our position in agriculture we were not offering the Soviets any special type of deal. The regulations for this program had remained unchanged since 1967.

Still another reason for my playing up the significance of the United States offering the Soviets access to the well known CCC Credit Program (GSM-4) was because I had advised a few legislators of the proposed action. Congressman Jamie Whitten, chairman of the sub-committee for agriculture appropriations, Senator Gale McGee, chairman of the sub-committee for agriculture appropriations in the Senate, Herman Talmadge, chairman of the Senate committee on agriculture and his counterpart in the House—Chairman Poage.

The four chairmen of these respective committees and/or sub-committees were generally unresponsive. I felt Talmadge, McGee and Poage probably concurred in the proposed action. Whitten did not disagree but commented that the administration was moving pretty fast in dealing with the Soviets.

The matter of advising appropriate Congressional leaders "before the fact" is an absolute must, in my opinion. After all, a decision to obligate the assets of a government entity (CCC) even for a short period of time was a policy decision of some significance. The matter of the possibility of the Soviets buying more U.S. farm products was not a new action because about 3 million tons of grain purchased the year before (1971) was being shipped.

Butz, accompanied by a staff of four, the ad hoc group and myself and the deputy director, Office of East-West Trade, the Department of State, arrived in Moscow the evening of Saturday, April 8. The following day we accompanied Matskevich on a tour by plane of Crimea. We visited some state farms and were shown workers' homes, machine shops and schools. Enroute we were flown over some grain fields. One winter wheat field in which we walked was quite dry, and the wheat stands were not lush. After having said this it must be pointed out that not one of us from the United States had ever been to the Crimea before. Most of us, including myself, had never been to the Soviet Union before. I had no idea whether this situation was typical, normal or unusual. My judgment was no different than that of the average reader's opinion regarding the outlook for a North American wheat crop if he or she were dropped in a winter field in a rural Oklahoma township on the ninth day of April. The enormity of the Soviet agricultural sector is explained by D. Gale Johnson in his writings in the book *Prospects for Soviet Agriculture in the 1980s.* He states the total sown area in the socialized sector is divided approximately equally between the collective (producer cooperative assigned land in perpetuity) and state farms (state controlled corporation). These two types of farms according to Johnson have a total cultivated area of approximately 555 million acres, over 40 percent larger than the cultivated area in the United States.

The comment of one of the farm managers was identical to what one hears throughout the United States most any spring. I asked whether the stand of wheat—because of winter kill and/or poor germination—was sufficiently poor to cause them to dig up and plant spring seeded grains such as spring wheat or barley.

His answer was given by his turning his hand upside down and back again. This sign language is universal. It means maybe yes, maybe no.

He went on to explain.

"If we should replant and *not* receive germination moisture we get no crop. If we replant and receive germination moisture we might receive a good crop. If we do nothing we might harvest a fair crop; it depends on the weather."

(Incidentally, millions of hectares in that area were reseeded to spring grains. Germinating moisture was received in early May but excruciatingly hot winds prior to harvest in the month of August damaged the crop.)

Secretary Butz opened negotiations with the Senior Deputy Minister of Foreign Trade, Minister Kuzmin, on April 11. Following the opening ceremonies, I continued the conversations with Kuzmin. I described the GSM-4 Program. A few questions were asked by Kuzmin and his colleagues. Our side readily answered any and all such questions. After all, they had copies of the regulations before and had had the material for several days.

We offered to extend a line of credit with a maximum exposure not to exceed $500 million outstanding at any one time, and up to $750 million over a three-year period. We stipulated that we would only open the credit line upon receiving a commitment from them that they would buy grain from the United States through traditional commercial channels.

We further advised that the interest rate would be 6⅛ percent or the going rate on irrevocable letters of credit if opened on a U.S. bank and 7⅛ percent or the current rate for an acceptable foreign bank. Financing would be limited to the cost of the commodity f.o.b. U.S. ports.

We stated we would not finance the export of soybeans but that they were free to purchase U.S. soybeans from exporters on commercial terms.

Kuzmin turned down the offer. He said the Soviet Union—under any conditions—would not pay interest to the United States for the purchase of consumer goods such as grain. He immediately contradicted himself and said that they (the Soviets) may be receptive to purchasing U.S. grain if the United States would be in a position to offer 10-year credits at a low rate of interest, such as 2 percent. He was obviously familiar with PL 480 terms. I advised him that we would not be receptive to offering any special terms.

We mutually agreed to end the session but with a tentative understanding to meet again the next day. As we were leaving the conference table Kuzmin made one rather off-the-cuff remark about our large stocks of grain. I could not resist a pleasant comeback. I acknowledged that our granaries are full but the contents are more valuable than money in the bank.

We met in what was to be the final session the following forenoon.

Kuzmin and his colleagues had not changed their minds. They were not interested in buying grain from the United States under such terms.

Following this, the ad hoc group, the Department of State representative and I had a short meeting in the American Embassy. We gave consideration to flying home that afternoon rather than sticking with our original plan to return home two days later on April 14. We decided to *not* hasten our departure because it was unanimously agreed to not take action that would give the impression that we might be disappointed.

My written instructions as head of the delegation authorized me to reach agreement with the USSR within the guidelines as described—*with one caveat*. Prior to my leaving Washington, I was advised that I should not finalize any agreement—if negotiations should indeed have proven to lead in that direction—which had not happened.

I was convinced Kuzmin was not authorized to be forthcoming. This in a few words was full explanation of why I had not wanted to travel to Moscow on this so-called negotiating assignment. The reason for my lack of enthusiasm was because I simply did not know the full goal of the United States—nor was it essential that I should know. On the other hand, I knew I was being used as a pawn, which in itself may not be objectionable provided one's performance as a professional is not compromised due to lack of knowledge of overall goals.

It should be recorded that the North Vietnamese had begun the spring offensive in Vietnam with some material assistance from the Soviet Union. It was further felt the Soviets were rather keenly interested in a trade package with the United States, possibly including CCC credit.

On the other hand, most any layman realized cooperation from the Soviets was most desirable as the United States was trying to pull out of Vietnam. I was familiar with Kissinger's thought process regarding linkage. I learned more on this thinking from Senator Aiken—that great and wise sage from Vermont who loved to be called "Governor"—than I did from within the administration.

It is worth noting that Kissinger in his book *The White House Years* had asked his assistant, Hal Sonnenfeldt, on April 10, 1972—when Butz and I were in the Soviet Union—what negotiations with the USSR could be slowed down that were of substantial interest to the Kremlin leaders. According to Kissinger, the first item listed by Sonnenfeldt was "ensuring that the United States–Soviet talks in Moscow on grain sales yielded no results for now."

Kissinger went on to write that he approved this step—along with other recommendations. Once again my instincts proved to be well founded, because I obviously did not know the full goals of Kissinger and the President. The level of security classification is known as "on a need-to-know basis." Of course, I did not need to know! But big governments, not unlike big business, are the most successful and accomplish more when the chief executive officer (CEO) is able to instill the utmost confidence in the attitudes of the government's top appointees and/or executives.

Years later when Bob Bergland was secretary of agriculture under President Carter, he was commenting at a luncheon on the pressure he received from time to time from NSC. I explained to him that I too had been in government when the head of NSC (Kissinger) had discovered agriculture.

In the process of writing this book it is the reliving of events such as establishing the credit line for the Soviet Union that I become more satisfied with the title *Made in Washington*.

Following my return to Washington from Moscow I wrote a short report for Butz over the weekend. He incorporated my comments into a summary statement of his own for transmittal to President Nixon. I included in my portion of the report that Minister Kuzmin had acknowledged the Soviets' need for grain and frankly stated that purchases from the United States at the level of $250 million annually did not scare them. We (Butz and I) also recommended that the offer of GSM-4 credit remain open if they (the Soviets) were to agree to a multi-year supply arrangement for grain.

With the filing of this report, further activities on my part on the proposed credit line or additional cash sales ended until May 9, when on short notice from the Department of Commerce, I agreed to meet with Deputy Minister of Foreign Trade Alkhimov. He had participated in the Moscow conversations. His primary responsibility in the ministry, according to him, was in currency allocation.

Two members of the ad hoc group, Claude Coffman and Don Novotny attended the meeting with Alkhimov. Pulvermacher was not available but George Shanklin participated in his place. I requested Novotny to keep minutes of the conversations and to write a report for transmittal to Butz. He did so. The report was also sent to Secretary of Commerce Peterson, Kissinger and Peter Flanigan, counsellor for International Economic Policy (CIEP).

Alkhimov asked several questions about procedures having to do with GSM-4. Coffman fielded most of the questions with considerable assistance from Shanklin. Alkhimov again asked for more favorable credit terms. I advised him that the U.S. government policy was clear and unchanged. The terms for a CCC credit line were outlined in the GSM-4 regulations and there would be no exceptions to the provisions.

Before leaving, Alkhimov did inquire about purchases under the barter program, direct purchases from U.S. government stocks, and some relationship between natural gas and grain.

I responded to Alkhimov that I could not conceive of the barter program as being either useful or applicable and that whether purchases involved grain from government or private stocks, commercial exporting firms would do the selling.

Now years later, it seems to me the Alkhimov meeting was for the purpose of keeping the door open for further conversations on a possible credit line from CCC. I have no idea why barter and natural gas were mentioned—maybe feelers.

During this period in late April and early May in discussing the outlook for additional U.S. grain sales to the Soviets, I wrote out longhand notes which I referred to when I discussed the subject in the secretary's staff conference—with Senators and members of Congress and with agricultural press representatives. I later had those notes typed. As I now review them over 12 years later, the statements are fully responsive and accurate, even now.

I stated that the Soviet government officials sometime over the next several weeks would make a decision regarding the volume of grain and other feed ingredients they would import during the next 12 months. Further, in my opinion, the government officials at that time were probably faced with three options.

☆ They could choose to import a volume of grain that would allow the Soviet people a daily caloric intake at about the same level as at present. If this option were to be the policy, the import requirements would be x amount—largely determined by the crop conditions that would prevail during the balance of 1972.

☆ They could choose to import a volume of grain sufficient to increase livestock, poultry and dairy production consistent with their announced goals in the then current five-year plan, which would end December 31, 1975. If this were followed, their grain import requirements would be x amount plus an additional volume.

☆ They could choose a belt-tightening approach—as was followed in the decade of the 1960s. If this option were to be adopted as policy, their grain requirements from outside of their country would be nil, but the exact level of imports would again be determined by the crop and weather conditions as they prevailed in their country during the balance of 1972.

Butz and I agreed that, barring some unforeseen tragic weather situation, the Soviets probably would not formulate a firm policy regarding grain imports until August or September, 1972. This reasoning was based upon our feeling that the Soviets would postpone a policy decision until the size of their 1972 crop was more certain.

There was still another development about one week after Butz and I returned from Moscow. I was not aware of it until I read Kissinger's book *White House Years* several years later.

Kissinger went on a secret trip to Moscow. According to Kissinger's writing, he met with General Secretary Leonid Brezhnev on April 21 and was pursuing his theory of linkage as well as endeavoring to make the forthcoming meeting between President Nixon and Brezhnev (summit) a success. The summit was to take place about five weeks later.

On May 12, I had a visit with Butz on personal matters. I informed him that I wished to resign from government service and join Continental Grain Company in New York. And that if it was satisfactory with him, I would request him to forward my formal resignation to President Nixon in a few days. I mentioned to Butz that I wanted to talk with John Whitaker about my plans. Butz agreed.

Whitaker had been the best possible person to work with on any and all agricultural policy matters. He had always been 100 percent reliable in helping me secure answers to policy questions whether it involved responses from OMB, NSC or other places in the executive branch. It had been a wonderful and memorable working relationship.

In my conversations with Butz I stated that I was approaching a full six months with him in his official position. I further commented that I was satisfied with the changes in farm programs and trade policy we had been able to accomplish and that the actions were working toward strengthening our entire agricultural economy.

This matter of leaving government service and accepting employment in the private sector is a delicate matter—not because of any real conflict of interest as such, because people of integrity know full well the meaning of sensitive matters and by exercising good judgment need not become involved in any matters that have any chance at all of being suspect or sensitive. Unfortunately, one who has had a high profile is bound to attract attention and not all of it well intended.

As described earlier, the May 9 session with Alkhimov was the last meeting I had with the Soviets on the credit line proposal or any other subject. Prior to my resignation being accepted by President Nixon on June 7, I forwarded the draft of the proposed credit proposal—as it had been written by the ad hoc group—to Secretary Butz. It had been carried to Moscow by Claude Coffman on April 8 and as stated earlier was not shown to the Soviets because the conversations during the Moscow trip had not advanced to the stage of any expressed interest in the credit line nor additional grain purchases.

On July 8, President Nixon announced the negotiation of an agreement between the Soviet Union and the United States. The Soviets agreed to buy a minimum of $750 million of U.S. grain in the next three years. The United States agreed to establish a CCC credit line as provided in the GSM-4 Program. Not more than $500 million was to be outstanding at any one time.

Secretary Butz was to testify later before the House sub-committee on livestock and grains that the Soviet Union agreed to the regular CCC three-year credit terms at 6⅛ percent interest. The credit line and the non-concessional rate of interest was identical to that granted Rumania and several other countries.

Butz informed the house sub-committee on September 14 about the lack of interest expressed by the Soviets during the meeting in April regarding the provisions of the GSM-4 program. Butz went on to say the Soviets came to this country in late June and early July to negotiate further. Agreement was reached in 11 days with provisions as described and then announced within two hours on Saturday, July 8, by President Nixon.

Working concurrently in the United States with the Ministry of Foreign Trade officials who had negotiated the credit line with Secretary of Commerce Peterson and Butz was the head of Exporthkleb (the FTO responsible for Soviet grain imports). Exporthkleb is an action or functional entity; it is not a government policy agency per se. The FTO officials were in the United States at about the same time that the government credit negotiations in Washington were taking place—for the purpose of buying grain for cash and/or U.S. credit terms if such should be available.

Buy they did!

Over a period of about 15 days in July they purchased about 4.5 million tons of corn and a little over 7 million tons of wheat.

As described earlier in this book, domestic U.S. corn prices were identical with world prices. They were one and the same and had been for over a decade. Hence, U.S. exporting firms sold the U.S. corn to the Soviets at a price reflecting their (the companies') best judgment of projected free market price trends in the United States.

Not so with wheat!

As also stated earlier, CCC (USDA) had been involved in export price determination since being a signatory to the International Wheat Agreement (IWA) in 1949. CCC for at least two years as of that time (July, 1972) had generally been intent on maintaining the export price for wheat basis the gulf, f.o.b. position at about $1.63, ordinary hard wheat. This price in trade circles was often referred to as the "box price."

Question?

Would USDA continue to maintain the box price for the export of wheat into the future?

That was a key question. The answer was the chief variable factor for exporters in arriving at a wheat export price quote to the Soviets as well as to all other overseas buyers seeking price quotations.

I can only explain how Continental, one of the sellers, secured an answer to this question. Bernard Steinweg, senior vice-president of the company, requested Continental's Washington representative, Sam Sabin, to make an appointment for him (Steinweg) to see Carroll Brunthaver, assistant secretary of USDA, and president of CCC.

Steinweg testified on this matter July 20, 1973, before the permanent sub-committee on investigations of the committee on government operations, U.S. Senate. Steinweg told the sub-committee of his meeting with Brunthaver on July 3 when he had asked whether USDA would continue its policy of maintaining the current export target price of various classes of wheat for such a transaction (to the Soviets).

Brunthaver, according to Steinweg, said he would give this some thought and get back to him. Also according to Steinweg, that afternoon he was advised by Brunthaver by phone that the department would maintain its current export target prices.

It must be understood, the export target prices were maintained at what was deemed to be at world competitive price levels by lowering or increasing the export subsidy as free market prices fluctuated or changed. Most of the time, free market prices were higher than export prices, and thus the export subsidy was a payment to assure the United States be price competitive in world markets. It was not unusual for subsidy to be at a level of zero cents and at other times a few cents per bushel.

After about July 20 and following the purchase of about 12 million tons of U.S. wheat and corn, the Exporthkleb representatives returned to the Soviet Union.

After August 1 the buyers returned to the United States and bought from several companies 4.5 million more tons of U.S. wheat and corn, 1 million tons of soybeans, and small quantities of barley and sorghum.

Apparently, as later hearings and investigations revealed, six exporting firms participated in the business with the Soviets that year. Each company had been assured by USDA, according to the findings, that the export target prices for wheat would be maintained.

Total wheat sales were about 11.8 million tons.

Corn about 6.25 million tons.

Soybeans 1 million tons.

It is not my intention to dwell further on who did what during the year 1972, but several questions on why things unfolded as they did are deserving of exploration.

* Why did the Soviets buy so much grain?
* Why did they buy so much wheat?
* Why did they buy first during the month of July and then for a second time during the month of August?
* Why was not the U.S. intelligence better and to what extent did unfavorable weather in the Soviet Union influence their buying of grain from the United States, as compared to their desire to increase livestock production?

Now over a decade later, it is not possible for me to answer these questions with great accuracy. On the other hand, subsequent developments in Soviet agriculture and constructive writings by some of the better students in the United States on the politics of the Soviet Union go far in satisfying me why the Soviets acted as they did regarding their food situation in 1972 and the years following.

One student on East-West trade, Marshall Goldman, in his book *Detente and Dollars*, chose not to be helpful nor constructively analytical on the subject of grain sales to the Soviet Union. I received no help from him nor from his writings on the decision-making process in the Soviet Union regarding its grain imports. It has always seemed to me that second guesses and/or negative criticism of personalities requires only ink and not great brain power.

Conversely, the book *Prospects for Soviet Agriculture in the 1980s* by D. Gale Johnson and Karen McConnell Brooks sheds some light on factors affecting net grain production and use in the Soviet Union. For example, the authors explain heavy seeding rates of wheat and other grains in that country measured in terms of amounts of seed used per hectare of land or as a percentage of output is oftentimes unusually heavy as compared to seeding rates in the United States and/or Western Europe.

Johnson and Brooks in their book go on to refer to USDA and CIA estimates that in the lower yielding areas of the USSR the output-seed ratio is as low as four. The reader must be alerted, however, the Johnson-Brooks book was published in the 1980s. Such wisdom was difficult to come by in the advent of the 1970s. In fact, during that period, the concise book *Soviet Communism and Agrarian Reform* by Roy D. and Betty A. Laird was most helpful to me.

As a matter of interest, presently on my farm in Minnesota, my nephew generally harvests a crop of corn measured in terms as a percentage of output in relation to seed planted of 400. While the percentage of output of wheat and barley and other "small" grains—seed which is drilled as compared to corn which is planted with wider row spacing—requires much more seed per hectare.

I suspect the unbelievable low-grain yields in the USSR in relation to seed planted reflects low-germinating seed and thus large volume of seed planted per hectare. This causes me to reflect on the motto of the American Seed Trade Association, "First the Seed." I know of no other one criterion by which to assess a nation's degree of sophistication in agriculture production than its seed breeding, harvesting, processing and distribution enterprises. Viable strong perfect germinating seed planted in a properly prepared seedbed provides farmers the wherewithal before planting to decide the number of plants desired per hectare, and thereby the likelihood of maximizing yields.

Before commenting on the questions as to "why" the Soviets purchased a huge volume of grain, I want to again share the statistical background on USSR grain production and trade during the period 1967 through 1972.

During the three years 1967, 1968 and 1969, the USSR produced an average of 160 million metric tons of grain annually. The Soviets *exported* an average of 5.1 million metric tons each year.

In 1970 and 1971 they produced record supplies of grain—an average of 184 million tons—and *exported* an average of 4.5 million tons each year. Some well meaning students at that time thought they (the Soviets) may have stockpiled a fair amount of grain.

While Kissinger stated in *The White House Years* that the Soviets were confronting a catastrophic crop failure in the year 1972 the official crop production outturn later revealed was 168 million tons—the fifth largest Soviet crop on record. Kissinger was wrong!

The message from the statistical data!

Neither at that time nor since, as more statistics became available, was there or is there presently statistical substantiation to warrant the Soviets purchasing, on the world market in 1972, from all sources, including the United States, a volume of wheat in excess of 18 million tons and at least 8 million tons of coarse grains and oilseeds.

There were, in my opinion, three reasons.

☆ Their policy to increase the availability of meat, poultry, eggs and dairy products for their people.

☆ Insurance against unmanageable food riots and political unrest.

☆ Prolonged, devastatingly hot dry winds in July and early August.

I have a greater problem with the question Why did they buy so much wheat?

I guess there were at least four reasons.

* ☆ Internal transportation problems for movement of their own wheat.
* ☆ Tradition of feeding domestically produced wheat to livestock.
* ☆ Severe quality problems with their own wheat, such as badly shriveled kernels brought about by the hot winds.
* ☆ Favorable wheat import price in relation to corn and other coarse grains.

The answer as to why the Soviets bought in July and then again in August is quite simple.

I believe the July or "first round" purchases of about 12 million tons from the United States reflected the Soviets' policy to expand livestock and poultry production. But another factor may have entered into that decision. The Johnson and Brooks analysis leads me to believe that the heavy replanting of spring wheat and barley, probably with low-germinating seed, greatly taxed the projected stockpile or carry-over of grain, particularly wheat.

The August wave of Soviet buying was probably in response to the hot winds and heat wave which apparently withered a portion of the spring planted crop. And a portion of the impetus to buy during the second round of dealings had to be caused by the Kremlin's desire for still more insurance against political demonstrations. I believe this latter reason explained the purchase of 1 million tons of soybeans in August of 1972.

Why was the U.S. intelligence not better on reporting and interpreting the intensity of the Soviets' desire to upgrade the quality of the diets of their people through greater availability of meat, poultry, eggs and dairy products?

That is a matter I cannot answer. It is a political question and falls in the province of NSC, CIA and/or the political section of the Department of State. There has been ample finger pointing already regarding the shortfalls within USDA in projecting the economic impact of burgeoning exports. I do not intend to add to the "after the fact know-it-all attitude." I do hope, however, that the CIA is more astute in handling worldwide covert activities than was the agency in predicting the intensity of the changing attitude regarding quality of diets for the citizens of the Soviet Union.

Exporthkleb expended about $1.3 billion for U.S. grain and soybeans during that buying campaign in the late summer of 1972. Over 18 months were to elapse before shipment was completed.

Other nations were also increasing their purchases. Japan, the miracle market for our farm products as described in Chapter 3 increased its purchases from the United States that year in an amount *greater* than the total value of the Soviet purchases.

In fact, the export sales to the Soviet Union accounted for about 25 percent of the increase in total export sales through that 12-month period July 1, 1972, through June 30, 1973.

The EC increased purchases by an amount greater than the amount of the Soviet Union sales.

One little publicized happening was unfolding in the world. Most of Asia was harvesting a short crop of rice. As a consequence, several nations bought more wheat as a substitute. India, for example, entered the market as a buyer—after several years as a non-importer.

Africa was suffering from a prolonged drought.

The United States had devalued the dollar thereby making U.S. grain and other farm products cheaper in terms of importing nations' local currencies.

The volume of fish meal—a high-protein livestock and poultry-feed ingredient—was down because of a lower fish catch off the coast of South America.

In addition to the large unpredicted volume of grain purchases by the Soviet Union, one other policy matter received a great amount of publicity and criticism, the wheat export subsidy paid by CCC.

The export subsidy per bushel on the 430 million bushels of wheat purchased by the Soviet Union during July and August, 1972, averaged about 35 cents per bushel. The subsidy on July 3 when the Soviet buying commenced was 5 cents per bushel and had been increased to a high of 47 cents when the subsidy program was terminated in September. The higher subsidy reflected most of the increase in free market price at gulf ports through the several weeks following July 3.

By September of that year the increased subsidy had become an emotional issue. As one case in point, those responsible for the subsidy program in 1963 when U.S. wheat sold to the Soviet Union had been subsidized over 65 cents per bushel were now crying "foul ball."

Traditionally, when government policies affect food prices or prices received by farmers for their products, rational judgment is thrown to the wind. The summer and fall of 1972 was no exception to this tradition.

Now, over a decade later, I find the pros and cons as to whether or not the export subsidy for wheat should have been discontinued long before the program was actually terminated equally compelling.

Before going further with an analysis of the pros and cons of earlier termination of the program, I want to remind the reader of one unpublicized annual event. The agricultural appropriations hearings before the sub-committee for agricultural appropriations in the House.

Chairman Whitten each year reminds the secretary of agriculture, the under secretary, the assistant secretaries and several bureau chiefs of their responsibilities as dictated by the Congress to offer U.S. farm commodities for export at competitive prices. He has performed in this manner for 30 years. During the Nixon years—my last tour of government service—when Whitten became short of breath—Mark Andrews at that time a Republican Congressman from North Dakota would take up the charge and trounce the government witnesses from groin to rib cage.

Does this annual humiliation have an impact on USDA export policy?

Of course it does!

I do not know the "weight of importance" Butz or Brunthaver attached to the annual Whitten-Andrews lectures—as the policy to continue the "box price" for the export of wheat in the summer of 1972 was decided. I never discussed the matter with them.

While I state the arguments for ending the subsidy before actual sales were made to the Soviet Union are as equally compelling as are arguments for maintaining the subsidy through the summer—if I had been in government at that time, and with less than full knowledge of all world political developments—and with less than full appreciation of the agricultural goals of the Soviet Union—I would have voted in favor of continuing the wheat export subsidy program at that time.

As I see the issue, there were sound reasons to have terminated the export subsidy program on July 3, 1972. I list some of these reasons on the assumption that the level of export price of U.S. wheat to the Soviet Union was neither agreed upon nor even insinuated by *any* U.S. government official. I make this assumption but I obviously do not know whether or not that assumption is accurate. On the basis that wheat export price of U.S. wheat was not agreed to by any U.S. government officials, I mention some of the reasons favoring a discontinuance of the subsidy program July 3.

☆ If there had been concern in the minds of USDA officials, whether or not the private sector (grain exporting firms) was prepared to risk offering large quantities of wheat for export—in the absence of government guaranteed export target prices— that doubt should have been dissipated when Steinweg advised Brunthaver on July 3 that Continental had been requested to sell

Exporthkleb 3 million tons of corn and was prepared to do so. As related before, the export price of corn was free of government interference. The point is that if the wheat export subsidy program were terminated, identical free competitive market forces as determined by the exporter would establish the wheat export price to be quoted.

* Presumably, federal outlay of funds would be reduced if the export subsidy program were terminated.
* World wheat prices would increase, thus causing a higher percentage of wheat farmers' incomes to come from the marketplace.

Some of the reasons favoring a continuation of the wheat export subsidy program July, 1972 were:

* The wheat carryover, June 30, 1972, was estimated to be near 1 billion bushels, the largest for a decade. Exports for the ending 12-month period had dropped to 575 million bushels due to work stoppages and strikes; this compared to 739 million a year earlier. Any action by government officials that could be interpreted as further discouraging wheat exports would be difficult to explain.
* Statistically, for at least four weeks (by the end of July) after the Soviets began to buy wheat, there was no sound evidence that world demand would be sufficiently strong to greatly "bull" the wheat market. The Soviets' August buying surge coupled with India's buying caused the price scales to tilt. Even then the People's Republic of China (PRC) had not yet purchased U.S. wheat.

Again, it is to be remembered that when the sub-cabinet ad hoc group under Ambassador Winthrop Brown prepared economic background papers preparatory to the normalizing of trade with socialist countries by President Nixon June, 1971, the goal was to be as even-handed as possible on matters of concern with the Soviet Union and the People's Republic of China.

During the latter part of August the Chinese made their move and purchased 400,000 tons (14.7 million bushels) of wheat. Shortly after this, USDA terminated the export "box price."

I never discussed the significance of the first U.S. wheat sale to China (Continental Grain Company did not make the sale) with any of the U.S. government officials at that time. I did believe then and continue to think today that it was an example of an evenhanded policy to have allowed China ample time to purchase wheat at the "box price."

In the light of projected wheat exports to the PRC—at that time—and subsequently with that country becoming a major and in some years *the* major importer of U.S. wheat, the export subsidy for wheat to China and for that matter to all destinations during that period may have proven to be a sound investment in market development and world stability.

I felt in 1971 that China had the possibility of being a logical importer of our wheat—on a price basis. That hypothesis has proven to be correct. From the standpoint of our nation's ability to earn foreign exchange from such sales it presents a logical argument for the United States to further develop the market for wheat in China.

As one not in government, that late summer of 1972, I was relieved to see the subsidy program finally ended. From the philosophical point of view, the 23 years of its existence offers a lesson for current and future government administrators, namely, "When you (government officials) commence tapping the federal treasury for benefits of a group or groups—please develop plans to end the expenditure and involvement."

Easier said than done!

Cliff Pulvermacher and I talked many times of how we might simply end the wheat export subsidy program. An acceptable economic and political climate never presented itself—until after we both left government. And then it was only possible as the world market, as made up of unprecedented volume of buying by many nations, caused the subsidy program to crumble. Even though Pulvermacher and I, along with several in government at that time including Brunthaver, were bruised, the happenings in the marketplace made it all worthwhile.

Our final comment on wheat subsidies needs mention before moving on with related historical actions. Further discussion of CCC subsidy payments for American flag vessels will illustrate that bad ideas never really disappear—they only sleep for awhile.

I mentioned the questionable and excessive payments for the export of durum as a technique to pay for the higher cost of American flag vessels—as engaged in 1964 by the Johnson administration. I also discussed how the ghost of that circuitous decision showed its ugly head in 1971 and 1972. In my naiveté, I thought the issue finally was dead. Not so. In 1983, during the Reagan administration, Secretary Block authorized payment of about $30 million for shipment of a portion of the heavily subsidized wheat flour to Egypt in higher-priced American flag vessels. A relatively high proportion of the vessels should undoubtedly be classified as "rust buckets."

The Block action illustrates three things.

* Bad ideas do not disappear; they only lounge undercover until new officials come around.
* Government actions assisted by federal funds quickly become entitlements.
* A CCC subsidy to implement a policy (quite often questionable in itself, such as the wheat flour sale to Egypt) causes other interest groups to stand in line to collect their handouts.

Reverting back to the happenings following the grain sales activities and to wrap up that specific period, some mention must be made of the national media and the political rumblings in Washington, D.C.

During my entire career as a government official, head of an association and with an international food company, I had always talked freely and thoroughly with members of the agricultural media. I particularly worked at this when I was a government official—because my area of responsibility was with matters of great public interest to those involved in food and agriculture. I did not shun members of the general or non-agricultural media. They were simply not interested in day-to-day mundane agricultural policy issues.

As the events of 1972 unfolded, the general media involved itself with food and agriculture. A false and unfounded interpretation of a happening became an accepted norm for the next story. I discovered there was no way either to counteract or to correct such erroneous stories.

What does one do?

As Lyndon Johnson is quoted as saying, "You hunker down and take it!"

Several Congressional committees and their staffs investigated the Soviet grain sales and related activities. The Department of Justice, including the FBI, did the same.

Pages could be written on the findings of these hearings and investigations. The passage of time since then causes me to respond in all brevity to the chief unfounded charges by simply sharing the conclusions of the investigators on the allegations. They follow.

1) With respect to the allegation that grain exporters or the U.S. Department of Agriculture had inside information or advance knowledge of Soviet buying intentions, the Senate Permanent Subcommittee on Investigations, after a year of staff investigations which included complete access to the files of all prior investigations, and several days of public hearings, concluded:

. . . that the record does not reveal that anyone, either in the grain companies or in the government service, had any advance notice as to the Russians' intentions and hence capitalized on inside information. (Jackson Subcommittee Report, p. 60.)

2) The Comptroller General of the United States, after an investigation of the defendant grain exporters' profits on the 1972 wheat sales to Russia by the General Accounting Office, likewise reported to Congress that the grain companies "either did not have inside information of Soviet buying intentions or did not take advantage of any such information." (GAO Report [February 12, 1974], p. 10.)

3) With respect to the charge that the grain exporters might have used inside information to purchase cash grain or futures contracts in advance to secure windfall profits, the Jackson Subcommittee noted that five of the six defendants held *short* positions and the sixth had a mixed position in wheat from June 23 (just prior to the first of the Russian sales of July 5) through September. This was recognized as utterly inconsistent with allegations of advance knowledge. As the Subcommittee concluded:

> Persons attempting to capitalize on inside information about upcoming large export sales would be expected to purchase futures contracts and thus establish substantial *long* positions. (Jackson Subcommittee Report, p. 43; emphasis added.)

The GAO also concluded there could not have been inside information "because the grain companies' net position records did not show unusually large purchases before the Russian sales." (GAO Report [February 12, 1974], p. 13.) Both the Jackson Subcommittee's and the GAO's conclusions were emphatic: No one, either in the grain companies or in government service, capitalized on inside information.

4) With respect to the allegation that grain exporters improperly (or illegally) registered their export wheat for subsidies, the Comptroller General, although pointedly criticizing *government* administration of the subsidy program, specifically found that the *private grain companies'* practices "were not improper in view of [governmental] regulations which permitted them as a means of encouraging exports of U. S. wheat." (GAO Report [July 9, 1973], p. 31.) Contrary to allegations that the grain companies made "windfall profits" under the subsidy program, the Comptroller General found that the grain companies themselves "made purchases at escalating prices which

were not fully compensated for by subsidies. . . ." (GAO Report [February 12, 1974], p. 21.) And the Department of Justice, after a review of still another investigation of the grain companies' subsidy registrations by auditors of the Inspector General of the Department of Agriculture, found no indication whatsoever of criminal fraud against the government. (Department of Justice Memorandum, dated July 5, 1973, entitled "Investigation of Matters Related to the United States–Soviet Union Grain Sale Agreement," summarizing Justice Department and FBI findings, reproduced in Jackson Subcommittee Hearings I, Exh. 17 at p. 246.)

5) Finally, with respect to the allegation that Clarence Palmby revealed information obtained as a government employee to the financial benefit of Continental or the other companies, the Justice Department's twice-affirmed conclusion (after a reexamination of their own prior findings in response to a specific inquiry from the Jackson Subcommittee) was that:

> [I]t should be noted that neither the Subcommittee's hearings nor our earlier investigation adduced even a scintilla of evidence that Mr. Palmby provided inside information to Continental Grain Company or in any other unlawful way placed that company in a favored position in the Russian Grain transactions. (Letter of Assistant Attorney General, dated March 4, 1974, to Senator Jackson, quoted in Jackson Subcommittee Report, p. 25.)

My first writing on this historical period was undertaken before Senator Henry Jackson, chairman of the permanent sub-committee on investigations, had died. Those comments were quite pointed and somewhat caustic. Now after his death I delete those words and offer only a summary judgment such as "The Jackson Hearings contributed very little or nothing to the national welfare. Such is almost always the case when legislators use their elected position to further their own image for more serious consideration for national office."

One quote from still another Senator at that time who is also no longer living was made by the former Vice-President Hubert Humphrey. I had known Senator Humphrey since he was mayor of Minneapolis. We were members of different political parties, but from the time I had been ASCS committee chairman in Minnesota from 1953 to 1956, I had had a near perfect working relationship with him for a quarter of a century. We respected one another's integrity. He was always available to compare notes as deemed helpful by either one of us.

Senator Humphrey and Senator Bellmon (R.-Oklahoma) traveled to Moscow on their own fact-finding mission in December, 1972. I did not talk with either Senator before their departure—nor afterward for that matter on their findings in the Soviet Union. Senator Humphrey sent word to me in New York after his return that he was prepared to visit with me, but it was one of those well intentioned meetings which never materialized—largely my own fault.

The Senator at a press conference (which he loved to hold) had the following exchange:

Senator Hubert H. Humphrey
Press Conference
U.S. Capitol Building
December 12, 1972

QUESTION: Senator, you talked about the Democratic Party helping the poor. There seems to be a lot of grumbling from housewives about the side effects of the wheat deal—in prices of bread and meat. What justification do you see for the average American with the prices of their basic foods going up to help the Soviet Union out of this problem?

SENATOR HUMPHREY: We didn't help the Soviet Union. Now let's get this hogwash straightened out. First of all, we sold the Soviet Union grain at the price that was on the market. That is what you buy things for. Now the Soviet Union are dealers—and they are tough dealers. Frankly, the Soviet Union didn't have any more idea that they had a crop failure than we did. I am a South Dakota farm boy and I remember crops that looked beautiful on the Fourth of July that weren't worth harvesting on the first of August. When we used to get those southwest, hot winds that came across in the 1930's through those wheat crops of ours, it would just destroy them. And that is basically what happened in the Soviet Union. They had unusual weather patterns, a lack of moisture, hot winds, what they called a continuing high, heat, winds over a long period of time that destroyed a large segment of their wheat producing area. Now that is what happened and all this business of looking for scapegoats is good for the election, good for politics, but doesn't have anything to do with economics. Now I would like to be able to accuse for good partisan political purposes someone of making a fast deal. But the truth is I don't think there was any corruption. I think we lacked proper information. And one of the reasons we went to the Soviet Union was to do something about it. For example, we have two agricultural attachés for the whole Soviet Union. The Soviet Union is fifth from the bottom in the number of agricultural attachés. We have more in Britain than we have in all of the Soviet Union. And it is always difficult to get good crop information from them anyway. But we did get an agreement from the Minister of Agriculture that he would look with favor upon a joint team to improve crop reporting. Likewise, their crop reports are just not basically that good. If you think we have got a bureaucracy, you ought to try theirs for size. Ours looks like it is nimble and filled with spirit. There is just poor crop reporting. So I came away convinced that we can do a better job on crop reporting. I think we can do a better job on salesmanship. By the way, this whole country needs to get export oriented. We are just going to wake up one of these days and find out that we really need the people that can do trade and business. When you are in Moscow and you stay at one of these prestigious hotels, you will meet a West German about every other step. You will meet someone from France. And you will meet the Japanese all over the place. And occasionally you will run into some good American who will say, "Gee, have you seen the jewels in Leningrad?" We have got to get some people who have some get up and go and go out after this business.

The only matter which I wish I had discussed with Senator Humphrey was the Soviets' policy to increase their production of meat, poultry, eggs and dairy products. I know he understood well the impact of hot dry winds on ripening grain but I did want to discuss the still more significant political/economic policy change of improving diets of the Soviet people.

EXPORT CONTROLS AND OILSEED EMBARGO

Some students of politics and history maintain the most poignant expression to come out of the Carter administration was the comment made by Bert Lance before a Chamber of Commerce breakfast in Washington, D.C. In May, 1977. He said, "If it ain't broke, don't fix it!"

Even though the expression was probably not original with Mr. Lance, I like it. Furthermore, it describes well an attitude held by many in responsible government policy positions. And it seems to fit into the background of several of the government actions taken by the executive branch of the government over the four years prior to the Carter administration.

Throughout these writings I have emphasized the significance of more or less government involvement in the agricultural policy decision-making process. A debate on agricultural legislation in the Congress or between the legislative and executive branches of the government is not one of deciding whether or not certain restrictions will be applied to producers. It is rather a situation in which our government is giving us an opportunity to choose the kind and extent of freedom we shall have.

For purposes of comparison, I wish to describe the involvement of the federal government at the end of the Johnson-Freeman era as being zero. Not for one moment was the then government and its impact on farmers' decision-making processes at point zero. But to start this dialogue I will illustrate how the federal government relinquished some controls and hence on a measurement scale moved perhaps two points toward greater freedom, then moved in the exact opposite direction.

For example, the suspension of marketing quotas for wheat and cotton and the removal of penalties for over-planting specific crops in relation to their respective acreage allotments were moves toward greater freedom. Continuation of low-loan rates matched with deficiency payments reaffirmed belief in the consumers and users to send the right signal to producers. The decision of President Nixon in 1971 to normalize trade with the socialist countries resulted in producers gaining more freedom to plant and market.

In reality, that is the message of this chapter, "Growing Pains: U.S. Agriculture in a Global Economic Environment." This chapter is also one key to the subtitle, "Food Policy and the Political Expedient."

This not-so-proud series of events as far as agriculture is concerned commenced with edible oils, oilseeds and meal. As was mentioned in the previous subchapter, world weather conditions reduced the output of oilseeds in the Soviet Union, India, China, Australia and West Africa. Poor weather plagued U.S. oilseed crops in 1972. The Peru anchovy catch was very low.

A second devaluation of the U.S. dollar on February 15, 1973, increased demand for soybeans, soybean meal and other oilseed meals.

An extremely wet spring in the United States in 1973 delayed the planting of soybeans and corn.

On June 13, 1973, President Nixon imposed price ceilings on retail and wholesale prices. He also put in place an export monitoring system for agricultural exports. This was part of the general economic stabilization program. The President also requested new authority to control agricultural exports for the announced purpose of controlling the rise in U.S. food prices.

Two weeks later the Secretary of Commerce, Frederick Dent, with the approval of Secretary Butz, announced the imposition of an embargo on the export of U.S. soybeans, cottonseed and their products. According to the announcement, at that time, the embargo was imposed pursuant to the authority as contained in the Export Administration Act of 1969. (A more comprehensive discussion of this act is contained in Chapter 6.)

On July 2, 1973, the Department of Commerce announced an export licensing system for agricultural commodities as a replacement of the embargo. The licensing system was vague and allowed only a portion of contracts to be filled by exporters. Lawsuits contesting the party at fault for non-delivery continued for years.

On August 1, more modifications of the licensing system were announced.

On September 21, the Department of Commerce revoked the export licensing system.

The several government actions which had commenced with the second devaluation of the dollar on February 15, leading to the embargo, and then export controls for oilseeds and the oilseeds complex, culminating in revocation of the licensing system on September 21—government actions over a seven-month period knocked my scale-of-freedom example crazy. Government paternalism had replaced the choices of millions.

Furthermore, Mr. U.S.A. Soybean was never again going to ride as high nor as proud in the saddle of world commerce.

Why did it happen?

Several reasons, but in my opinion the real culprit was the Vietnam involvement and the failure of the U.S. government as constituted by the office of the president and the Congress to levy the necessary taxes to wage war, or as Governor Aiken said, issue a press release stating the United States had won and withdraw.

Of course, the second dollar devaluation antagonized the U.S. oilseed situation.

Naturally, fighting the Vietnam War "on the cuff" had taken its toll but it was unfortunate for our domestic economy and the impact on domestic food prices. Seemingly, events had made it mandatory to again devalue the dollar, February, 1973.

One other school of thought has been expressed regarding the policy action of the Department of Commerce and USDA in embargoing and then limiting the export of U.S. soybeans in 1973. Some marketing students postulate the theory that if an export reporting system had been in place and operating the precise statistics gleaned from such system would have convinced the government policy makers that supplies were ample to supply domestic and world requirements. Further, with such documentation, the reasoning dictates that prices for soybeans and oilseeds would not have boomed to such high levels. This after-the-fact theory is only hypothetical thinking.

Coincidentally, the need for more current information on volume of U.S. farm commodities which had been sold on any specific day for future delivery was mentioned on at least two occasions during meetings of the four agency heads in my office in 1970 or 1971. During a working lunch with Hardin, I also brought up the subject. Inaction on the matter—which would have required legislation—can best be described by the phrase, "If it ain't broke, don't fix it!"

The export monitoring system which had been announced on June 13, two weeks prior to the embargo was administered by commerce. New legislation, the Agriculture and Consumer Protection Act of 1973, made the reporting system mandatory. The Statistical Reporting Service, USDA, operated the new system for about one month, after which the function was transferred to the Foreign Agricultural Service where it remains until this day.

One philosophical comment should be made on the export reporting system. Because it came into being during the late summer—or early fall of 1972—it seems appropriate to incorporate those views at this time.

The reporting system came into being for several reasons.

☆ Producers and users want the most current information on the outlook for export of grains and oilseeds.
☆ Academia and government policy makers want the information.
☆ Marketers and a broad interest group of the public are always hungry for more information.

The reporting system only partially fulfills this need because the export sales report comprises a tightly bracketed spectrum of activity in a given period.

The system also has another characteristic which is worthy of note. When supplies are tight and prices are rising, the reporting system tends to overstate real commercial demand for U.S. commodities on a worldwide basis. When supplies are plentiful and prices are weakening, the system tends to understate the real potential for export business in U.S. commodities.

Even with all its weaknesses and shortcomings the export reporting system has filled some need and is an acceptable document in many agricultural libraries.

SCRIPT FOR INTERVENTION

If a script reader were to be given an assignment to advise on a theme for causing a free society to bleed—that advisor need only recapitulate the U.S. defense and foreign policy as it was carried out by our nation during the decade of the 1960s through the early years of the 1970s.

Our nation bled.

Formulators of agricultural and food policy in the United States, while being blamed by many for being too freewheeling as this hectic period was ending, found it impossible to take enough actions to fit the economic mold created by events far removed from production and marketing of farm products.

The printing presses turned out money to finance the nation's involvement in Vietnam. In turn, these dollars, so created, found their way around the world. The booming economic situation, because of the great increase in buying power, resulted in droves of people in several countries choosing to purchase more higher-quality food items such as animal proteins and vegetable oil.

During the year 1973, somewhat higher food prices in the United States really did not begin to ration use of grain and other feed ingredients for meat and poultry production. The year following, in 1974, price rationing, because of the 14 percent increase in the retail price of food, resulted in a drastic reduction in utilization of grain for feed in the United States.

The agricultural sector in the United States was performing well, as compared to the industrial complex, in generating more foreign exchange and would have done much better had the 1974 corn crop production year been more favorable.

The deficit spending in the United States, the devalued dollar and the unprecedented acceleration in consumption of animal products in many countries greatly antagonized the economic squeeze on households throughout the United States. And the resulting unhappiness became most vocal.

As mentioned, the final culprit making the economic impact much more severe across the nation was the late spring, summer drought and finally an early killing frost in 1974. These unfavorable conditions greatly curtailed the final outcome of the 1974 corn crop.

In fact, in a year in which a record feed grain harvest would have been welcome news, the coarse grain production dropped to 150.5 million tons down from 186.1 the previous year (1973).

Exports of both wheat and coarse grain were also down compared to the prior year, and this reversal of trend in export volume of 10 million tons of wheat and coarse grains (63.1 million compared to 73.3 the prior year) is the basis for the ongoing dialogue in my writings.

It seems appropriate at this point to step back and look at a profile of grain utilization in the world and in our own nation during that period in the mid-1970s. I want to look at grain used for livestock and poultry feed. The great increase in number and capacity of feed manufacturing plants was phenomenal. For example, as I looked at the grain-for-feed statistics at the end of the decade of the 1970s in a paper celebrating the twentieth anniversary of the U.S. Feed Grains Council, the utilization of grain annually for feed revealed:

ANNUAL UTILIZATION OF GRAIN FOR FEED

(in Million Metric Tons)

	1960	1970	1980
U.S.A.	110	130	140
EC-9	50	67	70
East Europe	30	50	70
USSR	40	90	120
World	260	413	536

(statistics are rounded)

(These figures would be still more dramatic if protein meals, oilseeds and competing carbohydrate ingredients such as manioc were included.)

The dynamics of the animal feeding industry was front page news in that period of 1974-1975, particularly in the United States, because global production of coarse grains in the twelve-month period ending June 30, 1975, dropped 45 million tons—559 million tons compared to 604 million. As stated earlier, the U.S. shortfall alone was 36 million tons. Most of the balance of the reduced harvest was in East and Central Europe.

At that time in the United States, the approximate breakdown in use of grain for feed by class of animals was about as follows:

Hogs: 26 percent
Poultry (layers, chicks, broilers and turkeys): 21 percent
Dairy animals (milk cows and replacement stock): 14 percent

Beef cattle (other than "cattle-on-feed"): 7 percent
Cattle-on-feed: 23 percent
Other livestock (ducks, geese, sheep, horses, goats and pets): 7
  percent

Because of run up in food prices in the United States antagonized
by world events, the three major television networks developed enter-
tainment documentaries. The major thrust of each in the grain-use
story was to depict the excessive use of grain utilized by "cattle-on-
feed."

Ironically, the accurate observation whereby the U.S. cattle industry provides the safety valve, which closes down and postpones grain
utilization until new grain supplies appear in greater abundance,
never really was told in an understandable manner to the vast public.

As a case in point, the world reduced the use of grain for feed
during that 12-month period by 36 million tons. Almost all of this
reduction took place in the United States and Canada—a large part by
less feeding of grain to cattle. The United States alone reduced grain
use for feed by about 30 million tons.

How was this reduction accomplished?

By market forces!

Higher grain prices contributed greatly to zero or negative returns
to cattle and to a degree to other livestock feeders.

It was economically painful to agricultural entrepreneurs but a
great tribute to our free livestock and poultry-marketing system.

The grain-use story in the world and in the United States attracted
many political interveners in the U.S. grain export market. In fact, the
three years, 1973, 1974 and 1975, offered a nightmare of jabs and
thrusts by government officials at the market—all designed to impact
prices or in one way or another influence the flow of grain from the
United States to several destinations.

The oilseed export licensing system had been revoked September,
1973.

The disappointing corn crop of slightly less than 4.7 billion bushels in October of 1974 contributed greatly to the USDA announcement
of a voluntary prior-approval system for export sales of wheat, corn,
grain sorghum, soybeans, soybean meal and soybean oil-cakes, effective October 7, 1974. Barley and oats were added on October 11.

The word "voluntary" was truly misleading. Exporters had
learned the meaning of having an embargo placed on the shipment of
commodities and the staggering financial losses inherent in a shipping

stoppage. So naturally the system should have been more logically termed "a sales system subject to government approval."

The so-called prior-approval system was terminated March 6, 1975.

BILATERALISM

A brief update on the Soviet grain production reveals that the country produced a record grain crop in 1973. For the marketing year ending June 30, 1974, the official grain production figures were 211 million metric tons. As a consequence, the total imports were 11 million metric tons.

The following year, 1974-1975, production dropped to 183.6 million tons and imports were 5.2 million tons. The Soviets obviously carried over a fair amount of grain from the good 1973 harvest. If they had not done so the Kremlin would have had big problems because world and U.S. grain stocks in 1974 and early 1975 were extremely tight.

As the 1975 crop production year unfolded, two things of major importance were happening. The U.S. wheat and coarse grain crop was progressing nicely. In fact, by end of harvest the nation had brought in 242 million tons—43 million more than the year before.

Across the ocean, CIA was saying the Soviet import needs could reach 40 million tons. It developed that the agency was too high but the Soviets did import that season a record 26 million tons, 10 million of which was wheat.

And so as the U.S. crop rebounded, a larger home was ready for the greater outturn. Total exports of all grains that 12-month period, 1975-1976, amounted to 81.7 million tons. Twice the volume of four years earlier.

To assume a happy supply/demand situation came into being is erroneous. The market during the period of that many months was a roller coaster neck-snapping affair. When a day or two of price stability seemed to be at hand some U.S. government official or agency or some other entity was prepared to come forward with a surprise.

Get this!

Richard Bell, assistant secretary of agriculture, stated that as of that date (August 9, 1975), U.S. grain sales to the Soviet Union included 10.3 million tons of wheat, corn and barley.

Two days later, August 11, Secretary Butz publicly called on all grain companies to withhold further sales to the Soviet Union until U.S. crop production figures were known.

One week later the maritime unions reaffirmed their intention to boycott ships loading grain for the Soviet Union.

On September 4, Butz stated that no additional grain sales would be made to the Soviet Union until the dispute with the maritime unions was settled.

On September 9, President Ford announced his intention to explore the possibility of a long-term grain agreement with the Soviet Union. The President extended the moratorium on grain sales to the Soviet Union until mid-October. The maritime unions agreed to load grain destined to the Soviet Union—as a result of negotiations between the President and George Meany.

The following day, September 10, Under Secretary of State Charles W. Robinson left for Moscow to begin negotiations for a long-term agreement. Richard Bell, assistant secretary of agriculture, accompanied Robinson. Bell was a long-time civil servant, but more importantly was well qualified to negotiate with the Soviets on agricultural matters.

On the same day, September 10, the State Department requested, through the embassy of Poland in Washington, that Poland halt grain-buying in the United States. This did not become public information until Jozef Danilczuk in the New York office of the Polish FTO, Rolimpex, on September 12 informed grain exporting firms that Rolimpex was no longer buying grain in the United States. Even then the embargo as such was only speculation.

Over 10 days later an AP story in the *Washington Post* stated that "informed sources" had confirmed that further sales to Poland had been suspended until a long-term agreement could be negotiated with the Soviet Union.

Rumors persisted that a secret government ban on grain sales to Poland was in fact "real." Grain prices were fluctuating widely on rumors and guesses.

A few of us in New York speculated over "coffee cups" on the protocol of a Senate or House agriculturally oriented Congressional committee subpoenaing the secretary of state for influencing farm prices in a less than public manner. This was only speculative gossip but I was somewhat surprised that some group of producers did not pursue the matter. (Henry Kissinger was now secretary of state and as such had been confirmed by the U.S. Senate and hence was subject to being called to testify before appropriate Congressional committees.)

While I make this remark—a bit with tongue in cheek—it is not far-fetched. Actions at that time, by high government officials, did have a serious impact on already volatile grain prices. Actions undertaken in secrecy were certainly foreign (no pun intended) to our open system of government.

On September 16, a State Department release announced the Soviets had agreed in principle to a long-term trade agreement for U.S. grains and on October 20 the White House released the text of the United States-Soviet grain agreement.

According to the text the agreement was to remain in force until September 30, 1981.

On October 10, President Ford announced he was lifting the embargo on grain sales to Poland because USDA was estimating record corn and wheat harvests.

Towards the last of November in 1975, Butz and the minister of agriculture of Poland exchanged letters involving a five-year supply agreement for wheat and corn.

SUMMARY

Over the four-year span as annual U.S. grain exports doubled from about 40 million tons of wheat and coarse grains to over 80 million tons (July 1, 1972 through June 30, 1976), the U.S. agricultural economy underwent growing pains of various sorts.

Wheat, corn, soybean and sorghum producers as one would expect reacted in various ways. For example, some, thanks to higher net returns, tidied up their financial base. Others cried, "Eureka, I have found it" and invested, thanks to relatively low-interest rates, in more land and machinery. Some of them did so with too much encouragement from banks and lending institutions. Anyone familiar with and traveling in the grain-producing area could feel the added prosperity of the period.

Feed manufacturers and the broad range of processors were forced to move rapidly to keep pace with the market volatility of the period.

Livestock and poultry producers had their problems adjusting to changing conditions during the four-year period.

Transportation interests had no choice but to increase investments in barges, hopper cars and other facilities—beyond in many cases—prudent judgment because the increase in tonnage to be moved was at hand.

International marketers found requirements for capital literally multiplied during some seasons within the four-year period. Cost of updating and expanding capacity at ocean ports called for excessive capital investment.

Many internal grain receiving, handling and buying entities felt the pinch of not being able to load and handle multiple units of hopper cars. Many miles of obsolete rail feeder lines became still less competitive with the overall grain movement.

Finally, the old cliche "necessity is the mother of invention" came into play during this period of agricultural history. The system did perform because the ingenuity of thousands of entrepreneurs with the profit motive in mind applied their resources and know how.

Two other observations are worthy of recognition—both disappointing happenings. The first development has to do with the national media and the misinformation engendered by many syndicated columnists with some encouragement from groups like the American Bakers Association (ABA). The second development was the reaction to higher world grain prices of the European Community agricultural policy officials.

What I found most disappointing was the bleating of much of the public media. I use the word "bleat" because it is a traditional descriptive term from the vocabulary of students in animal agriculture. It is a cry of a young calf or lamb while under some degree of stress or of humans making foolish, complaining talk.

Naturally, higher food prices upset consumers. Incidentally, food prices increased less than many other cost of living items such as medical fees, transportation and other items representing heavy inputs of labor—but substantiated truth is not as colorful as raw emotion.

The ABA, for reasons never very clear to me, chose to play up the possibility of the "bread a dollar a loaf" slogan. Its propaganda simply fueled an already erroneous over-publicized false claim that the U.S. wheat and/or grain sales to the Soviet Union were the sole cause of an increase in food prices.

The prices for fish, a non-agricultural food item, increased over 40 percent in a three-year period. My family is heavily involved in the fishing business, and I can assure the reader the higher prices for fish were not making the commercial fisheries wealthy—nor were fish retail prices riding the coattails of other food items. Furthermore, the U.S. interests were not selling fish to the Soviets.

One other thing which caused me to lose patience with the bleaters was the false message conveyed to the unknowing public that the United States would run out of wheat, hence flour and bread. On June 30, 1973—the end of the marketing year—the carryover of old crop wheat was over 440 million bushels. Our total use of wheat for food per year at that time was about 550 million bushels and the new harvest as of July 1 was already under way. Furthermore, the total wheat shipped to the Soviet Union during the 12 months, July 1, 1972 through June 30, 1973, amounted to 344 million bushels—far less than the old crop carryover at the end of the marketing year.

One other view expressed at that time and for years later by some well meaning economists—well meaning but naive—was the concept that sales of grain to the Soviets and the higher food prices in the United States were the chief cause of the high rate of inflation later in the decade of the 1970s. This theory I found to be near irresponsible because that argument disregards the printing of more than $100 billion worth of greenbacks in the United States to finance our ill-advised adventure into Vietnam over several years—as our officials chose to wage war without taxation to finance unpopular policy.

Finally, during the higher grain price era of 1973-1974 and a few months beyond, the EC officials chose not to capitalize on export marketing opportunities to the degree dictated by prudent management of their surplus grain stocks. As a consequence, they (the EC officials) received lower prices for their exported wheat than would have been the case if they had been more aggressive in selling. Then too, if they had been more eager sellers at that time, the pressure of a tight world grain situation would have been less severe on the users of grain in the United States, where the adjustment in use was taking place. In a manner of speaking, the slow and rigid performance of the EC officials is a commendation to the U.S. marketing system where price and stock management are based upon the views and actions of thousands.

CHAPTER 6

The Crucible for Global Food Policy

☆ ☆

INTERNATIONAL COMMODITY AGREEMENTS

"To assure supplies of wheat to importing countries and markets for wheat to exporting countries at equitable and stable prices" was the stated objective of the first International Wheat Agreement to be ratified by the United States Senate in 1949.

Wheat is the most important basic food commodity trading in world commerce. While a larger percentage of the world's population depends on rice as the most important food item, the volume of rice changing hands in world commerce has been relatively small compared to wheat. About 1 percent of the rice produced in the world enters world commerce whereas about 20 percent of the world's wheat production crosses the borders of nations.

The continent of Asia accounts for 90 percent of total rice consumption. On the other hand, wheat is the traditional food grain in the Western World and of increasing importance in Asia and Africa, particularly in the urban centers on those two continents.

Discussions aimed at organizing the international wheat market actually began in 1930. Depressed prices led to representatives of exporting countries discussing the feasibility of a system of export quotas as a means of increasing prices.

A second meeting of 11 exporting nations was held in London in 1931. No unanimity of thought developed.

A third international conference on the matter was again held in London in 1933. An agreement of sorts was reached but a workable effective instrument was not developed.

Many meetings were held during the world depression era culminating in a near type agreement in 1939. The Second World War in that year ended further such discussions.

During the war, Argentina, Australia, Canada, the United States and the United Kingdom did meet to discuss the world wheat and price situation. A memorandum of agreement was adopted. Perhaps the most noteworthy provision was the one establishing the International Wheat Council in London in 1942. The council has been in existence since that time and administers the International Wheat Agreement.

In a meeting of the International Wheat Council in Washington in 1948, an international wheat agreement was approved. The United States failed to ratify the agreement, and it did not go into effect.

One year later, another agreement was negotiated which was virtually the same as the one approved in 1948. The maximum price was $1.80 per bushel compared to $2.00 in the 1948 document, basis #1 Manitoba Northern, Fort William/Port Arthur, Canada. The agreement was ratified by governments, including the United States, and it went into effect August 1, 1949, for four years.

Similar agreements were put into effect in 1953 and in 1956.

The 1949, 1953 and 1956 agreements were quota-type treaties. They were based on the concept of guaranteed quantities. The export quota assigned to Canada was larger than the U.S. quota—203 million bushels annually and 168 million, respectively.

I was named by the U.S. secretary of state as the U.S. delegate to the 1959 negotiating conference. I was cautiously pleased to undertake the assignment of negotiating a new agreement on behalf of the United States. In preparing for the conference to be held in Geneva under the auspices of the United Nations (the first such under the UN), I discovered several things which had not occurred to me during my work career. It should be stated that I was open-minded at that time regarding any personal feelings on the merits or demerits of an international commodity agreement.

  ☆ Secretary Benson and his sub-cabinet were less than enthusiastic about the agreement. In their eyes, the document as such did not broaden the world market; it only attempted to divide the market as it existed. The Department of State favored an extension of the agreement.

* Top Canadian officials had traditionally oversold the market stabilizing influence of the agreement to wheat producers in the prairie provinces. Canadian officials were strongly in favor of an extension or renewal of the treaty. In fairness, it must be recognized that Canada did *not* offer its producers a wheat price support program comparable to the United States. Hence, the Canadian government had over-played the importance of the agreement from the standpoint of its lending strength to producer prices.

* The newly formed European Economic Community (EEC) favored commodity agreements, including the IWA.

* Australia was a strong supporter of IWA.

I worked with career people in USDA, most notable of whom was Arnold Garthoff, a loyal and dedicated agriculturally oriented diplomat, and with state department officials in developing a U.S. negotiating posture. It became increasingly clear that the U.S. delegate should seek an end to specific guaranteed quantities and removal of the quota provisions.

Ironically, over 50 percent of the wheat being exported from the United States was not being registered under the agreement. That volume moving overseas under P L 480 was outside of the pact. Those sales were concessional in nature and were made possible by government-to-government agreements.

The United Kingdom had not ratified the 1956 treaty, but as a result of pressure from Canada was ready to help negotiate the 1959 agreement. The U.K. delegate early on sided with the United States in favoring a discontinuance of specific quotas. Japan, a rapidly growing wheat importer also went along—early in the conference—favoring an end to the rigid quota provision.

Finally, the agreement negotiated in 1959 contained a provision whereby each importing country agreed to undertake to purchase from member exporting countries, while prices were within the price range, not less than a specified percentage of its total commercial requirements, and the exporting countries undertook collectively to supply all the exporting requirements of the importing countries. This mutual obligation applied throughout the price range of $1.50 to $1.90 per bushel basis, the more or less fictional grade, #1 Manitoba Northern.

During the closing days and hours of the 1959 conference one had to be impressed with the sentimental attitude or chumminess expressed by several of the long-standing participants in conferences having to do with wheat. This closeness in itself contributes to a few nations' near passionate zeal for a continuation of wheat agreements.

In briefing Assistant Secretary McLain for his presenting the document to the U.S. Senate Committee on Foreign Relations for consideration to ratify, I described the then new agreement as rendering the participating exporting countries an international club for member countries to garner sales with member importing countries.

The agreement was extended in 1962; the new price range was raised to $1.62½ at the minimum and $2.02½ per bushel at the maximum. This lasted until 1967 and also the following year, until July 1, 1968, but without the economic provisions (pricing section).

A final observation is worthy of note before looking at the wheat cartel attempt as contained in the International Grains Arrangement (IGA), 1967. The observation of note has to do with the attitude of Canadian and Australian wheat boards. In the absence of these two organizations it is doubtful whether an IWA would have ever been negotiated following the Second World War. An agreement was deemed most important to both groups, and seems to be to this moment.

THE INTERNATIONAL GRAINS ARRANGEMENT, 1967

The new arrangement emerging from the Kennedy round—general trade negotiations under the auspices of General Agreement Tariffs and Trade (GATT) included two legal instruments. One was a food aid convention and the second was a wheat trade convention. The wheat trade convention was not unlike the 1962 IWA but contained important changes in the price mechanism.

The reference wheat in the new arrangement was no longer the most cherished "cadillac of wheats," #1 Northern Manitoba basis Fort William/Port Arthur. The reference wheat became U.S. Hard Red Winter #2 (Ordinary)—the most commonly traded U.S. wheat—the high tonnage export grade and class.

In prior agreements, quality differentials to be used in calculations of minimum and maximum price equivalents had never been prescribed. In this new document, 14 specified wheats were agreed to and included in the convention. These additions were designed, according to quotes by negotiators, to ensure greater market stability through better price discipline.

During that period of time, and ever since World War II, the price of every ton of wheat trading in the world was established through one technique or another by governments. U.S. export price was determined by CCC. Domestic wheat prices, because of producer price supports, were higher than world prices. Subsidy payments were utilized by CCC to lower export prices and to keep U.S. wheat price competitive with wheats of other origins.

The new maximum price for the reference wheat (#2 Ordinary) was set at $2.13 and the minimum at $1.73 per bushel, basis the Gulf. Because the new minimum price was higher than the then prevailing free market price for Ordinary wheat at the Gulf, the Johnson administration responsible for negotiating the arrangement sought Senate ratification and Congressional authority to implement an inverse subsidy program—and thereby tax the export of wheat. The authority and ratification was granted, but with some delay. As a result of the delay, implementation of the new arrangement was postponed until late summer, 1968.

Delay in implementation became a meaningful happening because the few weeks left for the Johnson administration to be in power did not provide any meaningful volume of wheat export registrations. Export registrations for future shipment during the closing weeks of the old authority under the lower price were heavy—as one would expect.

Over nine years later, in 1976, John H. Parotte, executive secretary, International Wheat Council, in an address in Washington, D.C., described in a few words one reason, and a good one, why the International Grains Arrangement ended in failure.

Mr. Parotte said, "In my humble opinion, an international commodity agreement, if it is to be successful, must not operate so as to appear disadvantageous to any of the parties to it."

There are, in my opinion, several more reasons why the IGA was doomed to failure before the ink was dry.

The Johnson administration was outnegotiated in agriculture and specifically with cereals. I have always suspected the decision on behalf of the United States to agree to #2 Ordinary being the reference wheat was made by someone other than Secretary Freeman or Under Secretary Schnittker. The decision to do so was contrary to recommendations from grain trade organizations.

Treating this provision as kindly as possible one can say that the price of U.S. Hard Winter Wheat was unduly "exposed."

Various origin ocean transportation provisions were treated with naiveté.

The transportation provisions favoring Australia caused me to wonder, at the time, whether this concession to that country was in any way related to the fervor of President Johnson in his objective in maintaining the support of Australia on our side in Vietnam.

The decision of the Johnson administration to agree to a minimum export price in excess of domestic price and thereby necessitate an export tax was indeed a chancy goal. Had the pricing provision of the arrangement continued in effect for many months I believe the constitutionality of the tax would have continued to be challenged in the U.S. courts.

Historically, the world wheat situation is not a static affair. The year, 1968, as it unfolded, offered quite a different wheat supply/demand picture than the year earlier. Supplies for export were larger in several exporting nations and because of generally favorable world weather including importing countries the market had contracted. An agreement mandating higher export prices in face of the changed world situation was in trouble.

If artificially higher export prices as envisioned and agreed to in the agreement were to be maintained, each and every exporting member would have had to exercise maximum discipline—not only in pricing but also in holding additional stocks. They did not. The scenario unraveled about as follows.

Under Dr. Hardin in the new lineup in USDA, I was responsible for government activities involving agricultural exports. In the reorganization, the wheat export subsidy function was assigned to Clifford Pulvermacher, administrator of the newly organized Export Marketing Service (EMS). He reported to me. From the early days of my return to USDA, we were involved daily with wheat pricing policies under the relatively new IGA.

Several things happened during the first six months of 1969 which contributed, finally, to the United States piercing the minimum wheat export price—but not until strong attempts were undertaken with competing exporting nations.

* The 1969 U.S. and world wheat crop promised to be the third-in-a-row high production year.
* Less and less wheat being traded in the world was changing hands at the agreed-upon price levels. As an example: France sold milling wheat to Taiwan at a price of $12 per ton below the price being quoted by our exporters in Taiwan for comparable soft wheat from the United States. France also sold French feed wheat to Taiwan for 99 cents per bushel. This price laid down in Taiwan was about $17 a ton below the landed price of corn from

the United States or any other origin. The export restitutions (subsidies) paid by the EEC were greatly in excess of the actual net selling price. France, as an EEC member, was a signatory to the IGA.

* Wheat surpluses were increasing. World wheat trade, because of the larger stocks or carryovers in an expanded number of countries, now included a number of exporting countries not historically engaged in the export of wheat. As one example, at that time, was the Soviet Union sale of 10 million bushels to the United Kingdom at attractive prices—for delivery in late 1968 and first half of 1969. The Soviet Union was not a signatory to the IGA. This resulted in a direct loss of sales by the United States and Canada.

* As mandated by the farm program provision then in effect and with wheat stocks accumulating in the United States, Secretary Hardin had no legal choice but to further reduce the 1970 national wheat acreage production allotment. A decision on the matter, according to statute, had to be announced by August 15, 1969.

I intimated in a speech, delivered at Norfolk, Virginia, on June 20, that the days for the United States continuing to respect the rigid pricing provision under IGA were indeed limited.

Another happening added further "fuel to the fire."

Deputy Prime Minister Anthony of Australia had made a speech in rural Australia dramatizing the "advantages" Australian negotiators had captured for Australia nearly two years earlier in Geneva during the Kennedy Round (GATT) negotiations on cereals. His statement was not new information, but it received rather wide coverage in the United States. And the timing was such that Secretary Hardin and I, as well as others in the Nixon administration, were convinced that any further assessing of inverse subsidy for exporting U.S. wheat had to be ended.

After consultation with appropriate members of the Senate and House and concurrence within the administration, U.S. export wheat prices for all classes of wheat were established at reasonably competitive prices.

Thus the short-lived wheat pricing cartel ended.

Why? Because member nations chose not to or were politically unable to exercise the required discipline.

Over the years since that period, when we attempted to push the wheat export price uphill against all logical supply/demand forces, a lesson of economic truth presented itself. An increasing or expanding supply can only be utilized through lower prices. France demonstrated that economic truth by literally dumping a cumbersome inventory of soft milling wheat. Further, the world observed still another truth during the early years of the next decade, when world wheat stocks became tight, that at some price level, wheat becomes wheat for food purposes or at still higher prices grain becomes grain, the lesson should be clear to all.

Stated succinctly, *hungry* people can hardly tell the difference in taste of bread made from traditional high-quality wheats as compared to normally cheaper wheats. This truth in *no* way should be interpreted as a statement discouraging the production and marketing of the highest possible quality wheat—it only teaches that even the most prestigious government representatives cannot with success mandate a rigid price for a fungible commodity in contradiction of economic truth. National discipline, singularly or collectively, will not support such a policy.

THE 1971 IWA

A United Nations Wheat Conference was again convened in Geneva in January, 1971, to negotiate a replacement of the IGA.

The conversations ended in an extension of the Food Aid Convention, and finally, in a Wheat Trade Convention, 1971.

Howard Worthington, associate administrator of the Foreign Agricultural Service, USDA, was the U.S. representative. On behalf of the United States, he recommended incorporating into the agreement a pricing section to be included in the economic provisions not unlike the language contained in the 1959 and 1962 IWAs. Because Canada had changed its wheat grade standards, that country's delegate objected. Further, Canada would not agree to any grade of its wheat being the reference wheat. Likewise, the United States would not agree to any U.S. grade wheat being the reference wheat. Lessons learned from the IGA were too obvious.

After considerable debate, the 1971 IWA, as agreed to and ratified by the U.S. Senate, was free of economic provisions.

In the process of presenting the 1971 IWA to the Senate for consideration for ratification as a treaty, I appeared before a subcommittee of the foreign relations committee. Gale McGee (D.-Wyoming) was chairman of the sub-committee. During a conversation with him prior to the hearing, I quickly had come to the conclusion he would recommend ratification of the new agreement—but that he would also do something to embarrass the administration, Howard

Worthington or me. McGee performed as expected. He recommended ratification of the treaty to the foreign relations committee and in turn to the Senate. The Senate acted positively. He then presented to the Senate a sense of the Senate resolution which stated that the executive branch was hereby directed to negotiate economic provisions within the context of the IWA with other signatory nations. The resolution was adopted without opposition. I doubt if any Senator understood the meaning of economic provisions in an IWA. On the other hand, McGee should have because I had discussed the matter with him 30 months earlier when wheat exporting nations were disregarding the pricing provisions of the old International Grains Arrangement. The Senate action was, of course, without meaning because there was no way that signatory countries would convene to consider a proposal rejected a few weeks earlier. I considered the action a political heckling trick.

Unfortunately, Mr. Worthington did not live sufficiently long to appreciate the wisdom of the deletion of the economic provisions.

Had pricing provisions and related rights and obligations been incorporated into the 1971 agreement, they most certainly would have been disregarded by signatory countries—both exporters and importers. Certainly, had there been a continuation of a maximum and minimum pricing provision, the failure during the life of the 1971 treaty would have been on the high end of the pricing range.

Again, Mr. Parotte expressed it well in 1976 when he stated that the absence of economic provisions in the 1971 IWA was "a blessing in disguise."

The IWA has continued on and is in effect at this time, free of economic provisions. International cooperation in wheat has not disappeared. The council continues to provide an international forum for cooperation and review of the wheat market situation.

I learned through involvement with international wheat agreements that an international grain export pricing cartel will not hold together. Signatory exporting nations are not able, politically, to discipline themselves. In a majority of years, world grain carryovers are on the increase. In such instances, if exporting nations are serious about respecting an agreed-to minimum export price, they must either decrease production through reduced plantings or implement a policy of expanding storage capability—or both. Over a period of 50 years, the United States and, on one occasion (possibly two), Canada stood ready to decrease plantings and increase storage capability to attain price stability. Other exporting nations seemed prepared to negotiate an advantage for their respective nations or regions. I am not critical of this nationalistic attitude, but the U.S. delegate in keeping faith with economic realism dares not embrace dream world naiveté.

Conversely, signatory importing countries will not for any meaningful length of time pay a price to "club" exporting members greatly in excess of an offering price from a non-member nation. Experience to date teaches this truth.

Prior to completing this subchapter on international wheat agreements the subject of the world wheat price deserves further comment. Several recent happenings illustrate fuzzy thinking or lack of understanding of the price importing countries are prepared to pay for wheat—or *may* or may *not* be able to pay.

As a case in point, several Senators over the last few years have urged the formation of an international cartel. They, on occasion, have discussed the matter with Canadian officials—Senator Melcher (D.-Montana) and former Senator McGovern (D.-South Dakota) along with former Senator Bellmon (R.-Oklahoma) have been vocal on the subject. If one were to stretch one's imagination far enough and if at a given time naive administrations were in power on both sides of the border, I believe that by both nations withholding wheat from the world market a much higher price could be attained for a given volume for a short period of time—before importing nations adjusted their import policies and/or their internal human and animal eating habits. Over a period of time, and not a very long time frame, the United States and Canada would discover the world can get along without their wheat. One must remember Western Europeans feed a large volume of wheat to animals. The Soviet Union, in most years, uses about 60 percent of its wheat for uses other than food. Logic dictates that under a dream world cartel system the poor quality wheat in the world normally utilized by livestock and non-food uses will make pretty acceptable bread and other food products.

The McGovern pronouncements on the matter of such a proposed cartel is strikingly illogical or naive or both. In one moment he has been a bleeding heart, at our taxpayers' expense, for the developing countries and their food problems—whilst at the same time he expounds the merits of a formalized wheat cartel structured to gouge the very foreigners who wrench his heart.

Finally, our European friends have proven to the world that grain in the magnitude we would like to think is not necessary for the production of livestock. This matter will be discussed later in this chapter as we analyze the Common Agricultural Policy (CAP) of the EEC.

THE GRAIN EXPORT EMBARGO TO THE
SOVIET UNION, 1980

Prior to the decade of the 1970s, the most important legislative government action of interest to farmers and agricultural businesses was the omnibus farm program legislation. As discussed in the previous chapter, laws involving much broader interest groups began to be of great economic importance to the agricultural community—particularly as farm commodities took on added importance in the world of commerce and diplomacy.

For example, the soybean export embargo of 1973 and the de facto export controls of 1974 and 1975 illustrated the significance of the Export Administration Act.

Prior to the action of President Carter on January 4, 1980, as he invoked an embargo on the shipment of corn, wheat, soybeans and other commodities, I had thought the executive branch (President) of our government was more fully aware of the economic and diplomatic cost of unilaterally invoking broad economic sanctions against another nation—even though that nation was guilty of reprehensible conduct against another sovereign state.

When the USSR invaded Afghanistan near the end of 1979 and early 1980, many of us directly interested in exporting U.S. grain to the Soviet Union wondered whether President Carter would utilize executive authorities and thereby invoke economic sanctions against the Soviets.

I cannot speak for anyone else other than myself, but as an officer of Continental Grain Company and I believe well informed with the authorities available to the President, I did not think he (the President) would declare an export embargo of U.S. grain to the Soviets as authorized under the Export Administration Act.

The President, in my opinion—under the act—had unquestioned legal authority to embargo or suspend shipments as he announced to the public on Friday evening, January 4.

Congress had incorporated language in the Export Administration Act which stated that it is the policy of the United States to use export controls only after full consideration of the impact on the economy of the United States and only to the extent necessary—and to limit the authority to restrict exports for reasons of national security, for reasons of foreign policy and for reasons of short supply.

President Carter—for reasons of national security and foreign policy—directed the secretary of commerce, in consultation with the secretary of agriculture, as provided in the statute, to limit U.S. shipment of wheat and corn to the Soviet Union to 8 million tons during the 12-month period ending September 30, 1980. The President also directed exports of other agricultural commodities to that destination be suspended (including soybean meal and broilers).

Under the terms of a five-year bilateral agreement between the United States and the Soviet Union, the United States was committed to ship 8 million tons of wheat and corn each year to the USSR, with additional amounts as agreed upon in consultation between the two governments. In such consultation in the fall of 1979 (the prior calendar year), the U.S. government had authorized the USSR to purchase up to 25 million tons of corn and wheat for shipment during the 12-month period which was to have ended September 30, 1980.

As of January 4, 1980, when the embargo was declared, about 5 million tons had been shipped.

On Monday, January 7, President Carter directed that validated export licenses should be granted to the extent necessary to permit shipment to continue for that portion in excess of the 5 million tons already shipped but not more than a total of 8 million tons.

So as to put this volume of grain in a more meaningful perspective, the reader is advised that the world during the crop year 1979-1980 produced about 1,520 million tons of all grains. The United States had produced about 300 million tons and the Soviet Union about 179 million tons.

Prior to the suspension (embargo), the U.S. government had estimated the Soviet Union would import 34 million tons from all origins including the 25 million from the United States.

As mentioned earlier, I did not expect the President to embargo shipment of U.S. grain to the USSR. I was therefore taken by complete surprise.

In weighing the pros and cons as to whether or not the President would act on this matter, I misjudged the raw emotionalism which apparently was involved in the presidential decision-making process.

I thought the provisions of the Export Administration Act would not be invoked for several reasons among which were:

* There was enough grain available for export or to be harvested for export prior to the autumn of 1980 in other countries, particularly southern hemisphere nations, for the Soviet Union to make up most or all of the shortfall created by a U.S. embargo.
* On the basis of grain being available in other nations, I thought an embargo would be little more than an inconvenience to the

Soviet Union—*if*—and I repeat *if* the Kremlin wished to import grain in the magnitude expected.
* Unilateral economic sanctions involving non-strategic goods such as farm products had proven to be relatively ineffective in accomplishing foreign policy or diplomatic goals.
* I thought the language as contained in the Export Administration Act and the legislative history surrounding passage of the law—that language which stated—"It is the policy of the United States to use export controls only after full consideration on the economy of the United States and only to the extent necessary . . ." would come in for more serious consideration.
* It seemed to me that the futility of "going it alone," as experienced by three presidents with the Vietnam War, would be more fully weighed by President Carter.

My judgment was in error!

As of the close of business that Friday afternoon, January 4, 1980, corn and wheat market position of Continental Grain Company was even with the board. The company was neither long nor short—taking into consideration both cash positions and future contracts (contracts to buy and/or sell corn and/or wheat). Throughout the day on Friday the subject of the Afghanistan invasion by the Soviets was discussed—and the possibility of a U.S. grain embargo. The sentiment of most executives of the company was not unlike my own, but we obviously were wrong.

Following the announcement of the embargo by President Carter on television, Michel Fribourg, president and chief executive of Continental Grain Company, and I discussed the announcement of President Carter. Mr. Fribourg invited five of us to his home in New York City the following morning (Saturday, January 5). At least two other officers would have been included had they not been out of the country or away from the East Coast.

It was quickly established during the informal get-together on Saturday that as a consequence of the President Carter action the company (Continental) was at the moment *after* the announcement long about 80 million bushels (2 million tons) of corn and about 7.5 million bushels (200,000 tons) of wheat. The decision to be in a long position—or to own unsold corn and wheat—was not by design of the company; it was the result of a U.S. government decision.

As we pondered the alternatives for action, we did not discuss the President's announcement as such. He had made a decision on behalf of the nation to apply economic sanctions against the Soviet Union. The next step for the company was to develop a plan of action designed to minimize financial losses. For example, with consideration for the unshipped balance of the 8 million tons—which according to the President would be allowed to be shipped—there would be about 11 million tons of corn (430 million bushels) in the hands of all exporters in excess of what had been the situation prior to the announcement of the President. And about 4.75 million tons of wheat (180 million bushels). It was generally felt the price of corn when the markets settled down would be off at least 50 cents per bushel. If this conservative guess was realistic, Continental's projected loss on corn alone would be $40 million. Across the industry 14 companies (cooperative and proprietory)—assuming they were in about the same market situation—stood to lose over $200 million on the corn contracts. If our projected price drop of 50 cents per bushel was too conservative, the losses would be proportionately greater. Because Continental's major unshipped balance consisted mainly of corn, we concerned ourselves with that commodity.

A like scenario applied to other companies with varying amounts of unshipped corn, wheat, soybeans, soybean meal and broilers.

Later in the day on Saturday, January 5, Secretary of Agriculture Bob Bergland issued a press release detailing the economic impact of the President's announcement on the USSR and the actions to be taken by USDA to offset the financial damage to U.S. grain producers.

In the absence of actions to offset the decline in export shipments and the associated decline in commodity prices, the suspension on shipments of agricultural commodities would result in a loss in U.S. exports of about 13 million tons of corn (512 million bushels), about 4 million tons of wheat (147 million bushels) and about 1 million tons of soybeans and soybean products (37 million bushels). The secretary projected a decline in calendar year prices of about 15 cents a bushel for corn and 25 cents a bushel for wheat and soybeans (in the absence of further government actions).

If Bergland's projection on price declines for the calendar year was a reasonable guess, the 50-cent per bushel decline in the value of the 80 million bushels of corn in long position held by Continental as a result of the embargo was much too conservative a guess.

It was quite clear from the information being released in the nation's capital that very little, if any, consideration had been given to the immediate impact on the entire commodity marketing institutions. The grain industry had managed to survive the soybean export embargo of 1973 and the many interferences of the White House, USDA and the departments of State and Commerce—but this massive embargo was to be the granddaddy of all such actions.

As a result of about three hours of conversations it was decided the company would request Secretary Bergland and USDA to buy our export contracts with Exporthkleb at prices as contained in the contracts between Continental and Exporthkleb.

I was confident Bergland had ample authority through the CCC Charter Act—whereby the secretary is authorized to support the prices of agricultural commodities through loans, purchases, payments and other operations—to purchase the contracts. This was to be an unusual request and to a degree a "hat-in-hand" action but it was evident the magnitude of President Carter's decision was only beginning to be understood around the nation. Incidentally, Bergland was estimating a reduction in 1980 farm income on the order of $3 billion—over a 10 percent drop in net income—because of the action.

Apparently, other exporting firms were also in contact with Secretary Bergland and his top staff, because he announced he and his people would meet with grain exporters in USDA in Washington, Sunday, January 6.

As the meeting ended in the Fribourg home in New York on Saturday, it was decided that Myron Laserson, executive vice president of Continental's World Grain Division and I would attend the Sunday meeting in Washington. As we parted there was some speculation as to whether USDA would or would not agree with our request. I was confident the Carter administration would purchase the export contracts. I say Carter administration because I was sure any decision to expend such a huge amount of government funds would of necessity have to receive presidential consideration. My confidence in believing the administration would accede to our request was based solely on the negative and disastrous result of its *not* taking such action.

Very much on my mind at that time but not discussed in the Fribourg meeting was the likelihood or possibility of one or more of the grain exporting companies holding contracts with Exporthkleb declaring *force majeure* (an unexpected and disruptive event which may operate to excuse a party from a contract) on contracts to purchase grain from country elevators or with barge line operators to supply transportation for grain. It would have been difficult to over-dramatize the outlook for financial losses in fulfilling contracts through the marketing system. Literally thousands of people and entities were involved, commencing with producers who had sold grain for nearby delivery or for delivery into the future. And of course the soundness and workability of the futures market was at stake.

The Sunday meeting with Secretary Bergland and his top people in USDA developed as was expected. The government officials explained the action of President Carter. After this, a few of them listed the several steps being taken to "shore up" grain prices for producers, among which were changes in the reserve program which included increasing reserve release prices, waiving first-year interest costs for grain entered into the reserve and increasing annual storage payment for reserve grains. Bergland also stated CCC would be prepared to purchase up to 4 million tons of wheat.

Most or all of the 14 proprietary and cooperative grain companies holding grain and other commodity export contracts with Exporthkleb were represented and each spoke on his or her own behalf.

I have often thought this was one meeting between government officials and industry representatives which should have been on film. I am under the impression laypersons or even some media representatives look upon government/industry meetings as conniving sessions or at other times confrontational.

A running picture and recording of this session would reveal an "awakening."

Obviously, government had come forth with ongoing program changes designed to cushion the financial shock of the announcement for producers.

The "awakening" began to dawn as views and questions centered on the market disaster at hand. About 17 million tons of grain which had been destined for the Soviet Union were now unsold. The logistic nightmare was difficult to comprehend, because the entire mass of grain was in all stages of contract fulfillment. Much of it was in the form of futures—and you cannot export futures contracts. On the other hand, our marketing system provides the mechanism for the exporter to convert (sell) the futures contracts in an orderly manner and buy cash grain—hence, the price protection for all parties concerned. A considerable portion of the 17 million tons was in the form of contracts, with prices fixed with country dealers and/or producers. Transportation from the country to export locations had been arranged, the cost of which had also been fixed.

If the Sunday meeting had been on film, the viewer would discover that the firms in the export business contribute time and place utility. The risk inherent in performing this function gradually became clear to the government representatives participating in the discussions. A recording of this understanding would be obvious had the developing scenario been reduced to film.

Now, years after the fact, had the Carter administration chosen to not purchase the export contracts, I believe our grain-marketing system would have been thrown into a panic which may have required years to unravel. The detonator would have been the declaration of *force majeure* by some entity in the marketing or transportation chain.

While a horror story could be written about the negative impact of inaction, the reverse took place.

On Monday, January 7, Vice-President Mondale announced that President Carter was directing the secretary of agriculture to offer to purchase contractural obligations for wheat, corn and soybeans previously committed for shipment to the Soviet Union. The Commodity Credit Corporation was to assume the contracts at the contract price minus any costs that had not already been paid. Mondale further stated, "The purpose is to protect against losses, not to guarantee profits. This grain will not be sold back into the markets until it can be done without unduly affecting market prices."

To intimate this was a happy conclusion to an earthshaking happening would be gilding the lily. Rather, it was the best action to handle an awesome problem.

In summary on this page in history, several problems or developments deserve mention.

☆ The Carter administration had estimated—prior to the embargo—that the Soviets would feed 128 million tons of grain to livestock during the 12-month period. And as a consequence of the embargo, they (the Soviets) would be forced to reduce the grain fed to animals—on the order of a 10 percent reduction over the nine remaining months before new crop supplies became available. It is doubtful whether the Soviets lessened the use of grain for feed over 2 percent (2 to 3 million tons). Once again, through great cost, the United States learned unilaterally invoked economic sanctions do not attain desired foreign policy goals.

☆ In addition to the unsettling impact on the U.S. commodity markets, several longer trend developments resulted from the embargo, among which were (1) prices for the producers of grain and oilseeds in the nation dropped; (2) the marketplace momentum was broken; (3) federal budgetary outlays were greatly increased; (4) service industries were hurt; and (5) transportation entities as well as those involved with fertilizers, agricultural chemicals and grain handling suffered.

☆ President Carter was harmed politically.

✩ The credibility of the United States as a dependable exporter or supplier of farm products to world markets was once again severely injured.

One other observation continues to haunt me regarding this period in history. It involves the state of the art of animal feeding in the Soviet Union and the outlook for improved livestock nutrition in that country. This matter is intriguing because our agricultural sector is affected by level of grain and high-protein feed ingredients utilized by livestock and poultry in the USSR.

In Chapter 3, I discussed the U.S. Feed Grains Council and its work in several countries involving animal feeding. Since the mid-1960s I thought the Soviets would increase the quantity and quality of protein in poultry and swine rations. It is a *must* for them if they wish to have a more efficient animal industry. To accomplish this they will find it necessary to import more soybeans or soybean meal. I thought they would do so much earlier, but I am sure supply availability or restrictions on access to a dependable supply in the United States and to a degree elsewhere contributed to a delay in the Soviets making a hard decision to formulate higher quality poultry and swine rations on a sustaining basis.

Interestingly, the Soviets bought a sizeable tonnage of U.S. soybean meal from a U.S. company just prior to the embargo, the shipment of which was suspended.

Since that time, the Soviets have been importing soybeans and soybean meal from several origins on a more or less predictable basis. But their livestock rations—particularly poultry and swine—leave much to be desired from the standpoint of the animal nutritionist.

When I said in the previous chapter that Mr. U.S.A. Soybean is no longer high in the saddle, I had several U.S. government actions in mind which have crippled this valiant knight. The Carter export embargo was just one more debilitating government policy decision.

REAGAN-BLOCK AND PAYMENT-IN-KIND

Farmers, the media, agricultural business interests and the public generally were not unduly critical of President Carter when he embargoed the export of grain and soybeans to the Soviet Union.

During the meeting in Washington, D.C., on January 6, 1980, with Secretary Bergland, the grain exporters did not fault the Carter administration for suspending grain shipments. It may be stated that the industry could not very well be critical and at the same time request the administration to purchase the export contracts. There was truth to that statement. On the other hand, I was surprised with the number of former top government officials who immediately made laudatory statements supporting the action.

Most grain company executives simply stood aside and were noncommittal regarding the decision—myself among them.

I was also impressed with the attitude of many colleagues in the business world including bankers who generally commented that the export embargo will teach them (the Soviets) a lesson.

Within a few days after the embargo it was becoming apparent that Exporthkleb buyers were finding plenty of grain elsewhere and they were buying it for nearby and future delivery. Price was no great factor. On the other hand, grain prices in the United States plummeted; consequently, a premium for Argentina grain—over the U.S. prices—was not that costly to the Soviets.

Canada did not increase sales to the Soviets but did continue to ship as it had advised U.S. officials. Interestingly, though, Canada increased its acreage planted to grain in the spring of 1980 as follows: Barley up 23 percent, spring wheat up 4 percent and durum up 12 percent.

As the movement of grain in the world following the embargo became more clear, it was obvious that the Soviet Union, with minimum effort, could pretty much buy grain as desired.

From the political standpoint, it seemed to me our voters were telling President Carter we will watch and see whether the grain embargo, a classic example of an economic sanction, will attain desired results. Will the U.S. unilateral action result in the Soviet Union withdrawing from Afghanistan? If not, will the trade sanction cause the Kremlin political instability or the Soviet people to express unhappiness with the turn of events?

If the answer to these questions and other such political/economic queries was no, then the President would experience a deterioration in political support within the United States.

Past experience with trade embargoes had long ago convinced me this would be another costly and ineffective policy. After all, the Kennedy decision in 1963 required eight years to be "fixed."

As the calendar year 1980 progressed, it was apparent that candidate Reagan was given a bonanza type issue with farmers and the agricultural community.

Candidate Reagan said he would resume the sales of U.S. grain to the Soviet Union—if he were elected. The matter was a natural political issue, because President Carter was not able to demonstrate that the embargo had accomplished any economic or political benefits for the United States.

While this matter was not the major issue in the 1980 presidential campaign, it was an important one in several states.

Hence, within a 10-year period (1971 through 1981) two Republican presidents, generally described as hard-liners, took action improving commerce with the Soviet Union. In both cases the opportunity for such policy decisions was handed to them by Democratic administrations.

It seems a discussion of the 1983 Payment-in-Kind (PIK) program should logically follow the story of the 1980 Soviet grain embargo because the embargo was one of the major reasons for Secretary of Agriculture John Block and President Reagan implementing this drastic correction surgery for grain producers. There were other compelling reasons which I shall explain before making specific comments on the PIK story.

Throughout these writings, I have mentioned transition periods in our government—that period of several weeks following a presidential election and the inauguration of the new president. Our system, in reality, makes it possible for a new team to be in charge of the executive branch every four years. At the same time, a transition period causes an examination or a reexamination of agricultural and food policy as impacted by the president and his secretary of agriculture.

The period following the Reagan victory in November, 1980, and prior to January 20, 1981, was no exception. The transition papers in USDA were prepared by Secretary Bergland's people. Conversely, several Republican volunteers prepared summary papers on agriculture and food matters designed to be helpful to the secretary of agriculture designate and the new sub-cabinet officers. My contribution was peripheral at best; I did add to the writings on outlook for agricultural exports including foreign assistance authorities and farm income matters as impacted by farm program laws.

During the period prior to Inauguration Day, and for several months thereafter, I was troubled by the pronouncements originating in USDA but maybe even more I was concerned with the over-zealousness regarding the role of U.S. agriculture in the world of commerce. Inconsistency was creeping into Secretary Block's statements and actions.

In one moment Block repeated his belief in a market-oriented agricultural policy, but in the same breath expressed his lack of support for target prices or deficiency payments. Personally, I never liked the need for direct cash subsidies or deficiency payments, but when the choice is between payment of such in some years to maintain income to grain and cotton producers as compared to higher loan rates the choice is easy. Thirty years of experience with price support programs had illustrated that high loan rates and a market-oriented policy are at absolute loggerheads. The Food and Fiber Commission findings in 1967 confirmed this fact. The Republican party transition papers on food and agriculture dwelt on this obvious truth.

One other international economic trend was obvious to the knowing but quite clearly did not come in for serious thought as USDA foreign trade and domestic farm policies were being developed under Secretary Block. The worldwide phenomenon of which I speak was the problem being caused in many nations by excessively high interest rates and burgeoning external indebtedness. I feared this obvious lack of concern or lack of understanding in USDA would lead the nation's entire agricultural sector into an economic reversal.

My worries were well founded!

The Agriculture and Food Act of 1981 as enacted by the Republican-controlled Senate and the Democrat-controlled House and approved by the President was a near disaster. While Secretary Block and the Reagan administration continue to blame the Congress for the political disservice to agriculture in enacting the law, I maintain the executive branch could have insisted on provisions more in keeping with reality.

I shall explain!

The Act of 1981 reflected naiveté, poor judgment and lack of dedication. Each descriptive shortcoming is deserving of comment.

I use the word "naiveté" because the new administration in 1981 seemed to take for granted that the exports of U.S. farm products would simply continue to increase. There appeared to be a lack of understanding of the cyclical nature of world production of agricultural commodities. Rather, there was a feeling of euphoria demonstrated by too many of those in top positions with the desire to travel to far off places for the expressed reason of "promoting exports"—at best a term with mercurial meaning. Granted, the Carter-Bergland administration enjoyed a first-class honeymoon in foreign trade of farm products. Dollar value of U.S. exports during the four years increased over 50 percent reaching in excess of $43 billion in the 12-month period ending June 30, 1981. World grain use in the four-year period had increased over 10 percent. Net farm income had also fared very well. The actions of the new group in 1981 gave the impression they believed this trend of increased trade and larger utilization would continue— almost regardless of price levels. This is why I use the term "naive."

A demonstration in poor judgment was illustrated by Secretary Block in his giving the impression that he did not understand the concept of target prices versus higher commodity price-support loan rates. I have already discussed the role of target prices (deficiency payments). Certainly, a policy favoring target prices is not a sacred position. But waffling on the need for such contributed to still higher loan rates in the Agriculture and Food Act of 1981. In development of farm legislation Congress excels in enacting legislation containing higher and higher loan rates. Apparently, it is an issue that—in its members' eyes—sells well back home. In all candor, the alternative to such pressure is the target price concept designed to keep price supported commodities more price competitive. Failure to push the concept in 1981 resulted in price support loan rates being established at levels discouraging the export of U.S. commodities, encouraging more production and greater exports in and from several competing nations and dampening world use of grain for feed. The global economic downturn coupled with these poor-judgment actions in the United States caused the export dollar value of U.S. farm products in the 12-month period 1982-1983 to be less than 80 percent of the record established in 1980-1981.

Price support levels for corn offer an illustration of what happened during the Bergland and Block periods.

The corn loan level for crop year 1975-1976 was $1.10 per bushel. Five years later, the last year of the Carter-Bergland period, the loan was $2.25—more than double. Exports were booming; domestic use was increasing. But more importantly, many held the view that the newfound prosperity emanating from expanding exports could only improve. The 1981 law placed the minimum non-recourse loan rate for 1982, 1983, 1984 and 1985 at $2.55 for corn (with authority for the secretary to reduce the level the last three years by no more than 10 percent if the average market price falls below 105 percent of the loan level).

Domestic and overseas users of corn were further discouraged to purchase and utilize corn by the manner in which the Farmers Owned Reserve (FOR) was administered (the program heretofore known as the reseal program). Payments to farmers for storing corn under FOR were paid in advance. Hence, the two-year storage payment of 52 cents per bushel had the same result as that much increase in the loan itself.

As an aside, I identify with farm program administrators because, through experience, I know how difficult it is to please anyone—not to speak of everyone—in arriving at annual provisions. In this instance, however, judgment dictates the level of non-recourse corn loan rates simply got out-of-hand. Further, the scheme to administer the reserve or reseal program as a price-boosting mechanism rather than a supply safety net reflected poor judgment and was quite inexcusable. The results offer absolute proof of how price support programs can be administered to bolster farm income in the nearby period short run—but at great financial penalty to farmers against longer-term farm income.

I mentioned a lack of dedication on the part of the Reagan administration in the development of the 1981 law. Perhaps a more fitting definition of the shortcoming would be "less than top priority to a sound agricultural policy."

To an observer during that period in 1981 it was obvious that the matter of tax cutting legislation was of chief importance to the executive branch. In fact, it was quite obvious concessions were being made to some legislators to secure support for tax-cutting provisions. I have no way to compile the total of these deals as a charge against financially sound farm policy.

In meaningful terms and more often than not the real contribution of a secretary of agriculture and the sub-cabinet officers should be measured by that which they successfully prevent from happening rather than that which they propose. This sounds like the mutterings of a cynic, but an entire book could be written on the subject of "that which was defeated or deleted."

Made in Washington is not an accidental title for these writings. In my opinion the chief legacy flowing from the Agriculture and Food Act of 1981 will be the classic example for students to better understand how the legislative process and unsatisfactory administrative regulations and procedures can work toward rewarding producers in the short run with proceeds properly charged against future earnings and opportunities.

A description of the 1981 legislation and the manner in which it was administered seemed to be a requirement as a lead-in to a discussion of the Payment-in-Kind program developed by Secretary Block and embraced by President Reagan for the grain crop to be harvested in 1983. It was only natural that a bad law (Act of 1981) should spawn a less than pleasant antidote (PIK).

The most negative characteristic of PIK was the concept that it was entirely oriented toward production and production costs. The very nature of the program was damning to the users of grain (the demand side), including the livestock industry—within the United States and overseas. While many dairy, beef and hog farmers produce much of their own feed requirements, the very announcement of a most financially attractive grain production-cutting program immediately changed price relationships.

Conversely, the negative features of the 1981 law and the administrative actions had worked against an expansion of the use of U.S. grain, domestically and overseas. Lip service was given to the desirability of market-oriented policies but a costly PIK which penalized utilization was in opposition to natural market forces.

A long list of negative features and outgrowths emanating from the creation of PIK can be enumerated. Among such are excessive cost to the government, inadequate stocks in CCC inventory to distribute to participating producers and thereby necessitating some producers to place quantities of 1983 production under 1983 crop price support loans and then have these loans forgiven as their PIK entitlements. This became known as "plant for PIK."

Analytically, it is not difficult to identify with grain and cotton producers and certainly with program administrators in performing drastic surgery aimed at reducing production so as to prevent a prolonged period of huge surpluses in the hands of CCC—such as that which existed for several years in the late 1950s and early 1960s. Only future events and passage of time will render a decision on the wisdom of the administration implementing the PIK program. An assessment of the success or harm from PIK must include an examination of the impact on many interest groups other than grain and cotton producers among which is the livestock industry, the soybean and other oilseed industry, overseas users and all agricultural businesses servicing agricultural—no small number of which were rendered insolvent.

Three other important policy matters are inherent with PIK. Each in its own way is likely to haunt the nation's agricultural sector.

* PIK gave the wrong economic signal to some producers. In reality, the negative happenings as described earlier which gave birth to PIK should have convinced producers that a broader use base is absolutely necessary or a cutback in production will be required—or both. To the extent that proceeds from PIK are used to expand production via increased investment in production inputs, the aftermath may be even more severe.

* Trade talks with the EEC, Japan and other countries with the message that the United States enjoys an economic comparative advantage in the production of grain and cotton lost much luster because of PIK. Spokespersons for the nation will find it increasingly difficult to explain federal expenditures for aid to

agriculture in excess of total farm net income. I found it hard enough when such aid was less than 25 percent.

☆ The number three policy matter has to do with payment limitations. While this matter is discussed in greater detail in Chapter 7, "Market Forces or Intervention," the flagrant disregard for the limitation concept as had been dictated by Congress must be acknowledged as I complete the discussion of PIK.

Many of us, myself included, cringe to see limitations on opportunity included in programs designed to lend stability to agriculture. But after much deliberating and considerable debate within the Congress over several years and between many involved with agricultural policy—I am firmly of the opinion that farm program benefits should operate as a crutch or as an assist to a farm unit, lending stability to a rural community and our nation—not as a reward for an amassment of wealth or huge agricultural holdings. More in the next chapter.

FOOD POLICIES IN CONFLICT

European Economic Community

It seems only natural to discuss the European Economic Community (EEC) and the Common Agricultural Policy (CAP) under the general chapter heading of "The Crucible for Global Food Policy." It is logical because the CAP has had a global impact on commodity prices and on patterns of trade.

Trade relations between the United States and the EEC, along with the changing attitude between the socialist countries (including USSR and China) and the United States, have monopolized my energy over the last quarter of a century. Hence, it is only natural to delve into the agricultural policies pursued by the EEC. I shall do so with the goal of being analytical rather than hostile toward their protectionist actions as they have unfolded.

During the Eisenhower administration the six European countries—France, Germany, Italy, The Netherlands, Belgium and Luxembourg—were strongly encouraged by American diplomats to establish the European Economic Community, otherwise known as the Common Market. There were many reasons for this encouragement but a few are naturally obvious. Above everything else the new association being born should, in the minds of our diplomats, insure a more stable peace, a more prosperous Europe and a much more dependable ally.

During the 1950s and into the following decade, the United States gave lip service to the impact the new customs union of the EC-6 would have on international trade, but such thought or concern was largely peripheral. The U.S. foreign policy goal was to encourage a viable economic union of the six.

Students of agriculture acknowledged that Europe had an awesome task with structure reform of those engaged in agricultural pursuits.

For example, as intimated in Chapter 3, Italy's meat output was about 11 percent of that per person working in the same enterprise in Benelux (Belgium, The Netherlands and Luxembourg). In France it was less than 30 percent and in Germany less than 40 percent. Capital intensive farm enterprises were commonplace in the Benelux countries.

The problem of farm structure in much of Europe, as the EC was being organized, dated back to feudal times and to outmoded inheritance laws leading to splitting of farms from one generation to another. As one would expect, structural reform was essential to attain the goal of lowering the percentage of the work force engaged in farming. Dr. Sicco Mansholt, of The Netherlands, as the minister of agriculture of the EC-6 for many years and later president of the EC, wrote in the Common Market Farm Report as late as April 1971 that "There are roughly 6 million farms in the EC-6 on about 170 million acres of farm land, or an average of less than 30 acres per farm."

Dr. Mansholt developed his own plan for structural reform, a costly program designed to move people off farms, improve individual productivity and modernize the entire agricultural sector.

Many leaders in Europe, including Mansholt, believed harmonizing agriculture was the keystone to a successful Common Market. Stated another way, others maintained that a harmonized agriculture was the glue able to hold the community together. This attitude from the beginning (in the late 1950s) was the password of the U.S. Department of State.

I had great appreciation for the efforts of European leaders to reform agriculture by consolidation of fragmented farm units, by offering payments to encourage the retirement of older farmers, by education and retraining techniques to speed up transfer to other occupations and by programs designed for farm modernization. Such ambitious schemes are at best very costly and, of course, long term in nature.

In the early 1960s, as grain prices in the EC moved toward harmonization and always upward which meant import levies (the lubricant allowing the target prices, intervention prices and threshold prices to function) were also increasing. And to make it more troublesome for the United States, the EC was becoming a factor in world markets outside of the six through unbridled restitution payments (export subsidies).

During the decade of the 1960s, in my role with the U.S. Feed Grains Council, I was disappointed with the lack of concern of U.S. diplomats as the Europeans increased grain prices, import levies and export subsidies.

Upon my return to government in 1969 and during the subsequent 40 months, there was the beginning of a greater realization of a worsening conflict in policy between Common Market agriculture and that of the United States.

Gradually, through the years, an increasing number of our diplomats appreciated the pending conflict between the higher variable import levies and the U.S. interests. My opposition to such blanket increases was never meant to be negative toward European unity. I simply believed action being taken by the EC-6 agricultural leaders would prove to be self-defeating.

I believed farm prices supported substantially in excess of world market prices would have two negative effects on structural reform.

  ☆ The high guaranteed prices not only enabled but encouraged the marginal operator or the older farmer to continue at a poverty level of existence.
  ☆ The high commodity price guarantees become capitalized into increased land values. (Where have we heard of this before— note the next chapter.)

In reality, the policies the EC farm leaders followed caused many land owners to be largely destitute but enabled them to see the value of the estate increasing.

One publication in France, *Statistiques et Indictateurs des Regions Francaises*, states the average value of arable land in France rose nearly 300 percent in the period 1959 through 1969. This was during the decade of EC grain price harmonization.

In reality, the CAP and the manner in which it was financed defied sane economic principles. Unrealistically high guaranteed prices acted as a deterrent to industrial expansion. As a consequence, industrial and service industry job creation was thwarted in addition to slowing down agricultural structural reform.

On the subject of world commerce in grain and other farm products, the EC became and remains a disruptive force. Restitutions (export subsidies) on occasion are higher than net prices received by the EC member countries. This system of wasteful export subsidies maintains artificially high consumer prices within the community, discourages utilization and consumption and penalizes developing countries attempting to export such products as sugar because world commodity market prices are depressed as a result of the dumping of EC farm products.

From the standpoint of the trading interests of the United States, it should be remembered that a quarter of a century ago as the EC was organized, several countries of Europe were the leading buyers of U.S. grain—both wheat and corn. At that time, the United Kingdom (joined the EC in the early 1970s) was the largest importer of U.S. corn. Italy was importing corn free of duty. The Netherlands nearly so and West Germany was a large importer but was levying a "skimming charge."

To complete the circle on U.S. corn sales to the expanded EC-10, the reader should be advised that such exports have dropped to virtually nothing. In fact, production and use trends points to the EC becoming a net exporter of corn rather soon—because of several reasons, among which are:

* Use of corn and all grains because of the high fixed prices is discouraged. Tapioca (cassava) from Thailand and other tropical countries enters the EC countries free of the variable import levy system and is an acceptable substitute. The same can be said for corn gluten feed and other by-product feed ingredients from the United States.
* The almost constant reminder of U.S. government officials of the serious impact on world trade of the EC export policies results in still greater substitution of EC wheat in livestock rations as a replacement for imported corn.
* The man-made abnormal price relationship between high-protein feed ingredients as compared to high-carbohydrate ingredients (grain) results in a larger use of protein in rations than competitive world market prices would dictate.
* Meat, poultry and dairy products priced artificially high in the EC because of higher feed ingredient prices discourages consumption, particularly by lower-income people.

As mentioned earlier, a major U.S. policy thrust following World War II was to encourage the formation of a united Europe. I have no argument with this goal. But an unrealistic price protective CAP was not and is not necessary to attain this goal. In fact, I believe it will prove to be a deterrent to European unity. Over $10 billion in subsidies per year is funneled into agriculture. Food prices are at least that much more costly because of the high guaranteed price schemes. It does not require any great amount of imagination to comprehend the number of jobs that could be created if the $20 billion were available to the industrial sector. Rural structural reform could likewise move along at a faster rate.

Artificially high grain prices have acted as an incentive to greatly expand grain production, particularly in France and Britain. As stated in Chapter 2, the world needs more agricultural production—wherever it can be grown—if it is produced efficiently. It is only helpful to world food requirements as it is marketed competitively—not in a manner disruptive to world markets. Because of the extreme two-price system—high in Europe and a much lower export price—utilization is discouraged within the EC.

The key question as we continue to cooperate with Europe on matters of trade including agricultural commodities is Were the artificially high EC grain prices necessary to build and maintain a more united Europe?

No, and the United States should have been more aggressive through greater use of the international institutions we support. This did not need to be a belligerent undertaking—only a thoughtful, deliberate, clear-cut exercise. The suggested exercise I am about to describe is not a new idea. I recommended such procedure in the early 1970s, but it fell on deaf ears. I shall explain why that happened after I outline the steps which should have been followed.

The United States, the EC and most of our trading partners support the General Agreement on Tariffs and Trade (GATT).

The objectives of GATT as expressed in the preamble are as follows:

> The Governments of . . . , [r]ecognizing that their relations in the field of trade and economic endeavor should be conducted with a view to raising standards of living, insuring full employment and a large and steadily growing volume of real income and effective demand, developing the full use of the resources of the world and expanding the production and exchange of goods, being desirous of contributing to these objectives by entering into reciprocal and mutually advantageous arrangements directed to the substantial reduction of tariffs and other barriers to trade and to the elimination of discriminatory treatment in international commerce, have through their representatives agreed as follows: . . .

In my opinion, the variable levy system is not compatible with this objective.

Article XXIII provides the procedure for arriving at an adjustment of a complaint by a contracting party (signatory nations).

Why didn't the United States challenge the chief feature of CAP—the variable levy system?

I do not know all of the reasons, but it was generally felt by those responsible for U.S. foreign policy that the variable levy system was necessary to attain a Common Agricultural Policy (CAP). And in their view, a CAP was the keystone for a united Europe.

As I discussed this matter at all levels of government in the United States and in member European countries, I developed a bit different conclusion. I discovered there is a woeful lack of understanding—particularly in the minds of diplomats—with the role of price in the distribution of goods—or in the production process.

I can explain this quirk by an example—lowly as it may seem.

In October, 1966, as head of the U.S. Feed Grains Council, I invited five grain and cattle producers from France to visit small- to medium-sized cattle feeding operations in the United States. Most of the enterprises we visited were in North Dakota. The installations in that state utilized several grains (including barley) in their feeding operations. The senior gentleman heading the visiting team was M. J. Deleau. In addition to his being a French farmer, he was also president, EC Cereals Consultative Committee.

During the week we spent in North Dakota we visited two auction cattle sale barns. One barn was auctioning feeder cattle (destined for feedlots); the other barn was selling finished and grass-fed cattle to processors.

On two successive evenings following the two sales we discussed—late into the night—the variation in prices between top-quality feeder cattle as compared to low-quality feeders. The same for the variation between well finished steers and heifers as compared to those of equal weight but carrying less finish.

Our friends from France had a mental block which I found hard to understand. Incidentally, their chief interest in addition to seeing feeding installations was to observe the manner in which cattle prices are determined in the United States. The mental block or my failure in communication was their disbelief in the system taking place to arrive at a selling price. Continually, they asked the question "Who is deciding the price?"

This episode is related—not to downplay the mental sophistication of our guests from France, but our demand-responsive method of discovering cattle prices—and the obvious recognition of quality differences was truly foreign to their tradition.

Government involvement in the price discovery system for farm products in the EC is so deeply ingrained that any mention of freeing up the system is terrifying to those who have nurtured tradition for generations and centuries.

Prior to ending the discussion of CAP, it should be noted that the United States—through the years—with more or less support from other agricultural exporting nations—did negotiate and conclude several documents with the EC aimed at containing the variable levy system but not directly challenging it.

In 1962, a standstill agreement was concluded with the EC on corn, sorghum, ordinary wheat, rice and poultry. At the same time a separate agreement was concluded as to quality wheat.

Later in the same year (1962) the United States negotiated with the EC under the standstill agreements, as a result of the imposition of variable levies on poultry. The results really were to no avail and the United States did retaliate under Article XXVIII of the GATT.

The quality wheat agreement provided for negotiations to commence at the latest by June 30, 1963. This date was extended many times. To my knowledge, there have never been any serious negotiations on this matter—nor do I expect any.

The true folly of the CAP as put into place by the six EC countries and later extended to the expanded Common Market is the false assertion that higher guaranteed prices (target prices, threshold prices, intervention prices accompanied by more lubricant, higher import levies) are necessary as a keystone to hold the EC together. It is a false premise because other means of financial support to EC agriculture could have been put in place which would have been much less disruptive to economies around the world. If this had been done structure reform could have been accomplished more rapidly and at a much lower cost. And still of greater significance, more resources would have been available for job creation in the industrial and technical sector. Sadly, Europe is trailing in this latter field.

Being somewhat repetitive, it must be stated again that the major impact of the undisciplined increase in guaranteed prices is to make wealthy people out of landowners and thwart restructuring, penalize consumers, discourage traditional imports, increase subsidization of exports, retard growth of the economies of developing countries, stagnate job creation by industry and absolutely contradict announced defense posture. I mention the contradiction with defense posture because as more international public opinion has been brought to bear on the EC and its CAP—the Community takes the easy way out and dumps food into the Soviet Union at a fraction of the cost paid by its own consumers. Food items such as beef, sugar, butter and wine (remember how milk and honey flow).

What is doubly ironic about its contradicting defense policy is that the goal to maintain a common defense policy—the United States and the EC—more than any other U.S. desire contributed to the U.S. foreign policy of embracing the high variable levy system. Certainly, if we did not embrace it, we gave our tacit approval.

Now, over a quarter of a century after the creation of CAP, where are the United States and the EC headed with their respective agricultural policies? What is the future impact of the CAP on the economies of other nations?

The United States from time to time has engaged in scare or heckling tactics. All of them based on the premise that "If you continue to utilize government funds in an unrestrained manner to distort trade, we will also do so."

In the late 1960s and the early 1970s, the United States on a selected destination basis subsidized the export of lard and broilers to retain a percentage of an export market developed by the United States on a competitive market price basis but grabbed by the EC through payment of undisciplined subsidies. The pressure of public opinion in the United States finally compelled the United States to withdraw. A logical question presents itself. How can the EC continue such tactics? The answer: "That is their system!" Superior technology has nothing to do with the overproduction of such food commodities as beef, broilers and sugar. High guaranteed prices bring forth production without regard to domestic demand or requirements (at that high price).

The U.S. sale of wheat flour to Egypt at a cost in subsidy of about $100 million to the U.S. Treasury in the winter of 1983-1984 was another such attempt to regain a U.S. market which had been taken over by the EC through heavy export subsidies.

I am skeptical at best of the pay back of such head-on confrontations. A case can be made that the Egyptian exercise resulted in the EC showing some greater discipline. On the other hand as mentioned earlier, the Europeans simply denatured more of their wheat and diverted it to feed use and thereby reduced their requirement for imported corn.

On a broader front, I have strong feelings regarding future actions the United States should take and an equally strong attitude on policies we should not adopt.

First, and related to what appears to be nearby problems, we must retaliate with all out severity if the EC establishes quota or applies the variable levy system on corn gluten and/or other by-product feed ingredients. We must act against its bringing more such items under its levy system. If we do not, the EC is likely to bring the import of soybeans and soybean meal under its "system."

The rationale for our action is sound. Naturally, EC's imports of non-grain ingredients has increased. Distortions (contrary to the objectives of GATT) created by the EC caused this to happen.

(It should be recognized that to the extent our own U.S. government has subsidized or continues to subsidize an increase in the production of corn processing by-products such as direct or indirect subsidies for alcohol-based fuels the strength of the U.S. argument is eroded.)

Second, the possibility of attacking the variable levy system and thereby bringing the entire matter to a head could only be constructive if the United States gains support and cooperation from developing member countries of GATT as well as a long list of industrially developed nations. Passage of time has greatly eroded the viability of this procedure. I do not rule out this step even if it should result in strong trade retaliation. There may be an overriding need to mount such an exercise. That strong reason may spawn the need to test the very effectiveness of GATT. For example, the hesitancy of the United States to contest the variable levy system has gone far in creating a lack of faith in GATT to discipline nations or regions engaging in world commerce. I share that lack of faith but I do not want to return to jungle type tactics in international trade.

Third, I am unalterably opposed to the United States following policies designed to compromise the price differential between U.S. and EC commodities. Compromisers have, from time to time, suggested that the EC and the United States should sit down together and agree to bring their respective commodity prices into harmony over a period of years. This attitude reflects something less than realism. We must at all times remember that the U.S. government is directly involved in supporting the price of a relatively small percentage of the farm commodities produced in our country. This is the exact opposite of the situation in Europe. The heavy involvement of the European officials in the EC is the very action which is contrary to the spirit and the objectives of GATT. Furthermore, all peoples of the world will likely be better fed in a more open trading world as compared to a tightly rigged global market.

Some have reasoned that the CAP would break down with its own weight—because of excessive cost and because of disgust in the industrial sector. At times I have shared this view, but I fear any meaningful policy change is far into the future.

I am sure the United States should maintain a policy designed to supply farm commodities to importing nations without interruption. I further believe we should continue to encourage the Europeans to take actions designed to create jobs, lower unemployment and stimulate technical advancement. By so doing maybe Europe will dismantle its greatest economic deterrents—the CAP and the excessive subsidies.

Japan

Japan and other Far East countries have become so significant to the world of commerce that extra attention to the food policies of Japan and that area of the world are critically important to agricultural interests in the United States. I explained in Chapter 3 some market development activities carried on in that country by the U.S. Feed Grains Council. But the economic vitality in that area of the world is so striking I wish to devote several pages to an examination of the Japanese policies.

It seems commonplace to discuss those policies and activities and in the same breath add the expression "and in other Far East countries."

There is a logical explanation as to why this happens, and it is consistent with economic developments in Asia over the past third of a century.

Tokyo and in reality Japan is the pace setter. Students of history often use the expression "All roads lead to Rome." They did!

In modern times in the Far East, "All roads lead to Tokyo!"

Japan has built a large and powerful economic sphere of influence. Anyone who does not recognize and appreciate this truth is simply asleep at the controls.

This being the case, it is incumbent upon us to not only understand the food and trading policies of Japan but also the reasons for those policies.

I expect the United States-Japan relationship since World War II is one of the brightest pages in the history of U.S. diplomacy. On the other hand, the political economic policies of the two countries have been closely dovetailed because of self-interest of both nations. Japan with a land area equivalent to the state of Montana now has a population of about 120 million (compared to about 90 million a quarter of a century earlier).

The military umbrella supplied Japan by the United States has contributed greatly to that nation's ability to develop its sphere of economic influence. That influence is greater and far in excess of what many would expect with limited land area and natural resources. In reality, the nation has capitalized on its shortage of agricultural land and other natural resources. Japan has actually benefited by buying farm products and other raw material (including iron ore and petroleum). The country has built its industrial and financial base on world trade. And with each passing year has become a more prominent economic power in the Far East.

From the standpoint of U.S. agriculture, the development of trade with Japan has been a high-priority item. I described several developments in that country in Chapter 3 as I outlined some of the activities of the U.S. Feed Grains Council within the country. Westernizing the eating habits of the Japanese has been the key to trade in farm products between the two nations.

The success of the eating habit change is illustrated by the trends in importing agricultural commodities. Total farm product imports into Japan from all destinations are now about $21 billion annually whereas U.S. agricultural imports (largely tropical products) from all destinations are slightly less than $18 billion for a 12-month period.

To put this in a more meaningful perspective a few general comparisons may be helpful.

At the time of my first trip to Japan in 1959 (25 years ago) that nation was importing from the United States corn and sorghum equivalent to the total corn produced in Blue Earth County, Minnesota, plus six townships of the adjoining Watonwan county. Twenty-five years later (present time) Japan imports corn and sorghum from the United States in an amount annually equivalent to more than the corn production of the entire state of Minnesota.

Each year, Japan has been importing about 6 percent of the U.S. wheat production and around 8 percent of the U.S. soybean crop. Specific percentage of the U.S. crop destined for Japan varies each year—largely dependent on the magnitude of annual production of each commodity in the United States.

With this volume of sales to that country the non-agricultural observer may be inclined to believe trade matters between the two nations involving farm products may be without problems. Not necessarily so! A closer look at the farm situation in Japan deserves analysis.

Prior to World War II, Japan was largely an agricultural country. What may be surprising to many is the fact that presently about 20 percent of the work force is engaged in the production of farm products. Approximately 18 percent of the population lives on farms. Many rural family members have off-farm employment. But latest figures indicate the agricultural work force totals about 5 million. Average farm size is slightly more than 3 acres.

From the northernmost prefecture of Hokkaido to the tropical tip of Kagoshima—a span of over 2,500 miles—the rural people are living examples of ambition and hard work. The 15 million acres devoted to agriculture are among the most intensively farmed land in the world.

Farmers in Japan are a potent and powerful political force. Because of this, the guaranteed price established by the government for domestically produced rice is about five times higher than the U.S. target price for rice produced by U.S. farmers (depending on the yen-to-dollar currency relationship one wishes to use).

In many countries, particularly in Asia but to a degree in the United States, rice and the rice price issue is truly political. Hence, it is fair to say rice is a political commodity. Naturally—in that rice is still the most basic food item in Japan—the prices of other competing crops are likewise notoriously high as compared to our prices. This includes all vegetables and fruit.

Recently, the country has been offering incentives to divert some acreage from rice production to other crops such as forage, vegetables and wheat. The acreage is not large (in our standards), and the financial incentive to switch to other crops is figured in so many yen per 1/10 hectare.

As one would expect of this heavily populated land and with politically potent farmers, about 25 percent of Japanese disposable income is expended for food compared to slightly more than 18 percent in the United States.

The high rice price and the tradition accompanying rice as the backbone of the Japanese diet contributed greatly to their official policy for the import of wheat and the price at which wheat—both imported and the relatively small amount produced domestically—is made available to flour millers.

The food agency on behalf of the Japanese government imports wheat and sells it to the flour millers at a price which equates out to about $10 per bushel. You may call the differential between the imported price and the resale price as a "skimming charge" or a "markup." Either term, in my judgment, is correct.

Japan's wheat import policy has come in for limited discussion officially between U.S. and Japanese government representatives. The United States has not, to my knowledge, made a major issue of the high skimming charge levied on imported wheat.

Oh, it has been mentioned on many occasions!

On the other hand, the United States has been critical of Japan's rice-pricing policy, particularly when the unrealistically high price was creating a surplus, which in turn the Japanese wanted to dispose of overseas. Their converting much of it to animal feed did not endear them to officials in the United States. This practice was unusually sensitive as many Japanese industrial products (such as automobiles) penetrated the U.S. market deeper and deeper.

Obviously, Japan could buy much goodwill in the United States by allowing wheat to be made available to millers free of the skimming charge.

Will this happen?

I would not recommend anyone holding his or her breath until it does!

Naturally, corn, sorghum and soybeans entering Japan free of duty make that country a most dependable outlet for those commodities.

Terms of entry for grapefruit, lemons and oranges have gradually improved but required considerable prodding through the years.

Students of foreign trade look upon quota restrictions as the most brutal of all trade impediments.

High import levies (specific and ad valorem) can truly impede trade, but hopefully the level of duty may at the proper time be a candidate for negotiation (reduction).

A quota in itself is so final. Because of this, I have felt for several years that Japan is making a mistake in continuing the quota restriction on the import of beef. The Japanese are truly fond of good beef. But because of the quota restriction and extremely high cost of domestic beef production enterprises, quality beef is an expense account fare. Per capita consumption is very low. The beef price situation is further aggravated by their outdated distribution system.

The reader may feel the Japan beef situation is none of our business. I think it is!

Japan is a great force in the world of trade and in the case of the United States sells considerably more dollars' worth of goods in the United States than the country purchases from us.

U.S. industry has not and does not have much of a market in Japan. This being the case the lopsided trade balance must largely be held in check through sales of farm products. That is why I think Japan would be well advised to terminate the quota restriction on the import of beef. Even under a free entry system (undoubtedly with a high levy) a large market would require years to develop.

I wish to end this dissertation on Japan with the observation with which I began this discussion.

Japan has been and continues to be a most important trading partner. The country is a growing economic force in Asia and the world. From the standpoint of U.S. agriculture, the nation's importance as a trading partner is magnified. In reality, our selling farm products to Japan and buying industrial items has made it possible for both nations to become more prosperous and much more understanding of one another's social mores and customs.

☆☆☆☆☆☆☆☆☆☆☆

CHAPTER 7

☆☆☆☆☆☆☆☆☆☆☆

Market Forces or
Intervention

☆ ☆

Over the past 50 years the technological progress in agricultural production in the United States has been nothing short of phenomenal. Likewise, the changes in grain handling, transporting and storing have progressed with innovation and capital investment. Feed formulation over the 50 years developed into an accurate and precise science. Animals and fowls for food and animal products, such as dairy products and eggs, bear little resemblance to their ancestors of 50 years ago. Such has been the agricultural development story in America since the depression era of the 1930s.

Through the half century of development, the processing and marketing of commodities has changed even more than production techniques. This then is the core of my attempt to finalize these writings. The choice between allowing market forces to determine volume of food categories to be produced and marketed versus government intervention is central to the summary I wish to develop.

Several learned professionals remind us that those who disregard lessons of history are bound to suffer from the same mistakes repeated over and over again.

I have reviewed happenings over the past half a century impacting—in the short run and at times for a longer number of years—the level of prosperity of U.S. agriculture and the success of the industry in its role of servicing the food requirements of Americans and people in other countries. I have mentioned many types of government intervention influencing level of investment flowing into agriculture. We have described the painful steps of global food policy development.

Out of all this history and development I want to draw some conclusions on the outlook for the future of U.S. agriculture. I wish to isolate areas of emphasis if the agricultural community is to again attain momentum that was taking place during the decade of the 1970s. We should have learned through mistaken emphasis—some repeated. Most likely we have. But unless we bring into focus those areas of mistaken emphasis we will only repeat them over and over again.

THIS TERM "EFFICIENCY"

One of the most over-used terms in discussing farmers in our country is the term "efficiency." The term means different things to all of us. In my opinion, the term has been somewhat of a catchall. I want to discuss it.

One school of thought dictates that "efficiency" means the accomplishment of or ability to accomplish a job with a minimum expenditure of *time* and *effort*.

I reject this definition as applied to farmers and their relative productivity!

After having been away from day-to-day living in rural America and now returning for a few years, I feel particularly keen about the loose meaning given the word "efficiency."

Over the last generation a new concept has come into being across the Corn Belt and the Wheat Belt and I am sure across other agricultural producing regions.

Capital investment has replaced time and effort of humans. Machines—big machines—have replaced human power.

But we have not changed our mind-fix on the meaning of the word "efficiency."

Herein lies a contradiction.

To me, "efficiency," as the term applies to farmers, agricultural businesses and industrial complexes, means the accomplishment of or ability to accomplish a job with a *minimum* expenditure of *time* and *effort* and with a *maximum* return on *investment*. Whether that investment reflects owners' equity or borrowed capital is inconsequential to an accurate definition of the term.

Cabinet officers, sub-cabinet members, elected officials at most every level continue to blithely placate agricultural producers by expressing the view that U.S. farmers are the most "efficient" in the world.

If we accept the narrow definition of the meaning of the term, the statement is absolutely correct—beyond a doubt.

If we believe my more comprehensive definition is more accurate—there has grown up a relatively high percentage of inefficient farmers in America. This is indeed worrisome!

The problem is not confined to farming. It spreads across agricultural businesses and other industrial activities. The chief difference is the fact that only in recent years the glaring negligence of consideration to return on investment in agricultural production has become the number one financial and management question with farmers and their lending institutions.

Of course, high interest rates sparked this problem.

Why did this happen?

Quite simple, really!

In far too many instances, the attitude has prevailed that if farm managers or employees can double or greatly increase their productivity in terms of *time* and *effect* through added investments in land, machinery or facilities, their relative efficiency is increased.

Not necessarily so!

Relative efficiency will only be increased if the added productivity will pay the interest on investment, supply income to maintain cash flow and/or yield a competitive return on owner's equity!

This terminology opens the door to a whole new set of definitions for some areas in rural America which must be considered.

Recently, I have become aware of several farmers having real financial problems. In each case they have obligated themselves to make large interest payments on money borrowed for the purpose of buying machinery or an adjoining farm or to use as operating capital. In three instances the farmers in question had signed contracts for deed of land they are now farming. In each case the price paid per acre is perhaps 25 to 30 percent greater than the price at which the land would change hands today. And in each case the current net owner's equity in the land at today's value is about zero. I am sure this is not an unusual situation. Many similar examples are commonplace as regards indebtedness on farm machinery.

What caused this reversal or downturn in owner's equity in far too many individual farmer's enterprises? Each case is different but many are similar. In our type of cyclical economy it was bound to happen but several things were at work; all of which added to the severity of the loss in value of land and used machinery.

In my field of acquaintance with farmers in the Corn Belt and the manner in which farm owners and operators and their families acquired equity, a common thread of similarity prevails. In most instances, each one took advantage of the relative decreasing value of the dollar.

With minimum exaggeration, it can be stated that farm land in the early 1930s was near zero in value. The nation was attempting to pull itself out of the depression. Dollars were dear. Through sacrifices in family living, frugality and calculated risks many acquired land and others more and more land. As economic recovery gradually took place, wars were fought, the dollar became less dear and land prices increased at a rate in excess of inflation itself.

This over-simplified example describes the manner in which most family estates were created across the Corn Belt. The upward trend in the price of farm land in a near uninterrupted spiral for half a century seemed in the eyes of many to be a sure-fire formula to prosperity.

The bubble burst!

Why?

Many factors contributed to the shock; no one reason is necessarily the culprit. I shall list several.

* A prolonged period of high interest rates with no apparent end in sight has pushed a substantial number of farmers into a negative income situation.

* Financial institutions—both the cooperative credit system and proprietary banks—were too eager to loan money with far too little consideration for the individual farmer to make interest payments, retire a part of the principal and provide for family living. I am aware of professionals in units of the farm credit system being financially rewarded on the basis of volume of business accomplished (money loaned) as compared to percentage of principal repaid on an ongoing basis—a sure policy for disaster.

* The too rapid increase in price support rates in the Act of 1981 has already been discussed. The manner in which overseas utilization of our farm products was discouraged by this law is not a proud chapter in our market-oriented economy.

☆ The super-duper export suspension and embargo of 1980 also had a severe impact.
☆ Finally, it seems only logical to understand that as U.S. farmers have become more dependent on export markets as an outlet for their production—those same farmers have become more vulnerable to world economic conditions—ironically, the general prosperity within the centrally controlled economies the same as the free world.

I have discussed the economic plight of a percentage of producers of grain, oilseeds and other major commodities we export because the manner in which this problem is handled is *key* to the United States recapturing a more dominant position in world marketing. If we attempt to cure the distress of the 20 percent or thereabouts that may be in a financially precarious position—by sweetening the price support system (loan rates)—we will only slip farther into the abyss of lost markets, still more limited opportunity and prolonged hard times on the farm.

We gained improved access to foreign markets—in Asia, socialist countries in Europe, the Soviet Union and China—to mention only a few.

We can do much better in servicing overseas markets. But we dare not continue to piddle away our advantages and opportunities.

That is why I have dwelt in detail on the meaning of production efficiency. It means the accomplishment of or ability to accomplish a job with a minimum expenditure of *time* and *effort* and with a *maximum* return on investment. It has been a costly lesson. Bigness is not necessarily synonymous with efficiency.

TRIAL AND ERROR

Preparatory to summarizing policy recommendations designed to once again bring growth opportunities to our nation's agricultural plant, I looked backward for the purpose of weighing past federal government involvement in the production and marketing of a long list of commodities.

I reminded myself of trial and error tactics which proved to be excessively costly to the government—of little or no comfort to consumers—and painfully upsetting to producers.

One such trial and error exercise was the Irish potato price-support program of the late 1940s. Tons of this perishable commodity were ultimately utilized for fertilizer. Ironically—because of price-support elegibility specifications—consumers purchased lower grades for consumption as the higher quality potatoes were pledged to CCC as collateral under the loan program. The experiment ended in failure.

Still another venture ending in failure was the price-support program for hay and pasture seeds and winter cover crop seeds.

It is not constructive to be negative on past trials and experiments undertaken to improve farm income and creating havoc with specific interest groups (including producers). To not recognize the economic weaknesses and in many cases actual disservice rendered by such a foray into historic production and marketing systems is being blind to reality.

Several major farm commodities or items have been subjected to one form or another of government price support. Among this category are "big-ticket" items such as beef, hogs, chickens and turkeys. Only the pressure from the producers of these products caused major government interference in the marketplace to be short-lived.

In observing various methods utilized by the federal government to "stabilize" farm income through interference in one way or another with price mechanisms, one common thread of predictability is certain. Government-made prices through the various facets of price-support programs can increase farm income for a year or two; after which the realities of the marketplace take over.

The latest and most glaring example illustrating this point is the painful development leading to the PIK corn program. I select corn for this example but the outcome of a trial-and-error approach is only indicative of an economic truth.

As related in the earlier chapter the price support corn loan rate was increased over a seven-year period (from the year 1975-1976 to 1981-1982) over 250 percent.

What was the outcome?

The net farm income going to corn producers was enhanced!

It was not income through use.

It was income equivalent to an advance on future years earnings.

And what was doubly harmful, the higher guaranteed price—as established by CCC—discouraged use in the United States and overseas. Furthermore, the higher floor price as financed by CCC created a price support for all the corn and other grains in the world destined for international commerce.

Of course, a costly PIK shored up market prices but did nothing to improve the possibility of U.S. corn farmers earning higher incomes in future years—because the use or demand base was actually eroded rather than increased.

Hence, I repeat!

Prices made in Washington enhance farm income in the short run. After which the forces of the marketplace (both domestic and export markets) must come to bear.

How?

Loan rates are reduced. Even after 50 years of experience this truth has not changed.

The damage done to the U.S. corn industry through foolish action of U.S. government officials in increasing corn loan rates out of all sane proportions may require several years to rectify. The correction can only be accomplished through recognition of simple economic truths.

I do not know who coined the expression "You can lead a horse to water but you cannot make it drink."

If ever a homily describes the corn situation and the extent to which the utilization of such is affected by fixed prices, the refusal of the horse to drink does the job.

The CAP of the EC supplies several textbooks of information on how not to broaden the use base for grain.

The United States has had over 50 years of experience in illustrating the impact of artificial prices on farm income. Scores of attempts have been made in jazzing up income, only to discover the proceeds represent an advance on future years' income.

So goes the pattern of trial and error with minimum attention to past actions found wanting.

MARKETING VERSUS SUPPLY MANAGEMENT

Some elected government officials, a few commodity groups and some general farm organizations seem to believe the true service of USDA to U.S. agriculture is best gauged by the level of agricultural programs. The greater the expenditure—the greater the true contribution to the nation's farmers. Some spokespersons become vehement on this issue.

I reject this attitude. To think thus is non-visionary.

Charles Shuman, president of the American Farm Bureau (AFBF) in 1959, is quoted in *The Nation's Agriculture* as saying "Two-way trade between nations is one of the best ways to promote peace, yet everywhere we turn there are barriers to the exchange of goods. We can produce more (farm products) than domestic consumers will buy—we must have stable, non-subsidized foreign markets—they can be developed."

Mr. Shuman was right!

We have developed export markets. The most notable expanding export markets for U.S. farm products were developed in the Orient (Japan, Korea, Taiwan, Indonesia and others). The second most significant was the Soviet Union and "bloc" countries. Both regions increased their purchases from the United States because we were price competitive and logistically capable to ship and deliver in a dependable manner. Furthermore, both regions were prepared to improve the diets of their people by increasing the availability of animal proteins and vegetable oils.

As stated throughout this book, we did better year after year for a quarter of a century until 1981. Maybe we did too well—too well because an increase each year in the dollar value of U.S. farm exports was taken for granted.

I constantly think back to the best days of the eight years I spent as the head of the U.S. Feed Grains Council—the 1968 Williamsburg conference. The storm clouds were already appearing at that time—in the United States. I mentioned in Chapter 3 the concern expressed by Ioanes on the meaning of higher fixed prices in Europe and in the United States. His worries were certainly justified.

Leaders in government—both the legislative and the executive—seem always to be tempted to recommend or set price support loan rates (equivalent to guaranteed prices) a little bit higher—always a little bit higher. In many cases, those same spokespersons knew the long-term negative benefit to farmers and all of agricultural interests—and even though such action is likely to be costly.

One other pearl of wisdom was shared with me in the mid-1960s by Fred Maywald, who at that time was head of the Grain Division of Farmers Grain Dealers Association of Des Moines. His comments have little bearing on the subject at hand—but philosophically a great deal.

Mr. Maywald informed me of the positive earnings of his division for the fiscal year just ending. The earnings from merchandising were several times those of storing grain for CCC. This had not been the situation in the few years prior. Maywald exclaimed that for reasons hard to explain this was highly pleasing to him.

I understood the delight experienced by Maywald because he was talking about real or cash income earned for farmers from entities utilizing corn and soybeans—the end products of which were finding their way to the tables of consumers.

Before recommending specific actions which I deem necessary to place U.S. agriculture in a starting gate for a long sustained drive toward greater prosperity, I wish to tell of still another wise comment made by an entirely different personality in the spring of 1984.

Kenneth Horn, a specialist in tree care and removal, had just topped and removed an injured tree for me. We were having coffee. He had inquired about the general health of farmers. I shared the observation that some farmers were enjoying the best of times— while others were in severe financial difficulty. I explained the financially over-extended situation of far too many in farming. I mentioned a percentage of those in tough financial straits would survive; others will not.

Horn replied, "Isn't that our system?"

After-the-fact I have thought about that remark. I can neither add nor detract from it.

Specifically, if one applies lessons learned from past experiences with farm legislation designed to improve farm income there are actions and provisions that should be considered as constructive. Others have been proven to be politically expedient and disadvantageous to the agricultural economy.

GOALS TO ACHIEVE

The preamble of omnibus farm legislation reads like a grand and noble goal to be attained by the statute. I thought it was always written thus as an epistle for appeal to many interest groups—particularly producers and consumers.

Unquestionably, the first and major goal of farm legislation is to *assure the nation a dependable supply of food.* Second, the law should *afford opportunity for producers to maximize incomes.* Third, *overseas customers and users of our farm products must be assured of dependable supplies.*

In achieving the goal of satisfying overseas desires for our food and other agricultural products, we have taken for granted that as the world economy expands the volume of U.S. farm commodity exports will likewise increase. Experience gained since World War II pretty much substantiates this premise. But over the past three years we have learned this is not an automatic happening. Many forces are at work thwarting this development (of automatic growth). Not the least important are our own laws and the manner in which they are administered. In the attempt to accomplish the goal of maximizing farm income the Act of 1981 and the manner in which it was administered eroded the use base of grain—both domestically and overseas. Because of a too rapid increase in loan rates (price supports) the U.S. livestock industry was actually penalized. The grain reseal program or Farmer Owned Reserve (FOR) was administered in a manner which contributed further in involving CCC in the price mechanism. And as already explained, other grain exporting nations were handed a greater incentive to increase production and the export of grain—all because of our own U.S. laws.

Concisely stated, the Act of 1981 failed in accomplishing all three goals of acceptable farm legislation.

* Consumers were shortchanged because livestock production was discouraged.
* Producers were harmed—particularly in the long run—because the provisions of the act discouraged the use of grain. Frankly, the law was completely production-oriented at the expense of marketing and utilization.
* Overseas customers were actually forced to look elsewhere for more of their grain and oilseed requirements.

If a scenario were to be written on how *not* to continue a market-oriented agricultural policy, one need only describe the Act of 1981 and the manner in which it was administered. In that the demand side was neglected and penalized and growth of farm income in future years was deaccelerated.

Much has been written about provisions to be included in farm legislation if the three goals as stated are to be attained; and I believe they can be achieved. For example, on the matter of export earnings—as stated many times in this book—the United States did capture a growing percentage of the export market, only to see that percentage dwindle. The loss was largely due to the faulty policies of the United States itself.

Because the U.S. agricultural sector accounts for about 20 percent of the nation's gross national product (GNP), 20 percent of the employment and 20 percent of U.S. foreign exchange earnings—the absolute requirement to keep the nation price competitive in world markets is a priority of the highest order.

We have had more than ample experience with various agricultural programs. Those policies and provisions which have been found wanting must be discarded.

To accomplish the three goals as mentioned, I recommend the following in ongoing legislation.

* ☆ Establish a planting base on each and every farm producing commodities eligible for price support such as grain, soybeans and cotton. Discontinue all specific commodity acreage allotments (except for tobacco).
* ☆ Establish the level of price support loan rates as a percentage of prices received by farmers from the market (not unlike the formula used for soybean loan rates). Discontinue any reference to cost of production in all farm program legislation.
* ☆ Set target prices for grain and cotton at a level somewhat above loan rates but in relation to the same formula as utilized in the second recommendation. Subject target price payments (deficiency payments) to a realistic limitation such as $15,000 per farm.
* ☆ Continue provisions for reseal programs or Farmer Owned Reserve (FOR).
* ☆ Provide authority for land diversion payments aimed at securing maximum conservation benefits on a longer term basis.

The recommended provisions seem relatively simple; hence, a more detailed rationale seems appropriate.

I recommend commodity acreage allotments be discontinued and replaced with a planting base on each farm. The reasoning is simple. In a final effort to allow farmers maximum freedom to plant those commodities each year best suited to increase farm income through maximum efficiency in production costs, I believe it desirable to free each and every one from historical planting patterns. This action is not unlike the suspension of wheat and cotton marketing quotas in the 1970 Act. The establishment of a planting base is a simple procedure readily determined by information already available in county Agricultural Stabilization and Conservation Service (ASCS) offices. Such bases will likely be necessary to administer land diversion provisions.

Price-support loan rates must be set at a level affording competing grain exporting nations such as Canada and Australia and South American nations, less financial incentive to expand at our expense. This type of flexibility can best be attained by setting the specific level each year as a percentage of the most recent five years such as 75 to 80 percent with authority to ignore the high and low year. The rationale is not to knock down prices but to keep the U.S. competitive in world markets—and to maximize farm income from the marketplace rather than from CCC (which is not a market). Naturally, I recommend against any reference to cost of production because the determination of the specific cost of production of a commodity cannot be done with any degree of accuracy. Furthermore, the attempts of USDA to accomplish this unenviable task, by the very nature of the exercise, will recognize irrigation costs (in some areas) and work toward perpetuating what may be non-competitive production practices and a waste of natural resources.

I recommend the inclusion of a payment limitation provision on deficiency payments. To not do so, in my opinion, is unacceptable public policy. While I suggest the limitation be established at $15,000 per farm unit, the precise level is in reality a "fine tuning" matter. The principle of such a policy is of utmost importance.

An explanation as to why a payment limitation on deficiency payments is necessary can best be explained through a general classification of farms by size in terms of annual cash receipts. Naturally, this is not a precise science but the breakdown in annual cash receipts by size reveals an interesting profile of the nation's farmers.

I repeat that a breakdown of farm size in the nation via cash receipts is not an undertaking in precision; but again it is the principle I am attempting to illustrate.

In establishing the principle I assume the following:

☆ About 15 percent of our farmers account for slightly more than 60 percent of cash receipts each year. As of 1983 this category comprised about 360,000 units. Cash receipts for this group totaled about $102 billion. Average cash receipts per unit for the farms in this category were about $285,000.

☆ About 25 percent of another group of our farmers account for about 28 percent of the cash receipts each year. In 1983 this group consisted of about 600,000 farms and the total cash receipts were about $46 billion—28 percent of the total and averaged about $77,000 per unit.

☆ About 60 percent of the remaining farmers are part-time operators—generally with off-farm jobs. In 1983 this category accounted for over 1.4 million units. Total cash receipts were about $16 billion—10 percent of the total and averaged about $11,000 per farm.

I note a publication released by the Council for Agricultural Science and Technology (CAST–report #98, September, 1983) utilized a table of farms by volume of sales in 1981. The number of farms in each of three categories is quite different—according to the table. Thus, I repeat the classification of farms by size based on sales is not an exact science. On the other hand the message is the same. The CAST table revealed the following:

Numbers	Large Farms (Sales $200,000 and Over)	Medium Farms (Sales $40,000 to $199,999)	Small Farms (Sales Under $40,000)	All Farms
Number of farms	112,000	582,000	1,742,000	2,436,000
(Percent of all farms)	(4.6)	(23.9)	(71.5)	(100)
(Percent of all sales)	(49.3)	(38.1)	(12.6)	(100)

It is important to remember that deficiency payments are income transfers. An authority to transfer income to large commercial farmers, without limitation, is nothing more nor less than an export subsidy mechanism. There are, therefore, two basic reasons why I object to the distribution of deficiency payments without limitation.

☆ Income transfers distributed to large commercial farmers, without limitation, exacerbates a trend making it still more difficult for new and young farmers to enter the farming business.

☆ Income transfer to large commercial farmers through farm programs further weakens the U.S. trade negotiating stance.

In my opinion, the objective of the target-price concept is to encourage younger farmers and/or middle income (in terms of gross sales) producers. The income transferred to this group by way of the target-price mechanism is not inconsistent with the goal of the old Homestead Act itself which was designed to lend stability to rural America. Regardless of farm program provisions or anything less than government edict, farming will continue to trend toward greater industrialization. My chief argument against open-end authority to make deficiency payments such as was utilized in the PIK program actually encourages the structural change toward more rapid industrialization. I fail to believe that such emphasis is within the charter or role of government programs.

The grain reseal program should be continued. In reality, this program has become known as the Farmer Owned Reserve (FOR). I use the word "reseal" because the provisions of FOR have been changed much too frequently. In fact, the program has been used as a price-support mechanism and at still other times as a political plum. I believe it is imperative to operate the program more similar to the old reseal program whereby on occasion a commodity loan was simply extended beyond the loan maturity date. The FOR provides the mechanism for producers to be dependable suppliers to domestic and overseas users of grain the year around. Properly administered, the program should be designed to encourage use expansion. Because of this there should be a national average price announced which when reached CCC terminates per diem storage (release price). At a still higher (announced) price, CCC should demand repayment of the commodity loan (call price). It is imperative that CCC not change the rules—once established and announced. Grain producers should be reminded the FOR or reseal program is a livestock feeder or industrial user "assurance program." The reason to have the privilege available to grain farmers (and it is a privilege) is to provide maximum marketing flexibility and to give comfort and encouragement to the livestock and poultry industry and industrial users of grain in the United States and in the rest of the world.

Land diversion authority is not an easy provision to discuss because a payment to farmers for not farming is one thing while a requirement to idle a portion of the planting base to be eligible for loans and deficiency payments (target prices) is something else. I believe both authorities should be included in legislation with one caveat. If or as the U.S. farm productive capacity continues to exceed demand—which is likely—and if paid diversion of a portion of the national planting base seems in the national interest—certainly we can do a better job, with all the professional expertise on conservation in USDA and throughout the nation in shifting the use of some land (shallow soils) to more appropriate uses.

In addition to the traditional provisions discussed, I wish to make reference to other items—some of which are a part of omnibus farm legislation and others are "think items."

I have discussed the Agricultural Trade Development and Assistance Act (PL 480) in Chapter 3. Unfortunately, as already related, this meaningful program is more and more hobbled by peripheral interest groups. This trend has resulted in PL 480 being much less virile as a market expansion tool and more a mechanism to attain some U.S. foreign policy goal. As a minimum in future legislation, the Cargo Preference Provision of the act should be deleted. This authority has not accomplished the goal of strengthening the U.S. Merchant Marine fleet. The ending of this section of PL 480 would save the taxpayers of the nation about $100 million per year—or increase the overseas movement of that many dollars of U.S. farm products for the same expenditure of federal funds. The deletion of this authority should be a top priority item.

Still another section of the Omnibus Farm Legislation should be deleted and/or phased out as rapidly as possible, namely the manufactured dairy price support program. In my opinion, over the past 30 years there have been three times when the program could have been ended—with minimum impact on dairy farmers and the milk products industry.

Those periods were near the end of the decade of the 1950s, again in the mid-1960s and in 1970. Legislation, of course, would have been required, and I am fully aware that there was no organized public clamor to accomplish this task. That is all history, but with new scientific developments in the dairy industry and with a multiplicity of products now being manufactured by dairy processors, the time has come for market forces to allocate resources in this industry. The most significant scientific development to which I refer is the breakthrough of embryo transplants. This marvel of science makes it possible to literally multiply the birth of high-producing heifers from superior cows. There is no way that government can determine a fair price for production from such high-producing cows and at the same time be reasonably fair to taxpayers and their children. Nor should government be required to do so!

As an aside, I have always marveled why public policy should dictate the expenditure of tax money at the tune of $200 per year for a black and white cow and zero tax money for a black cow. I am being a bit facetious but I am pointing out the difference in cost to the citizens of the nation between the dairy industry and beef enterprises. In recent years, the manufactured dairy product price-support program has been costing CCC at least $200 per cow. The beef industry—in its wisdom—has remained free of government price-support programs. The time has come for informed national debate on the wastefulness of the dairy price-support program.

Finally, it should be recognized that the stated reason for the manufactured dairy products price-support program—according to the language in the statute—is to assure the nation an ample supply of dairy products. I maintain an ample supply would be produced if the law were to be ended. Further, and equally important for those of us engaged in agriculture, I believe producers would do well. Over a period of time, there would be adjustments. Superior breeding programs will speed up such adjustments with or without a price-support program. But I believe—beyond a doubt—thousands of market forces can accomplish such adjustments in a much more satisfactory manner than can a few program designers—be they heads of associations, government administrators or elected legislators.

I have never found the answer as to why so many of us fear the very forces which have made our agricultural sector so productive. I guess the answer lies in the weakness of human nature itself where many seem to favor designing farm programs based on historical facts.

Another "think item" has to do with corn and other feed grains such as sorghum. I believe a worthy goal to shoot for in future farm programs is an end to price support loans for the package of feed grains including corn and sorghum. A well administered FOR designed to keep the United States as the granary for the world via CCC offering to pay storage on a per diem basis to producers for a quantity not in excess of—shall we say 15 percent of the projected annual disappearance—would lend comfort to domestic and overseas users.

In developing this item a bit further, I want to share what I believe to be sound reasoning. I come by this thought with hands-on experience in at least a score of nations.

In not an unrelated manner, farmers, marketers and legislators often comment that "Soybeans are different!" I shall expand this thought with an illustration—the message of which is still germane to the subject at hand.

In one of the evening sessions between the members of the house committee on agriculture and USDA policy people—in late 1969—I was participating in an informal discussion of the soybean outlook with Chairman Poage and Secretary Hardin. Keep in mind that CCC owned a quantity of soybeans at that time but was slowly disposing of those stocks at a price in excess of the statutory minimum. It should also be remembered that Hardin (with my wholehearted concurrence) had lowered the price-support loan level for the crop being harvested at year end, 1969.

Hardin made the comment to Poage that in future legislation, soybeans may need to be subjected to acreage allotments similar to wheat and corn (restrictive planting). I do not know whether Hardin was being the devil's advocate or expressing what he may have believed to be a true possiblity. I assume the former. The response of Chairman Poage is the key to this exchange.

Poage said, "No! Soybeans are different!"

Why do people continue to express the view that soybeans are different?

They do so because it is believed there is great opportunity to expand the use of soybean oil and/or the end products derived through the feeding of soybean meal—meat, poultry, eggs and dairy products.

While several actions of our own U.S. government over the past 10 to 12 years hardly substantiate this view, I believe it to be fact.

This being my belief, I challenge the nation's agricultural policy makers to show intestinal fortitude by assuring livestock and poultry interests around the world that the United States believes there is almost unlimited demand for more animal products in a long list of nations. Of course, much of the demand is not *real*. But if we would concentrate country by country on steps to assist in making the demand *real*, I am optimistic of the outcome.

Further, the livestock and poultry industry in the United States would be a more predictable user of corn and other feed ingredients if CCC would declare an end to meddling with the corn and sorghum price mechanism. In addition, as I have visited with feed manufacturers and livestock and poultry producers in the Far East—and in some developing countries—I am impressed with their knowledge regarding the U.S. feed grain supply/demand situation.

Step number one necessary to encourage the animal industry in the world is for the United States to end policy surprises. Are we afraid to allow our customers (users of grain) to plan, to make investments and to build their enterprises on free market information?

I am not!

I say with absolute conviction that the world livestock and poultry industry—partially dependent on U.S. feed ingredients, including corn and sorghum—is much more likely to expand production in a progressive manner with less U.S. government interference with the price mechanism.

That is why I recommend an end to the CCC loan rates on corn, sorghum and other feed grains. The outcome has to be much brighter for producers under such a scenario than with the uncertainties of policies dictated by political expediency.

Hence, I understand fully the assertion that "soybeans are different." But by the same measure corn, sorghum, other grains used in feed formulation and other feed ingredients may also be labeled as being different.

I contend that, if—and I repeat if—producers and supporting enterprises really believe in feed grain global market development, then there should be agreement with suspending the major impediment discouraging expanded use in the United States and overseas. End the authority of CCC to lend uncertainty and unpredictability to prices!

DEMAND ORIENTED?

During the decade of the 1960s, when I spent at least one-third of my working days in the Far East and in Europe, the lack of interest in much of our industrial sector in overseas marketing was obvious. Automobile manufacturers through their actions told the world they (the auto makers) were not interested in exporting U.S. manufactured automobiles. In addition to their lackadaisical attitude, one had only to observe the bloated salaries paid their executives and over-rich labor contracts. The outcome in the U.S. auto industry was predictable. Exports dried up and in far too many instances the automobiles produced in the United States—for Americans—were less than quality competitive with imports.

It is not my intent to single out the automobile industry as an example of "how not to participate in global affairs." But the facts speak for themselves, and I want to make a point.

Still another industry which over-rewarded labor is the meat packing industry. In addition, the traditional big meat packers failed to modernize outdated plants. I mention the automobile industry and the meat packing enterprises because the trend in the entire agricultural sector is not unlike the two industries mentioned—albeit for entirely different reasons.

Commencing in 1954, when the United States through enactment of PL 480 notified the world that American agriculture was becoming a more active participant in an interdependent world, the nation for 25 years led the charge to improve human nutrition. Of course, the United States benefited, but buying nations also gained because both parties to a business transaction benefit or believe they benefit. Near the end of the decade of the 1970s, the U.S. government (executive and legislative alike) made some serious mistakes. Mistakes which were destined to cause agricultural producers and many of the businesses engaged in services serious financial hardship.

The similarity between the agricultural sector and the meat packing businesses is the manner in which rewards to labor had to be curtailed—first in some meat packing enterprises and now through reduced price guarantees (price supports) to farmers for grain.

It seemed to me the shortsightedness of government officials first showed its ugly head during the presidential campaign in 1976. During the heat of the campaign, President Ford and vice-presidential candidate Dole announced an increase in the 1976 wheat loan rate. The President had the legal right to do so, but that action seemed to commence an attitude that held sway for five years.

The attitude conveyed by such "Christmas present action" left me with the impression that officials in high places—both executive and legislative—believed they really created wealth on the banks of the Potomac. In reality the old adage "You can lead the horse to water but you cannot make it drink" was at work. It is possible to fix the floor price for wheat and corn at a higher level but you cannot force a user to buy it!

I fear that few people in high places in government circles fully appreciate the competitive situation in the world of commerce and the extent to which the actions of the U.S. government impacts major decisions influencing the international movement of agricultural commodities.

When the decision was made to embargo the exports of U.S. soybeans in 1973, do you believe the decision makers thought Brazil would double the production of soybeans in a decade—reaching an annual production of nearly 600 million bushels? Do you think they thought Argentina would boost its production to nearly 250 million?

I have often wondered also how legislators in their respective states or districts could answer with pride the extent to which Canada, France, Australia and Argentina smiled at U.S. government actions—as each competing country garnered a higher percentage of the world wheat market—operating under the tent of a more bloated guaranteed U.S. price.

Several major industries in the United States seemingly chose not to participate in global marketing, opting instead to satisfy domestic requirements, at a price.

I repeat again, the 1954 Act (PL 480) set the pattern for the United States in the world of commerce for a quarter of a century. In the early years, export subsidies were utilized in a limited manner to carve out a larger niche for U.S. farm products and to expand overseas use. One by one export subsidies were terminated and U.S. grain prices became world prices. In the early 1980s and to the present time the payment of subsidy to export is becoming quite a common discussion item. In most instances the huge restitutions paid by the EC is mentioned as an excuse for the United States to again go down the export subsidy route.

To do so would be shortsighted.

I dwelled on the target price concept as a means to support U.S. farmers and to lessen government involvement in the pricing mechanism (price supports). This is one method; there may be others.

The greatest weakness—history proves—with the target price concept is that it can be shortchanged by money managers. The Office of Management and Budget (OMB), seemingly for short-term fiscal management reasons, favors narrowing the gap between price received by producers and the target price by raising loan rates. Directors of OMB quickly learn how to increase prices in the short run and oftentimes insist on so doing. This action—if taken—deprives the target-price concept of its favorable aspects for the United States.

The question facing U.S. producers of price-supported commodities and the balance of the businesses servicing them is whether or not the U.S. policy makers will choose to take the appropriate actions making it possible for the nation to be more competitive. I believe the alternatives are generally well understood, but I am not so sure of the will to achieve growth.

Of one thing I am sure. A strong conviction to make and keep the United States competitive in world markets is absolutely imperative to accomplishing this goal. The strong conviction must emanate from the president of the United States.

Congress will not take the leadership in reaching this goal.

The president must stand ready to veto any legislation that undercuts the goal to make U.S. agriculture more competitive in the world of commerce. To not do so would cause our brightest and most productive sector (agriculture) to go the same road as has been selected by several industries—turning inward and depending on government appropriations.

My experience in working with Congress leads me to believe that many members of that body do not mind losing an issue or even a vote if they (Congressmen or Senators) have a culprit upon which to lay the blame.

This then is the job of the secretary of agriculture or the appropriate sub-cabinet official. While this may sound like an unenviable task, I can assure the reader it can be most rewarding. Because to fight for a principle and win, when the best of reasoning indicates the long-run benefits to the nation and the industry involved is most rewarding. Satisfaction gained—in spite of temporary criticism—is monumental compared to agreeing to a policy designed to further encumber taxpayers and straightjacket producers.

Some students of representative government maintain that the art of compromise is the key to the system.

There is much truth to this postulation, but there comes a point when compromise is over or beyond when a field is *mined*. To know where this point lies and still attain that which must be accomplished is the true art of governing.

INTERDEPENDENCY

To me the word "interdependent" means mutually dependent—or dependent on each other.

I choose to discuss this matter of interdependency as a summary to what has gone on before in these writings, because a more enlightened appreciation of the role of food and other farm products in the world is of paramount importance to a better understanding of the future of U.S. agriculture.

A truly interdependent world in which each person is mutually dependent upon every other person is a dream world situation. Maybe this naiveté was demonstrated by Wendell Wilkie in his book *One World*. In an idealistic manner he made the matter sound like an obtainable sort of utopia. If each and every country were of the persuasion that people would be better off in a free trading atmosphere, the Wilkie dream might be fulfilled. Unfortunately, sovereign nations have nationalistic goals determined by voters or dictators. Because of this, the *real* world is far from being an ideal and homogeneous planet in which to engage in commerce.

We have discovered a long list of macroeconomic factors in the world that have impacted the volume of farm commodities crossing the borders of nations. I am thinking of the changing value of the dollar (increasing), exporting practices of competing countries and regions, the debt situation in a long list of countries and perhaps of greatest significance to U.S. agriculture—the economic problems of developing countries.

I choose to not discuss these external factors in detail. I have decided not to do so in this book because I have wanted to concentrate on our own domestic agricultural policy and the extent to which that policy is influenced by short run political expediency.

Three examples come to mind as to why I believe a lengthy discussion of macroeconomic factors would lessen the focus on our own domestic policy decisions.

* I have noted particularly in statements emanating from the academic community or "think tank" groups—the increasing value of the dollar receives top billing as the chief negative reason limiting increased U.S. exports of farm products—or the chief reason for falling exports.
* The exporting practices of the EC, whereby restitutions are established with little discipline, are constantly mentioned by a long list of U.S. Senators and Representatives and also leaders in the executive branch—as the justification for the United

States to move further down the road of utilizing less than sound trading practices.

☆ The economic problem in a long list of developing countries—including devalued currencies—is touted as being the great stumbling block to an increase in the global movement of farm products.

Each of the three items is worthy of much discussion and analysis. Each example has influenced world trade and each has had a negative impact on the export of U.S. agricultural commodities. But I repeat again that these many external factors, singularly or collectively, do not provide justification for the United States to move away from a domestic sound economic farm policy. Neither do they (the external factors) provide ample fuel for the United States to invoke a multiple export pricing policy through the use of export subsidies.

Finally as I read excerpts from the Congressional Record I am impressed with comments in the halls of Congress recognizing the importance of international trade to U.S. agriculture. I also note the degree to which most of those statements are uttered with our own nationalistic welfare in mind. That is to be expected. On the other hand, if a major deterrent to a more prosperous global agriculture lies outside of the United States—then that is where our efforts should be focused—but always with the understanding our own domestic policies recognize the significance of economic health in each and every nation and region.

As a case in point an explanation of this rather profound statement is provided by Mexico.

Mexico is friendly to the United States. The nation is one of our most important trading partners. The country has great resources—including petroleum and a capable work force. And, unfortunately, a cumbersome foreign debt, but with strong determination to become a greater economic force in the world of commerce.

As this is written the value of the Mexican peso is 195 to the U.S. dollar compared to an exchange rate of 26 to the dollar three years earlier. We in the United States cannot possibly appreciate the internal adjustment in buying practices this situation forces upon the citizens of Mexico.

Yet, whether the country be Mexico, Venezuela or the Philippines—these nations along with the United States are members of and belong to this interdependent world. These sovereign nations are developing their economies and *they* along with many others hold out the greatest opportunity for expanding markets for our farm products—on a selective basis.

This can only happen (expanded exports) if we in the United States and other industrially developed countries increase our imports from them and multiply our efforts to assist and cooperate with total economic development within their borders.

Is this idealistic?

Yes, to a degree!

But an interdependent world becomes even more interdependent as the population increases to 5 billion with prospects of double that number in another 70 years.

I had fully expected to include at least two chapters in this book on the importance of agricultural businesses to the total U.S. community of agriculture. I have not done so because—as has been typical of public policy issues involving the entire subject of agriculture—it seems farm income issues continue in the forefront of any and all discussions of matters having to do with politics and our nation's food policy.

My glossing over the contributions of the business community to the total agricultural sector should not be interpreted as a non-recognition of that effort. Rather, a more detailed story of the significance of mundane matters such as return on investment, owner's equity, cost of borrowed money, risk and sound economic planning would only dramatize the enormity and significance of the total U.S. agricultural community.

Overall, a more intimate understanding of the contribution—to the national and global economic welfare—of all those industries involved in lubricating the production, marketing and distribution of food and fiber in the world only mellows the attitude of those involved in this great total effort.

Name Index

Schnittker, John, 163
Schoel, Egon, 81, 83
Shanklin, George, 130
Shulman, Ed, 110
Shuman, Charles, 203-204
Sonnenfeldt, Hal, 129
Stans, Maurice, 111, 119
Steagall, Bascomb, 4
Steinweg, Bernard, 134
Stevenson, Adlai, 7
Stolte, Darwin, 84-85
Symington, Stuart, 16

Talmadge, Herman, 124, 126

Thatcher, William, 1
Thye, Edward, 8, 10, 28
Tokoro, Hideo, 67
Truman, Harry, 2, 6-7, 9-10, 16

Vlastaris, Soto, 85

Wallace, Henry, 2, 14
Werner, Klaus, 83, 85
Whitaker, John, 103, 110, 113, 132
Whitten, Jamie, 126, 139
Worthington, Howard, 111, 166, 167

Young, Milton, 124

About the Author

☆ ☆

Clarence D. Palmby is recognized in the United States and in many countries around the world as an authoritative voice in the history and formation of agricultural policy and in the planning and implementation of market-oriented commodity programs.

For nearly a decade, Mr. Palmby was vice-president of public affairs for Continental Grain Company, New York, a major commodities trading organization.

Prior to joining Continental Grain Company, Mr. Palmby served for 3½ years with USDA as assistant secretary of agriculture for international affairs and commodity programs. He acted concurrently as president of the Commodity Credit Corporation.

On behalf of U.S. agriculture, he was instrumental in negotiating more favorable terms of entry for U.S. agricultural commodities into several nations and regions.

From 1961 to 1969, Mr. Palmby was executive vice-president of the U.S. Feed Grains Council with offices in Washington, D.C. As the chief executive officer of this association, Mr. Palmby contributed greatly to the increased export of feed grains and other feed ingredients produced by the United States. He was a leader in promoting the utilization of feeds and concentrates in livestock and poultry production.

During these endeavors and in his assigned government service role as an official of USDA, he gained firsthand knowledge of the grain, feed and livestock industries of European countries and of other countries such as Japan, Taiwan and South Korea.

Mr. Palmby illustrated his understanding of *marketing* as he developed the U.S. Feed Grains Council in Japan. He understood that the market for U.S. corn and sorghum in Japan could not increase any faster than the desire of the Japanese people to purchase the end products of animal feeding—meat, poultry, eggs and dairy products. Consistent with this understanding and philosophy, he designed educational and promotional programs in cooperation with feed manufacturers, food retailers and organizations representing livestock and poultry producers. He quickly developed a strong personal following in that country and in other nations which is still intact today.

From 1953 to 1961, Mr. Palmby served USDA in several capacities in Washington, D.C., and St. Paul, Minnesota.

He is a native of southern Minnesota and a graduate of the University of Minnesota. During his early years as a farmer in Minnesota, he was active in agricultural organizations and civic affairs in his home state.

Mr. Palmby received the Minnesota 4-H Club Alumni Award in 1954 and the Skelly Award for Superior Achievement in Agriculture in 1955. The government of Italy presented him with its Leader of Commerce Award in 1968.

He is a former director of the U.S. Chamber of Commerce and a former director and member of the executive committee of the National Grain and Feed Association.